Megastorms, California, and You

Megastorms, California, and You

Navigating Extreme West Coast Weather

R. W. Kerrigan, Ph.D.

The Dryas Press

**Megastorms, California, and You:
Navigating Extreme West Coast Weather**

ISBN: 979-8-218-23047-0 (pbk)
ISBN: 979-8-218-23048-7 (e-book)
Library of Congress Control Number: 2023916688

Cover photos by R. W. Kerrigan
 *Front: Half Dome in storm, seen from the top of Yosemite Falls, May 1973.
 Back: Rice, Kyushu, Japan.*

Published by The Dryas Press
P.O. Box 484
West Point, California 95255
www.TheDryasPress.com

For my forebears, and those who ensued

Contents

Preface   xi

Introduction to the Megastorm   1
     ...and to this book

Ch. 1   History: The Great Flood of 1861-62   5
     America's greatest natural disaster

Ch. 2   Understanding California's AR-megastorms   17
     What are they, what causes them, where do they come from?

Ch. 3   The Talkin' Water Blues   27
     How we imagine and describe storms and floods

Ch. 4   Physical Impacts of California's Next Megastorm   45
     An overview

Ch. 5   Infrastructure Impacts of California's Next Megastorm   61
     Loss of capabilities and services

Ch. 6   Impacts on California Transportation and Travel   65

Ch. 7   Impacts on California Energy and Fuels   81

Ch. 8   Impacts on California Water Infrastructure   105

Ch. 9   Impacts on California Communications   115

Ch. 10 Impacts on California Populations, Shelter, and Supplies   121

Ch. 11 Costs and Losses   131
     Consequences for property, wealth, business, agriculture, revenue

Ch. 12 Risks and Probabilities: 'All Bets Are On'   141
     What are the actual odds of experiencing an AR-megastorm in California?

Ch. 13 Planning and Preparedness for Individuals, Families and Households 149
    Empowering the grass roots (this means us)

Ch. 14 Preparedness for Communities 175
    Grass has many roots (us, again)

Ch. 15 Community-scale Roll-out 183
    First experiences and TTEs from Tahoe / Reno and Ventura

Ch. 16 State (and some Federal) Emergency Functions 187
    An introduction

Ch. 17 Lessons and a Perspective 195
    Some history, assessment and opinion

Ch. 18 On the Psychology of Risk 227

Ch. 19 What I Would I Like to See 241
    The author's suggestions, and advocacy, with a nod to USGS

Ch. 20 Banish Confusion 273
    Examining the root causes, including messaging, and resolving them

Epilogue 291

Acronyms and Abbreviations 293

Acknowledgements 299

About the Author 300

Preface

The roots of this book come from water. Early on the morning of February 14, 2019, an intense California rainstorm delivered approximately 4" of rain in one hour, according to a Caltrans (our highway department) spokesperson—an extreme event by any measure—onto wet ground and snow on my land and lands nearby. I was in the downpour watching as the massive water flow overtopped and damaged both small dams on my property, in spite of recent spillway and outlet improvements I'd made to them. The creek drains about one square mile of Sierra field, forest and orchard above the lower pond. Four inches of rain on one square mile would equal close to 70 million gallons of water; it took only minutes for a significant fraction of that to arrive at my ponds. Snow on the ground also quickly melted in the rain, amplifying the rainfall runoff. My big pond holds maybe 10,000,000 gallons on a good day, and was already full in spite of having the drains open, so you can understand the problem. Seeing water pour over the tops of earthen dams is frankly terrifying; wading onto one in an attempt to divert the overflow and keep damage to a minimum is also memorable. Similar scenes were repeated at many places in our area. Several important area roads, including our state highway, were closed for months, some even for more than a year, due to landslides.

Two weeks later, I heard a brief radio report on something called a megastorm. The phenomenon was unknown to me, as was the Great Flood of 1861-62, the West Coast's most recent megastorm and arguably America's greatest natural disaster in terms of scope. I decided to become better informed. Four years on, I'm still learning, while science marches on. I think it's timely now to offer this introduction to megastorms, the impacts—threats—they pose to the West Coast, and the risks we face. Those in a position to know sometimes refer to a future megastorm as the real 'Big One' facing California; the impacts could dwarf those of a major earthquake, and may happen sooner.

My own family roots reached the Sierra Foothills—now Amador and Nevada Counties—in 1850, in the early Gold Rush era. At some point—it might have been after the 1862 megastorm—our branch decamped for points west, where, two generations ago, they got to experience, and be uprooted by, the 1906 San Francisco earthquake. After a century, many of us have returned to the Foothills. A few years back, I took title to a small farm in the hills east of Sacramento and began spending more time here. My vantage point for the topic of this book starts here and overlooks the larger, diverse landscape of the Golden State.

We have written records from California in 1862, and we have geological records going many centuries further back, from sediments below lakes and the Bay and beneath the mouths of coastal rivers, telling us that the West Coast experiences a recurring series of megastorms, and indicating when and how often they have occurred. And we now have powerful computer models that carefully simulate global weather systems under past, present, and expected future climate conditions and trends, consistently forecasting that future twenty-first century weather, including megastorms, will be more extreme, and that big storms will be coming ashore more often.

In this book, I'll walk you through some history, some science, and then a series of expert assessments of the massive physical, financial and human impacts a storm event like this would have on present-day California. I'll give you a look at how such risks are being evaluated, and provide some insight into how and why different estimation approaches see things differently. For example,

> Huey says, "I have geological proof that there have been at least seven truly massive storm events that inundated California over the past 1800 years."

> Louie says, "Don't worry about it, I have statistics that prove each one of those was a once-in-a-thousand-years event. Ten-thousand-years, even!"

> Dewey says, "Swell, but the latest weather models indicate that we'll soon be having storms that severe, or worse, two or three times a century, on average."

Note that they are only arguing about when, not if.

If you are having a distinct reaction to those three conflicting assertions (really, Louie is the odd duck out here, but his cheerful take remains very popular), you are not alone. Unfortunately, some of our public agencies have appeared in recent years to be stuck on the wrong horn of this seeming dilemma. I promise that I'll explain the basis of those conflicting statements, and offer a broader view to resolve them, in a clear way that I think everyone is likely to understand. Misunderstanding could be dangerous, even deadly.

I also present chapters on individual and community preparedness, on official activities and frameworks, on lessons from other weather events, on some aspects of psychology that make it harder to deal with risks and threats, on some large and small ideas for how we as a state could move toward a better, safer, more storm-resilient future, and finally, to resolve any confusion, I'll end with a closer look at how misunderstandings and disagreement about actual storm risks have arisen, and how to get past those quagmires. There is good reason to feel positive, if we focus and act.

That said, the extreme storm impacts I'll describe are pretty sobering, and you may want to get in touch with your 'sterner stuff' as you take the descriptions of some consequences on board. I hope to inspire and motivate people, lots of them, to become better informed and prepared, and to support others around them in increasing local resiliency. I hope to stimulate conversations and discussions, and I hope that process will reach and persuade leaders, agencies and officials to place adequate, needed attention on these very real threats, and to engage with the public comprehensively. It may not be simple to know exactly how risks are, or will be, evaluated by agencies in advance, or as events unfold. In my research on preparedness in California I've found reasons for both hope and concern. It's prudent to give some weight to any cause for concern. It's reasonable to ask for clarity and commitment. It's wise for each of us to prepare.

—R. W. Kerrigan
   Summer, 2023

Introduction to the Megastorm

…and to this book

"The sky isn't falling… but one of these days, it for damn sure will." —*A. Little Chicken*

Extreme, dangerous West Coast weather events, now usually called megastorms, caused by prolonged and intense Pacific atmospheric river (AR) phenomena, are real, dangerous and, at least for now, relatively uncommon. The last megastorm here affected most of the West Coast, and the interior West, in 1861-62; we have written descriptions and scattered weather data for it, but not a detailed set of 'modern' measurements, so, to an unfortunate extent, it has been overlooked technically; it is not part of 'the record,' and so is forgotten generally.

Why do we forget? Storms and floods tend not to trigger the sort of visceral, adrenaline-fueled reactions that earthquakes, volcanos, or wildfire do.

"Rain is so familiar as to feel benign… floods cause less emotional distress than earthquakes." —Lucy Jones, 2018

Yet floods cause the most death, damage and destruction.

Looking at lake, bay and ocean sediments, we have a geological record of several other (wide-scale) megastorms and megafloods that hit here over the past 18 centuries. More narrowly, Northern California also had one in 1805, and several more in the preceding seven centuries. That is the reality.

Those facts are not widely known or accepted among the public. Furthermore, wild 'doomsday' or 'apocalyptic' predictions are typically met with intense skepticism, often with good reason; such presentations may be rife with sensationalism, hype, wild speculation, and alarmist rhetoric. That makes the writing of a serious report on unfamiliar but plausible natural threats and risks more challenging, particularly in view of the widespread psychological tendency to minimize, neglect or dismiss unwelcome and unfamiliar risks.

I have great respect for facts, and for well-supported expertise. The information in this book is based primarily on facts, for example the historical record; however, for estimation of present and future risks, I rely upon the technical reports and forecasts of leading experts. Those researchers and authors, whose work I have brought into this book, have my gratitude and perhaps they will earn yours too. There are different ways to make technical forecasts about what is likely to happen tomorrow, or 80 years from now, and I'll discuss those different approaches, how they have led to different perspectives... and the prospects for their reconciliation.

My role in this, as I see it, is: (1) to gather, distill and consolidate the sometimes-technical information that is unfamiliar to many people; sometimes I crunch numbers or connect dots; (2) to try to present this information in a clear and understandable way, without dumbing it down, or hyping or exaggerating it ('megastorm' is the strong term most often used by professionals in this field); (3) to explore some of the further implications of information that has been published elsewhere; (4) to occasionally flag information that seems to be missing, or in need of further evaluation, from the sources I've consulted; and (5) to help the reader find and consult those same original sources, and/or others, and draw their own conclusions. I have tried to present only facts as facts, and to avoid errors, but being only human, I'll ask you to take nothing on faith if you doubt anything you read here. Consult reliable sources (I provide several) and take your own fact-finding to a higher level. There is also a (6): sometimes I comment on things that concern me, or I advocate; those are my own views.

In short, I hope to be a good and faithful communicator of important information that may be hard to find or difficult to grasp. It is also necessary for me to address misinformation and any controversy, which I do.

Wherever you live in the West, this book can help you imagine something extremely dangerous on a scale that no living Californian has ever experienced... yet. It can inspire you to prepare and can help you get started on that. When readers and listeners are first exposed to this 'new' information, they often tell me they find it distressing. I think that may be an unavoidable first step in a process of becoming aware, motivated, safer and better prepared. At least, I don't know how to inspire people to minimize personal risks without first explaining the risks. As you read, keep in mind that several chapters toward the end of this book emphasize positive steps that everyone can begin to take, and preparations you can make, to follow a path toward preparedness and safety. I've also given a brief introduction to the frameworks responsible for the positive present and future activities you may expect from some federal and state agencies and local jurisdictions, and to contributions from experts who are involved with these issues. I've even outlined constructive ideas for a long list of small and large steps that the state, and others, could take to improve preparedness and public safety. I hope you, the reader, will retain that positive attitude as you explore this book, and if you need to think about emergency preparedness at arms-length, with a 'what-if?' puzzle-solving attitude, that's still a good start.

My hope is that you will find this book useful, and that you will in future enjoy a well-earned feeling of better preparedness, arriving in good time.

* * *

A list of defined acronyms and abbreviations can be found at the end of the book. Some good, primary sources are given below; full citations are provided in the relevant chapters.

- **USGS / ARkStorm** = Porter *et al.* 2011 study report from U.S. Geological Survey Team
- **UCLA / Swain** = Multiple recent research papers by Daniel Swain and colleagues
- **Dettinger, Ingram** = Two papers that appeared in Scientific American in 2013 [paywalled], plus additional research and programmatic papers and books or book chapters by these authors and their colleagues
- **The Big Ones: Lucy Jones, 2018. Hardback, Doubleday, New York**
- **Lake Sacramento** = A book available online in .pdf form; meteorological and hydrological insights into the 1861-62 flood
- **Rivers of Fear** = Printed book with contemporary accounts of 'living memory' 1986 Sacramento area and Central California floods
- **Spillway Emergency** = An e-book with informative detail about a 'small' potential disaster

[A note about online citations: some reports posted by news media are mutable or ephemeral. As another example, one state agency—Cal OES—replaced their entire website just before this book was finalized, breaking (rather than forwarding) all the cited links I had curated. As time passes, similar frustrations are likely to emerge. Wikipedia, in particular, as a source, is not a final authority, nor is it error-free, but it is a convenient <u>first</u> place to check for general information; citations to the original sources are normally provided, to allow verification and deeper review. Each article there is a curated composite of community, sometimes expert, contributed elements. Articles may be updated, or revised, so there is no immutability or version control. When I cite a Wikipedia page source, it's because I found a useful first overview or credited quotation there (or, sometimes, errors I flag). What you find at a future date may differ.]

1

History: The Great Flood of 1861-62

America's greatest natural disaster

*"That doomed city is in all probability again under water today…
I don't think the city will ever rise from the shock, I don't see how
it can."* —*William H. Brewer, Journal; entries from January and
February 1862, on Sacramento*

Some history, drawn from newspapers of the day

The situation in California, in late January 1862: After
a rainy, snowy November, from at least San Francisco north
and especially in Oregon and Washington Territory (including
modern Idaho), storms in California became extreme. At some
point in December the strongest storms began. It continued
to rain for 43 to 45 days straight, with several extremely heavy
downpours. The Carson Valley, east of the Sierra Crest, had
9 feet of rainfall in a few weeks; it normally receives less than
11 inches per year. Sonora also reported 9 feet of rainfall in
six weeks, apparently similar to the entire western slope of the
Sierra. For example, the New York Times reported that 9 inches
of rain fell on Grass Valley on January 7th and 8th, although
the paper added that such heavy rain seemed unbelievable.
The weeks of extended storm systems at first created a heavy
snowpack in the high Sierra, but warmer January downpours
melted the snow and sent the meltwater together with the
rainwater into the river systems. Rivers here rose far above flood
stage and low-lying areas were soon underwater. Communities
along the rivers, for example in the central Sierra, especially
mining camps such as at Oregon Bar, Poverty Bar and Long Bar,

and Knight's Ferry, Empire City, and Mokelumne City [just in the Amador-Calaveras area alone] were swept away with much loss of life. Deadly landslides were widespread in steep terrain, taking a heavy toll locally in Mokelumne Hill and seven lives in Volcano. Buildings were washed away in many places, including Jackson, with damage also in Sutter Creek, Amador City, and Drytown. People in normally dry Ione were trying to build boats. Many roads and virtually every bridge for hundreds of miles, or beyond, were destroyed, reportedly including a native bridge spanning the Mokelumne River at a height of 60 feet. The large American River was recorded with a high-water level rise of 35 feet, at Auburn. Scenes like these from the Central Sierra Nevada mountains were repeated throughout California and across the West.

Living Californians today (as I write this, it is 2023) have never seen anything like the catastrophic events of the winter of 1861-1862.

Rain falling everywhere west of the Pacific Crest flows downward, ultimately westward, from where it lands, much of it across the Sierra and into, then out of, California's Central Valley. Much of the land area in the Valley and its Delta is virtually flat, with an elevation at about sea level or only a few feet higher. A basin like the Central Valley will empty much more slowly than it can fill, because water moves so slowly across it, and because the only drainage to the sea is through the narrow Carquinez Strait near Benicia, Martinez, and Vallejo. 62,500 square miles, or 40%, of California must drain through that relatively shallow, steep-sided channel only half a mile wide at Crockett.

Some further history: In January 1862, the flooding rivers and lands supplying the Sacramento and San Joaquin rivers filled the Central Valley with water, creating an inland sea roughly 300 miles long and 20 or more miles wide "from the mountains on one side to the coast range hills on the other;" flood depths up to 30 feet "completely submerging telegraph poles that had just been installed" were reported; in Sacramento almost every home was flooded up into their second story, and many buildings were afloat. Virtually every other river valley in California was similarly flooded, including the areas north (like Napa), east (like San Ramon), and south (like Santa Clara) of the San Francisco Bay, as well as significant areas in Southern California including Los Angeles, Anaheim, and "vast areas of the Mojave Desert." In fact, the storms caused flooding or set rainfall records (after 160 years, many of those records still stand) from northern Mexico through Oregon and Washington Territory into southern British Columbia, and east into the Nevada, Utah and New Mexico (including modern Arizona) Territories.

In 1862 it took 6 months for the Central Valley to fully drain; note that parts of the Central Valley today are now up to 30' lower than in the 1860s, due to groundwater pumping and land subsidence, while the sea level has risen 8"; neither change will improve valley drainage (see Anderson *et al.*, 2018). It can take days for floodwaters to move on when the slope of the land is one foot per mile or less.

In the wake of the receding floodwaters, California in 1862 was a changed place. Much infrastructure was gone, including roads and bridges. One home in eight was gone, one-quarter to one-third of taxable property was destroyed. Many communities were rationing food and supplies. Most livestock in the Central Valley and much of Southern California perished (200,000 or 25% of cattle, 600,000 sheep and lambs statewide). After the first 14 days of flooding, vines, fruit and nut trees were dead. A newspaper reported that "Farmland [is] covered in a thick layer of sand destroying hopes of vegetation for some time." The State Capitol relocated to San Francisco. California was effectively bankrupt. Many people died, by some estimates possibly 5,000 out of a population of under five hundred thousand, or around 1% of the population, including more than 1000 Chinese, often living in riverside mining camps. For an impression of the impact of a river flood on a Sierra Foothills mining camp of this era, you can read Bret Harte's famous short story, 'The Luck of Roaring Camp.'

While other storm and flood disasters, such as at Galveston in 1900 or along the lower Mississippi in 1927, or in Hurricane Katrina in 2005, were extreme and devastating, the storms beginning in 1861 and the Great Flood of 1862 were larger in scope, flooding a much greater land area and impacting three countries and all of the western states and territories as far east as Idaho, Utah, and New Mexico; the loss of life (statewide) and subsequent restructuring of the economy in California were proportionally greater.

The storms of 1861-62 are often described as a 43- or 45-day event. More accurately, this describes a continuous period of rain in California that included the heaviest precipitation—the megastorm—bracketed by months of wet but less extreme weather in the fall and spring. The United States Geological Survey, in their 2011 study on this phenomenon, stated that they did not rely extensively on available precipitation records from 1861-62 because "…the 1861-1862 storm occurred at a time before extensive detailed and generally reliable measurement of precipitation, barometric pressure, and wind speeds…" Instead, we can form a picture of that wet season from dated reports of rain, scattered rainfall records, and observations on flood impacts. Broadly, Oregon experienced heavy precipitation in November, with flooding that reached its highest stages from December 3–8. In Northern California, there was rain and snow from late November into early December; then four distinct rainy periods between December 9 and January 17 (this was the megastorm, for Northern California). In Southern California, there was a continuous rainy period from December 24 to January 21. There were high floods there from January 22 into February.

Writings from people who survived the storms and floods of 1861–62 help us appreciate what the experience was like. William H. Brewer was a member of the first official scientific survey of the resources of the state, travelling widely on the land from 1860 into 1864, and writing a detailed account, via correspondence, of his experiences and what he encountered here. He was present during the storms and floods of 1861–62 and his account is of great interest for what it says about the weather that winter, the conditions on the ground, the impacts on people, communities, and activities, taxes, revenues, and finances, and much else. Brewer implies that some of his written records may have been among those lost in transit through the flooded interior of the state.

Reading Brewer's journal, the rains continued…

"San Francisco.
Sunday, January 19, 1862.

The rains continue, and since I last wrote [November 17, 1861] the floods have been far worse than before. Sacramento and many other towns and cities have again been overflowed, and after the waters had abated somewhat they are again up. That doomed city is in all probability again under water today.

The amount of rain that has fallen is unprecedented in the history of the state. In this city accurate observations have been kept since July, 1853. … This year at Sonora, in Tuolumne County, between November 11, 1861, and January 14, 1862, seventy-two inches (six feet) of water has fallen, and in numbers of places over five feet! And that in a period of two months. …

The great central valley of the state is under water—the Sacramento and San Joaquin valleys—a region 250 to 300 miles long and an average of at least twenty miles wide, a district of five thousand or six thousand square miles, or probably three to three and a half millions of acres! Although much of it is not cultivated, yet a part of it is the garden of the state. Thousands of farms are entirely under water—cattle starving and drowning. Benevolent societies are active, boats have been sent up, and thousands are fleeing to this city.

There have been some of the most stupendous charities I have ever seen. An example will suffice. A week ago today news came down by steamer of a worse condition at Sacramento than was anticipated. The news came at nine o'clock at night. Men went to work, and before daylight tons of provisions were ready—eleven thousand pounds of ham alone were cooked. Before night two steamers, with over thirty tons of cooked and prepared provisions, twenty-two tons of clothing, several thousand dollars in money, and boats with crews, etc., were under way for the devastated city.

You can imagine the effect it must have on the finances and prosperity of the state. The end is not yet. Many men must fail, times must be hard, state finances disordered. ... I see no help, and on whom the blow will fall remains to be seen.

San Francisco.
Friday, January 31.

We have had very bad weather since the above was written, but it has cleared up. In this city 37 inches of water has fallen, and at Sonora, in Tuolumne, 102 inches, or 8 1/2 feet, at the last dates [that is 30" more in the 12 days since the earlier entry]. These last floods have extended over this whole coast. At Los Angeles it rained incessantly for twenty-eight days—immense damage was done—one whole village destroyed. It is supposed that over one-fourth of all the taxable property of the state has been destroyed. The legislature has left the capital and has come here, that city being under water.

All the roads in the middle of the state are impassable, so all mails are cut off. We have had no "Overland" for some weeks, so I can report no new arrivals. The telegraph also does not work clear through, but news has been coming for the last two days. In the Sacramento Valley for some distance the tops of the poles are under water!

San Francisco.
February 9.

I wrote you by the last steamer and also sent a paper. I have sent a paper by each steamer for some time and will send another by this. A mail now occasionally gets in, but many letters and papers must have been lost. For papers and printed matter the "Overland" is a total failure. …

An old acquaintance, a buccaro, came down from a ranch that was overflowed. The floor of their one-story house was six weeks under water before the house went to pieces. The "Lake" was at that point sixty miles wide, from the mountains on one side to the hills on the other. This was in the Sacramento Valley. Steamers ran back over the ranches fourteen miles from the river, carrying stock, etc., to the hills. Nearly every house and farm over this immense region is gone. There was such a body of water—250 to 300 miles long and 20 to 60 miles wide, the water ice cold and muddy—that the winds made high waves which beat the farm homes in pieces. America has never before seen such desolation by flood as this has been, and seldom has the Old World seen the like. But the spirits of the people are rising, and it will make them more careful in the future. The experience was needed. Had this flood been delayed for ten years the disaster would have been more than doubled.

… the roads will long be impassable over large portions of the state.

San Francisco.
Monday, February 10.

Rates have risen here to three per cent a month lately, which shows how hard the money market is. It has been but one and a half per cent up to the last month.

San Francisco.
March 9.

The floods have still more deranged finances and make some action imperative. The actual loss of taxable property will amount to probably ten or fifteen millions, some believe twice that, but I think not even the latter sum. The Treasurer says that the next tax list will cut down the taxable property about one-third of the whole amount, or probably about fifty million dollars, as each man will get as much taken off on his property as is possible. I suppose the actual loss in all kinds of property, personal and real, will rank anywhere between fifty and a hundred million dollars—surely a calamity of no common magnitude! …

[It was raining on February 22–23; Brewer describes a trip toward the New Almaden Mine in Santa Clara Co.]

We took steamer to Alviso, at the head of the Bay of San Francisco, then stage for seven miles to San Jose. The roads were awful. We loaded up, six stages full, in the rain, and had gone scarcely a hundred rods when the wheels sank to their axles and the horses nearly to their bellies in the mud, when we unloaded. Then the usual strife on such an occasion. Horses get down, driver swears, passengers get in the mud, put shoulders to the wheels and extricate the vehicle. We walk a ways, then get in, ride two miles, then get out and walk two more in the deepest, stickiest, worst mud you ever saw, the rain pouring. I hardly knew which grew the heaviest, my muddy boots or my wet overcoat. Then we ride again, then walk again, and finally ride into town, having made the seven miles in four hours' hard work. The pretty village was muddy, cheerless, and dull beyond telling, but I called on Mr. and Mrs. Hamilton and had a pleasant time. [The next day, continuing rain forced the party to remain in San Jose. After several days Brewer gave up and returned north.]

I left here at 4 P.M. on Thursday, March 6, by steamer. Night came on before we reached the mouth of the Sacramento River, but it was a glorious afternoon and the views of the mountains were lovely before sunset. …

Early in the morning I went to a hotel in Sacramento and got my brakfast and brushed up for business [Brewer and the survey team had been unpaid for some time]. That dispatched, I had some time to look at the city. Such a desolate scene I hope never to see again. Most of the city is still under water, and has been for three months. A part is out of the water, that is, the streets are above water, but every low place is full—cellars and yards are full, houses and walls wet, everything uncomfortable. Over much of the city boats are still the only means of getting about. No description that I can write will give you any adequate conception of the discomfort and wretchedness this must give rise to. I took a boat and two boys, and we rowed about for an hour or two. Houses, stores, stables, everything, were surrounded by water. Yards were ponds enclosed by dilapidated, muddy, slimy fences; household furniture, chairs, tables, sofas, the fragments of houses, were floating in the muddy waters or lodged in nooks and corners—I saw three sofas floating in different yards. The basements of the better class of houses were half full of water, and through the windows one could see chairs, tables, bedsteads, etc., afloat. Through the windows of a schoolhouse I saw the benches and desks afloat.

It is with the poorer classes that this is the worst. Many of the one-story houses are entirely uninhabitable; others, where the floors are above the water are, at best, most wretched places in which to live. The new Capitol is far out in the water—the Governor's house stands as in a lake—churches, public buildings, private buildings, everything, are wet or in the water. Not a road leading from the city is passable, business is at a dead standstill, everything looks forlorn and wretched. Many houses have partially toppled over; some have been carried from their foundations, several streets (now avenues of water) are blocked up with houses that have floated in them, dead animals lie about here and there—a dreadful picture. I don't think the city will ever rise from the shock, I don't see how it can. Yet it has a brighter side. No people can so stand calamity as this people. They are used to it. …

It was rainy, dull day [March 7]. I left the city [Sacramento] at 2 P.M. Friday, and as I came down the river saw the wide plain still overflowed, over farms and ranches—houses here and there in the waste of waters or perched on some little knoll now an island.

San Francisco.
March 16.

We have had severe storms in the mountains, and for near two weeks the telegraph was stopped, but on Thursday news again began to come, and on Friday the word was that Manassas was occupied by Federal troops. …

We have had more heavy rains since I last wrote [March 9], and when we can get out again, if we get out at all, I don't know. It is time for the rains to cease, but they don't.

In Camp, near Martinez.
April 27, 1862.

Wednesday, March 26, Hoffmann and I started, with compasses, barometer, etc.—an unpleasant day and rainy evening. We went up to San Rafael, about twenty miles north of San Francisco…

On March 28 we were up early and were off to climb this peak [on Tamalpais]. A trail led through the chaparral on the north side. We reached the summit of the ridge, got bearings from one peak, and started along the crest of the ridge to the sharp rocky crest or peak. The wind was high and cold, fog closed in, and then snow, enveloping everything. We were in a bad fix—cold, no landmark could be seen—to be caught thus and have to stay all night would be terrible, to get off in a fog would be impossible.

We waited behind some rocks for half an hour, when it stopped snowing and the fog grew less dense; we caught glimpses of the peak and started for it. …"

* * *

From Brewer's journal entries it's clear that it was rainy or snowy in the months just before and after the most intense 'megastorm' period. But this extraordinarily wet winter was preceded by two very dry decades (later I'll describe this 'whiplash' pattern), punctuated by occasional storms and floods. Bret Harte wrote a piece, <u>Notes by Flood and Field</u>, that in the first half of the tale describes conditions near Sacramento in October of 1861, before the rains arrived. The narrator is a land surveyor…

> "It was near the close of an October day that I began to be disagreeably conscious of the Sacramento Valley. I had been riding since sunrise, and my course, through the depressing monotony of the long level landscape, affected me more like a long dyspeptic dream than a business journey, performed under that sincerest of natural phenomena,—a California sky. The recurring stretches of brown and baked fields, the gaping fissures in the dusty trail, the hard outline of the distant hills… There were no clouds in the flinty blue heavens…"

The second half of this tale finds the narrator, three months later, assisting in all-night rescue operations from a steamboat that is powering across the flooded lands of that same Sacramento Valley, under an almost starless sky, looking for survivors…

> "We are steaming over the obliterated banks [of the Sacramento River] far into the interior. Once or twice black objects loom up near us—the wrecks of houses floating by. There is a slight rift in the sky to the north, and a few bearing stars to guide us over the waste.
>
> As we penetrate into shallower water, it is deemed advisable to divide our party into smaller boats… It must have been about three o'clock, and we were lying upon our oars… and the light of the steamer is a solitary bright star in the distance, when the silence is broken by the 'bow oar'—
>
> "Light ahead."

California weather fluctuates over multiple time scales, from months to centuries. For perspective, here is one description of the pre-Gold Rush, pre-flood control era floodplain environment:

> "At the time of first European arrival, the Central Valley was a vast wetland, densely vegetated and flooded basically wall-to-wall each year by seasonal runoff." —Nicholas Pinter

Below is a brief description of the 1862 megastorm experience in Southern California, where thousands more square miles were flooded, per Ingram (& Malamud-Roam, 2013).

> "LA's Great Flood of 1862—50 inches of rain fell from late December 1861 to early January 1862; worst flood in the history of Los Angeles; thousands of cattle drown; fruit trees

and vineyards are washed away; **all overland routes to and from LA are closed for five weeks; only communication with the outside world is through the harbor**; in New San Pedro (Wilmington) the new federal barracks are washed out by the floods; in San Pedro the storms washed away the bulkhead at Alexander Bell's storehouse and sank Tomlinson's 2 lighters while they were still loaded with lumber (the floods are followed by a severe drought—the two disasters wipe out the southern California cattle industry and the days of the Dons and the great ranchos are dead)." [—synopsis from www.mysanpedro.org]

1861–1862 provided some very expensive lessons to early California settlers, experiences that the native Mi-Wuk and other peoples were quite familiar with through their history and oral traditions, but which, with our hindsight, were not well absorbed by the 'New Californians' in their drive to pursue the opportunities they saw in settling the lands of California and the western territories.

Recently there have been a number of studies on the 'history' of California weather, supplementing the oral histories of native people including the Mi-Wuk (there are several spellings of this tribal name), and establishing the hard evidence for dating several other earlier megastorms prior to 1861–62. As we shall see, such Atmospheric River or 'AR-megastorms' are infrequent but not all that rare.

This disaster really happened. At the time, and for a while, it was called The Great Flood. Well into the Gold Rush, with the Civil War focusing national attention to the East, amid explosive optimistic settlement and development of the American West, and the strategic push to secure and populate the Pacific Coast of the American nation, the events of 1861–1862 have largely been forgotten. Amnesia can be deadly, and I join with other writers who are trying to put this history back into our memory. When you compare a current map of California's population and infrastructure with a map of where severe storm impacts are likely to create flooding or other damage, serious vulnerabilities for the present and future become evident; you can see the result of our collective amnesia. Settlement of valley floodplains continues, sometimes encouraged by public policies.

* * *

Further reading

Ingram, B. Lynn. California Megaflood: Lessons from a Forgotten Catastrophe. Scientific American, January 1, 2013. https://www.scientificamerican.com/article/ atmospheric-rivers-california-megaflood-lessons-from-forgotten-catastrophe/

Ingram, B. Lynn, and Frances Malamud-Roam. 2013. The West Without Water. University of California Press, Berkeley.

Hunsaker, Leon, and Claude W. Curran. "Lake Sacramento" —Can It Happen Again? Copy Quick and Academy Printing, Grants Pass, Oregon, November 2005. https://cepsym.org/history/LakeSacramento_book.pdf

Pinter, Nicholas, *et al.* 2018. Flooding in the Sacramento Region. Pp. 236–245 IN Geology of Sacramento, California, United States of America; Cities of the World Series. A paper released as part of the XIII IAEG Congress and AEG Annual meeting held in San Francisco, 17–21 September 2018. https://aeg.memberclicks.net/assets/ docs/Cities%20of%20the%20World%20-%20Sacramento%20-%202018.pdf

Anderson, Robert, *et al.* 2018. Land Subsidence. Pp. 245–246 IN Geology of Sacramento, California, United States of America; Cities of the World Series. A paper released as part of the XIII IAEG Congress and AEG Annual meeting held in San Francisco, 17–21 September 2018. https://aeg.memberclicks.net/assets/ docs/Cities%20of%20the%20World%20-%20Sacramento%20-%202018.pdf

[Note: If you search for more information on the Great Flood of 1862, you may encounter misinformation. If you had consulted the (community contributed) Wikipedia article on the Great Flood of 1862, before it was corrected very recently in 2023, you would have found it to state that:

> "However, the series of storms that led to the Great Flood of 1862 averaged precipitation levels that **records show only occur once every 500 to 1,000 years**."

But ‘records’ don't ‘show’ this. The misinformation (more than just a very misleading statement) quoted above has two errors, which I discuss in Chapter 20 and elsewhere. For now, I'll just encourage you to be aware, and read widely, relying upon trusted sources; don't take every written statement at face value.]

2

Understanding California's AR-megastorms

What are they, what causes them, where do they come from?

"The air moves like a river and carries the clouds with it; just as running water carries all the things that float upon it." — *Leonardo da Vinci*

To understand the winter of 1861–62 in the West, and other extreme past and future West Coast storms, we need to understand two concepts: 'atmospheric rivers' (or ARs) and 'megastorms.' This chapter covers both.

For the western USA, a megastorm is an uncommon type of storm system or event that delivers <u>extremely</u> high levels of precipitation, mostly rain, over an unusually long period of time, over a broad regional area, causing "truly massive floods" as scientist B. Lynn Ingram put it in 2013.

> "Historically, the most dangerous storms in California have been extreme events resulting from weather patterns known as Atmospheric Rivers or the Pineapple Express*> (warm, heavy storms that strike in winter, producing intense rainfall over large areas). When these storms fall on existing snowpack, flooding can be exacerbated." (—California's Flood Future, CA Department of Water Resources, 2013)

There is no single, precise technical definition of when a storm pattern reaches megastorm scale, but they are larger phenomena than the storm events of the 20th century.

In addition to precipitation, a megastorm may produce hurricane-force winds with more speed and power than almost any other 'western' weather system. It may also produce coastal storm surges much like a hurricane does, although probably less dramatically. The term 'Atmospheric River Storm' can be used, but landfalling atmospheric rivers (those reaching the Pacific coast) lasting two to several days actually can be fairly common and relatively small (or sometimes large) events; the more common, smaller AR storms deliver much of the needed water that the American West receives. About half of California's total precipitation is delivered by atmospheric rivers. The biggest events involving ARs are the AR-megastorms: a long-lasting sequence of extremely wet storm 'pulses' (some describe this as a continuous string of atmospheric rivers). A winter megastorm weather pattern can last anywhere from two or three weeks to at least six weeks, or longer, and can occur bracketed by a wet fall season and a wet spring.

In this chapter I'll take a closer look at atmospheric rivers, and then introduce you to an important study of a megastorm-scale AR event similar to the massive storms of 1861–62.

Atmospheric Rivers

Atmospheric River systems, lately prominent in weather news reporting, were only discovered, named and understood beginning *ca.* 30 years ago. They are narrow, flowing bands of extremely wet air crossing the ocean, mostly at about one to two miles above the surface. Ours here are not more than a few hundred miles wide, and can stretch across much of the Pacific Ocean. They are now tracked in real time and used in weather forecasts; they can be seen up to seven to eight days in advance of reaching the West Coast. Big atmospheric river flows can be dangerous: landfalling AR storm systems (including at megastorm scale) can bring huge volumes of water onto the West Coast, at average rates as high as <u>27 times the rate of water flowing out of the Mississippi River</u> for ARs still over the ocean, (that's equal to the flow of 2.6 Amazon Rivers for our southern friends), and at least <u>20 times</u> the Mississippi flow for ARs crossing the coastline (per CA Department of Water Resources). In megastorm events, extreme flows like this may continue to occur repeatedly for weeks, not just hours or days.

In 2019, a new scale for measuring the 'size' of ARs, and the magnitude of their impacts, was introduced. You'll be hearing more about this in winter weather forecasting, so I'll explain it a bit further. The method looks 72 hours into the future, offshore, and determines how much water is flowing in an AR, how fast it's moving, and how long it will continue (up to the 72-hour measurement limit).

"The Center for Western Weather and Water Extremes (CW3E) at the Scripps Institution of Oceanography released a five-level scale in February 2019 to categorize atmospheric rivers, ranging from "weak" to "exceptional" in strength, or "beneficial" to "hazardous" in impact. The scale considers both the amount of water vapor transported and the duration of the event."

The width of the AR plume is a third parameter that determines the geographical impact scope of the approaching AR, but not the local intensity of impacts, and is not used in the CW3E scale, although regional-level emergency managers presumably take note of it along with the somewhat unpredictable storm track.

With this five-category scale, public awareness of impending AR events on the West Coast may now be moving toward the level that hurricane awareness has reached in eastern North America. Here is how the press release from CW3E at Scripps described the impacts of the newly defined AR categories:

"The atmospheric river scale ranks ARs as follows:
- AR 1 (Weak): Primarily beneficial. For example, a Feb. 2, 2017 AR hit California, lasted 24 hours at the coast, and produced modest rainfall.
- AR 2 (Moderate): Mostly beneficial, but also somewhat hazardous. An atmospheric river on Nov. 19-20, 2016 hit Northern California, lasted 42 hours at the coast, and produced several inches of rain that helped replenish low reservoirs after a drought.
- AR 3 (Strong): Balance of beneficial and hazardous. An atmospheric river on Oct. 14-15, 2016 lasted 36 hours at the coast, produced 5-10 inches of rain that helped refill reservoirs after a drought, but also caused some rivers to rise to just below flood stage.
- AR 4 (Extreme): Mostly hazardous, but also beneficial. For example, an atmospheric river on Jan. 8-9, 2017 that persisted for 36 hours produced up to 14 inches of rain in the Sierra Nevada and caused at least a dozen rivers to reach flood stage. [Author's note: that one also caused damage to my own small dams and spillways.]
- AR 5 (Exceptional): Primarily hazardous. For example, a Dec. 29, 1996 to Jan. 2, 1997 atmospheric river lasted over 100 hours at the Central California coast. The associated heavy precipitation and runoff caused more than $1 billion in damages." [Author's note: My neighbors remember that 1997 storm; they were watching a Caltrans crew trying to save our vital local highway bridge.]

At this time there is no upper limit on the size of a Cat5 AR. Computer models have predicted storms at double the intensity of a typical AR 5 storm, perhaps arriving before the end of this century. Note that the most extreme AR storm values occur in climate models when greenhouse gas emissions continue under current 'business as usual' trends.

Here is a quick take on the <u>historical</u> frequency (ignoring climate trends) of large AR storms reaching the West Coast, and their costs:

> "Typically, the Oregon coast averages one Cat 4 atmospheric river (AR) each year; Washington state averages one Cat 4 AR every two years; the Bay Area averages one Cat 4 AR every three years; and southern California, which typically experiences one Cat 2 or Cat 3 AR each year, averages one Cat 4 AR every ten years."
>
> "Atmospheric rivers have caused an average of $1.1 billion in damage annually, much of it occurring in Sonoma County, California, according to a December 2019 study by the Scripps Institution [of] Oceanography at UC San Diego and the U.S. Army Corps of Engineers, which analyzed data from the National Flood Insurance Program and the National Weather Service. Just twenty counties suffered almost 70% of the damage, the study found, and that **one of the main factors in the scale of damage appeared to be the number of properties located in a flood plain.**" (—Wikipedia, paraphrasing the CW3E / Scripps press release)

For recent perspective, in the 2022–23 wet season, 31 atmospheric rivers hit the American West Coast through the last week of March. Seventeen crossed the California coastline; see Dettinger's comment below that a typical average annual expectation based on representative observations prior to 2013 would be for nine ARs to hit California. Fortunately for us, only one of the 31 (at the Oregon-California border) reached the AR 4 intensity 'Extreme' level. Still, the first, December-January string of ~12 of those ARs here caused a reported $1 billion in immediate damages; by March, not only numerous fatalities and injuries but $5 billion in damage from the continuing storm season were being reported; this 'snapshot' of events is from the point in time (now) where the huge Tulare Basin is continuing to flood and fill, and the record Sierra snowpack has not yet begun to melt in earnest.

Where do megastorms fit into this AR framework? Based on 1861–62 descriptions, scientists now believe that a megastorm can be a sustained atmospheric river event that delivers repeated pulses (a sequence of ARs, or 'storms') of high-category impacts, including apparent AR 4 / Cat4 and AR 5 / Cat5 storms / pulses, with a continuing duration that lasts for weeks (potentially several) rather than days.

Although atmospheric river storm systems can affect much of the American West Coast and beyond, California may be a highly affected area for two reasons: these systems frequently come ashore here, particularly in Central California, and the Sierra Nevada mountains and other ranges to the north and south cause them to drop much of their moisture here. As wet air is pushed up mountain slopes, it cools, and cannot hold as much moisture; the excess falls as rain or snow precipitation. (Certain conditions in the Central Valley can cause more rain to start dropping while the AR is crossing Valley itself.)

Atmospheric rivers and their effects continue to be identified in more remote parts of the Earth, for example:

> "When temperatures in Antarctica soared to 38 degrees Celsius above normal—around 70 Fahrenheit—in March, a teetering ice shelf the size of Los Angeles collapsed. Scientists don't know what role the extreme temperatures may have played in the event, but the heat rushed in through what's known as an atmospheric river, a long plume of moisture that transports warm air and water vapor from the tropics to other parts of the Earth." —CNN, 14 April 2022

The USGS ARkStorm Study Report

In 2011 the United States Geological Survey (USGS) released a report, "Overview of the ARkStorm Scenario," on a 2010 study project involving more than a hundred scientists and experts, trying to understand megastorm-scale AR-event patterns and their potential impacts on modern California (Porter *et al.*, 2011). The free report is available online (see below), and I recommend looking it over. Much of the information in this book is drawn from the USGS study report.

The USGS team joined real weather data from two strong 20th century storms to try to reconstruct a single storm similar to the real megastorm of 1861–62. The 2011 USGS ARkStorm digital <u>simulation</u>, of a huge and catastrophic storm, is thought to have described an apparently smaller megastorm than the actual 1861–62 event. Based on geological evidence, some earlier California megastorms in the past 1800 years have been even larger, particularly the one dated to AD 1605.

If what you read in this book sounds incredible, remember that the experts working on the ARkStorm project only accepted and reported a storm scenario that they believed to be plausible. Leading experts call more events like this inevitable.

Study team member Michael Dettinger and colleagues wrote in 2012:

> "The [ARkStorm] storm scenario … was designed to be larger overall than the largest 20th century events in both Northern and Southern California. Nonetheless, **it probably is**

not as large as the largest observed storm, that of the winter of 1862."

This quote from Dettinger *et al.* is worth noting:

> "In designing ARkStorm, care was taken to avoid creating an implausibly severe storm."

Referring to their modeled ARkStorm, Dettinger was quoted in a 2023 New York Times article: "1862 was far worse than this [the ARkStorm]."

Lucy Jones, Chief Scientist for USGS on this project, said this about the ARkStorm simulation:

> "The model is not an extremely extreme event."

In related work, Dettinger and colleagues also used weather models that looked at potentials for future megastorms. From a comment in a 2013 Scientific American article:

> "In six of the seven climate models, the average rain and snow delivered to California by future atmospheric rivers increases by an average of 10% by the year 2100." [Note: Later studies by other teams suggest 23% as a future average precipitation increase for Northern California, in some places reaching over 40%.]
> "All seven models project that the number of atmospheric rivers arriving at the California coast each year will rise as well, from a historical average of about nine to 11. And all seven climate models predict that **occasional atmospheric rivers will develop that are bigger than any of the historic megastorms.**"

Feel free to re-read that last sentence. "Any…megastorms," plural, appears to refer to the events of the past 1800 years of known geological history. These authors estimated that the A.D. 1605 megaflood was 50% bigger than <u>any</u> of the others (six to 12 are indicated, looking across regions) since A.D. 1–200, including the 1862 Great Flood.

Please note the use of the word "scenario" in the title of the ARkStorm study report. The ARkStorm model storm is not a past or future event, it is a simulation used to create a description, or scenario, of a realistic event, similar to (but smaller than) the real one in 1861–62, to help us understand how an event like this, which might happen in any winter, would behave. It is a one-off description of an event, which does not itself forecast the event (however, other approaches, which I'll discuss later, do offer some probability-based forecasts). Storms similar to that of the ARkStorm scenario have happened repeatedly in the past, and these also show up in most or all computer simulations of <u>future</u> weather.

The 2011 USGS study report is a fairly thorough first attempt to put hard numbers on the kinds of physical effects (like precipitation) that California would experience, and then to extrapolate from there to predict the kinds of immediate and lasting damage the state and its people would suffer. Finally, it attempts to put some dollar costs on the losses that people, institutions and society would endure, and the numbers are frankly staggering. Add in years of lost tax revenues and economic ripples, and you will appreciate that entities from renters and homeowners to businesses, financial institutions, the insurance industry, and even governments may take hits so severe that a wave of financial disruptions, including bankruptcies, is a reasonable possibility. I'll draw freely from this USGS report to paint a picture of what to expect. There are some important gaps in the 2011 report; I'll note them when those topics come up.

The 2011 USGS report, and an accompanying warning video released by USGS, were both wake-up calls as well as a first / new realistic set of planning tools for society. Some print and radio articles have brought some of this material forward to the public, but it has remained largely unknown and is sometimes misunderstood, or misrepresented. The spirit of this book is to promote understanding, awareness, planning and preparation from the ground up, beginning on the basic level for which we all can take personal responsibility.

* * *

Further reading

Porter, Keith, *et al.*, 2011. Overview of the ARkStorm scenario: U.S. Geological Survey Open-File Report 2010-1312, 183 p. and appendixes[http://pubs.usgs.gov/of/2010/1312/]. [= USGS 2011 ARkStorm study] [Note: USGS dates this publication from January 14, 2011; Porter cites it as from 2010.] https://web.archive.org/web/20131220004346/http://pubs.usgs.gov/of/2010/1312/of2010-1312_text.pdf [or] https://pubs.usgs.gov/of/2010/1312/of2010-1312_text.pdf

USGS ARkStorm warning video: https://www.youtube.com/watch?v=8P-N-HA9iS8

USGS: Good ARkStorm summary; includes video link: https://www.usgs.gov/programs/science-application-for-risk-reduction/science/arkstorm-scenario

Supplemental ARkStorm study overview and materials from Anne M. Wein, a USGS study coordinator: https://www.usgs.gov/centers/western-geographic-science-center/science/arkstorm

Dettinger, Michael D., F. Martin Ralph, Mimi Hughes, Tapash Das, Paul Neiman, Dale Cox, Gary Estes, David Reynolds, Robert Hartman, Daniel Cayan & Lucy Jones. Design and quantification of an extreme winter storm scenario for emergency preparedness and planning exercises in California. Natural Hazards volume 60, pages 1085–1111 (2012). https://link.springer.com/article/10.1007/s11069-011-9894-5#Fig14

ARkStorm: California's other 'Big One'. 2011. Science Daily. https://www.sciencedaily.com/releases/2011/01/110117142512.htm

Dettinger, Michael D., and B. Lynn Ingram. Megastorms Could Drown Massive Portions of California. Scientific American, January, 2013. [Online title; spelling error in link URL; formerly paywalled article at:] https://www.scientificamerican.com/article/megastorms-could-down-massive-portions-of-california/
     [Note: print version of article was titled "The Coming Megafloods"]

Pinter, Nicholas, *et al.* 2018. Flooding in the Sacramento Region. Pp. 236–245 IN Geology of Sacramento, California, United States of America; Cities of the World Series. A paper released as part of the XIII IAEG Congress and AEG Annual meeting held in San Francisco, 17–21 September 2018. https://aeg.memberclicks.net/assets/docs/Cities%20of%20the%20World%20-%20Sacramento%20-%202018.pdf

Ralph, F. M., *et al.* [9 authors]. 2017. Dropsonde Observations of Total Integrated Water Vapor Transport within North Pacific Atmospheric Rivers. J. Hydrometerorology 18 (September): 2577–2596. https://cw3e.ucsd.edu/wp-content/uploads/2017/07/Ralphetal2017-JHMDropsondes.pdf

* * *

Note on storm event terminology

In this book, the terms megastorm and AR-megastorm both refer specifically, and only, to the largest Pacific Atmospheric River event sequences making landfall along the West Coast of North America. That is how the term 'megastorm' is now commonly used. UCLA researchers including D. L. Swain *et al.* in 2018 called the biggest type of AR storm event a "severe storm sequence," but as of 2022 this research team is now using the term megastorm. The term 'ARkStorm' has been popularized as a <u>generic</u> name for megastorms in recent years, but strictly speaking that name refers only to one particular computer simulation (thus, a defined scenario) that was extensively studied for planning purposes by a United States Geological Survey (USGS) study team in 2010–2011. However, the media being the media, the very catchy term 'Arkstorm' is being used generically and will certainly be (mis-)used and heard as a popularized proper noun in much future reporting. Researchers including Huang and Swain (2022) have recently rebooted the ARkStorm study objectives in a project they call ARkStorm 2.0, with an initial focus on two new selected storm simulations called 'ARkHist' and 'ARkFuture.'

*The weathercasters' cute term 'Pineapple Express' trivializes a potentially powerful weather system that can sometimes have catastrophic consequences. (For me, it's like calling a firing squad a 'snappy military drill team.') DWR Climate Change Program Section Chief Elissa Lynn stated in 2020 that "A Pineapple Express, the name California **used to give these storms**, are [sic] just one type of Atmospheric River." In any case the fruity term only applied to the warmest AR events, those that tend to melt snowpack rather than bring snow. Some ARs are colder. I suggest avoiding the term except possibly when you're talking to the grandparents.

The term 'megaflood' refers to how a megastorm impacts low ground and those on it. The seat of government in Sacramento, several large populations, property and infrastructure worth trillions of dollars, and many news media, occupy low ground, so you may see more news reporting about a megaflood than about extensive severe storm effects elsewhere. Between the floodplains and snowbound mountain summits are many elevations where other potentially serious storm impacts will occur but may receive relatively less public attention. This book sees them.

Technical Note on atmospheric water measurement

[Technical notes are <u>not</u> 'required reading'… but if you want more insight into the new five-category scale for ranking AR storms, here is a brief, basic note on water content and flow rate, *i.e.*, the IVT concept, that partly defines the expected impact strength of an AR.]

The standard measure of IVT (Integrated Vapor Transport, a moisture-flow rate) is stated as (an atmospheric flow of) kilograms of water per meter per second, or kg/m^-1s^-1 (in spreadsheet format; otherwise 1kg/ms). 1 kg is 2.2 lbs. The meter (m) in this IVT unit, for example as used for West Coast weather forecasting, is a 1-meter (39.4") line running level and perpendicular to the long axis of the AR filament, so a line running roughly NW to SE across one meter of the AR. In terms of impacts, for landfalling ARs we can consider a 1 m straight line roughly parallel to, and typically along, the coastline. Since landfalling Pacific ARs move across the coastline onto land, an important IVT measurement is the number of kg of water vapor coming onshore across that 1-meter coastal line in one second, or, in a forecast, approaching that coastal line. If, hypothetically, that storm wind was blowing onshore at an unrealistic, <u>very</u> slow 1 meter per second (2.2 mph), the IVT measurement would also correspond to the amount of water in a 1 square meter column of air (like the air above a big Hula Hoop™) rising some miles above the coastline**. More realistically, for example with winds of 40–60 mph, in the <u>mildest</u> Cat5 AR, in the air crossing a 1-meter line drawn on the ground, 1.375 tons of water would be zipping overhead "between your outstretched elbows," roughly (on sustained average) every second; the minimum Cat5 IVT is 1250 kg of flowing atmospheric water crossing over a linear meter, per second. As now defined, there is no upper limit to the amount of atmospheric water flowing in an AR 5 storm.

**The quantification of precipitable water in a column of atmosphere uses an older measure called IWV, no longer preferred for measuring ARs: "Integrated water vapour (IWV) is the total amount of precipitable water in an atmospheric column between the Earth's surface and space." (—Makama & Kim, 2020). In fact, the square meter is the standard column cross-sectional area for expressing IWV. IWV is a mass quantity, not a flow rate. "Taking into account the density of liquid water [thank you, metric system!], the IWV expressed in kg/m^2 is equivalent to the Total Precipitable Water (TPW) expressed in millimeters of liquid water [which is to say, the depth on the ground, if it had all precipitated down in an instant]." (—OSCAR / Space). The relationship between IVT and IWV depends upon the velocity of the flowing air, as noted above.

Interesting fact: the average water content (like IWV) of the Earth's atmosphere has increased by about one pound (0.41 kg) per square meter column of air for each decade since 1988, according to Lawrence Livermore National Laboratory. More on this later.

3

The Talkin' Water Blues

How we imagine and describe storms and floods

> *"Extreme rainfall is a signature consequence of a warming climate, and <u>it is happening more frequently</u>. The deluge in South Florida is just the latest instance after <u>1-in-1000 year rains</u> struck over the past year in areas including Dallas, St. Louis, eastern Kentucky and Yellowstone."* —CNN, April 13, 2023

The way in which we think, talk and write about storms and floods affects our ability to understand them. Take a moment to consider the 'logic' in the reporting quoted above.

You will find it <u>very</u> helpful, while reading this book, to think of a so-called '100-year-storm / flood,' or 200-, 500-, or 1000-, as a <u>predicted volume of water falling as storm precipitation, and as a level of runoff water, and its flow / flood behavior</u>, rather than as an event that relates to a calendar. It's hard to make this mental adjustment, given the common terminology, but it's important, and you'll be glad you did. Pros do this but seldom explain the distinction. Also, the question of "which 100 (or 1000) years?" is crucial, suggesting that we may soon need to scrap the 'X00-year' terminology altogether. In this chapter I explain these points further, because it is <u>really</u> hard to read about weather, storms and flood, and understand clearly, until we straighten out a few wrinkles in our language and our thinking.

Flood terminology

One of the unfortunate things that makes it hard to talk clearly about storms, floods, risks and probabilities is the 'hundred-year' language. So, right now, let's try to forget the words 'year,' and any label that has the word 'hundred' or 'thousand' in it, for at least a few pages. That can be challenging [!] but I know this book will be much easier to read and understand if we unlearn our 100-year and 1000-year thinking. Really, _much_ easier. This chapter will explain why.

A storm is a weather system that drops some amount of water, as rain or snow, at certain places, with a certain rhythm or tempo, over a certain period of days. Related to that is the idea of the AR 1 (Cat1) to AR 5 (Cat5) scale for AR storms, introduced in Chapter 2, which describes an amount of atmospheric water, moving somewhere at a certain rate, and expected to last for a certain number of days; <u>it doesn't mention years at all</u>.

When that water hits the ground and begins to flow in streams, rivers, and channels, many things will determine what is happening, but ultimately, volumes of water will flow at certain rates; the level or stage of water in the river will be high or higher depending on both the storm and features of the river. That volume of water can be measured in gallons, acre-feet, or cubic miles. That flow rate past any point can be measured in units including cubic feet per second (cfs). These measurable facts <u>don't refer to years at all</u>.

When there is excessive water running off across the land, it can flow over the banks of rivers, over or through levees, and even over dams. As areas begin to flood, those areas can be measured in acres, or in square miles; depths and durations can also be measured. Predictions can be made about which areas are most flood prone, and maps of flood zones can be prepared. In fact, such maps are now common. But current maps are exclusively marked with time / probability estimates, rather than with an objective measure such as 'this zone will flood if 20 cubic miles of rain falls on the Sacramento River drainage during a 15-day period,' in part because rhythms and patterns of rainfall, and other conditions, are variable, and hard to pigeonhole. You could simulate and map a defined model '20 cu. mi. / 15 day' flood. You could define a hypothetical 'Cat4' flood (for example, the NOAA Weather Prediction Center uses a 1-to-4 category scale for ad hoc area maps of short-term excessive precipitation threats). You could call some <u>old</u> 1% AEP estimate (see below) a Level 1 storm or flood. Options for naming and scaling floods were and are available.

However, the 20th century USA settled on an approach centered on a potentially confusing concept requiring probability guesstimates built on various assumptions, using methods that had various limitations and potential weaknesses. Below, I'll start with the history and concepts, then with some of the problematic issues, and then, briefly, some consequences of those issues. By the end of the chapter you'll have some background context for the expert megastorm impact descriptions that follow, for what to expect, and for the value of individual preparedness.

How did we get here, and why?

Back in the day, U.S. Army Corps of Engineers manuals on "Standard Project Flood Determination" from 1952 and 1965, documenting federal procedures for the design of dams and other flood control structures, barely mention estimation of recurrence intervals or the probability of any event. Briefly, the process of defining an 'SPF' (standard project flood) or a design flood involved looking at some decades of 20th century precipitation and flow / flood data for an area, especially the numbers logged during periods of from six to 120 hours, <u>and then picking something that looked like a reasonable (or affordable) flood expectation to design for</u>. Officially, these manuals state:

> "[For a number of reasons] it is not considered feasible
> to assign specific frequency estimates to SPF determinations in
> general." [Please also see note at end of this chapter.]

The big push to prepare flood susceptibility and probability maps for the USA began with the National Flood Insurance Program (NFIP) authorized by Congress in 1968, and later a part of FEMA. Here's the briefest description of what happened. NFIP was designed to serve the interests of mortgage lenders, insurers, and developers, and arguably of home- and property-owners, by standardizing how financial risks to property, due to floods, would be defined and managed. Why? In parallel, the Army Corps of Engineers (USACE) sees one purpose of effective flood control infrastructure as being "to encourage wise **use** of the floodplain." (—Draft CVIFMS Plan, 2015). The U. S. Bureau of Reclamation, a dam builder, exists to <u>reclaim</u> 'wasted' arid and flood-prone lands for use and development. From one perspective, NFIP encouraged flood-risky development, as long as someone (the Federal Government) universally defined the risk (and assumed the cost of any errors).

To manage business risks, you need to estimate predicted losses per year, or per contract (<u>the risk to a 30-year mortgage is literally part of the NFIP flood zone definitions</u>). A legal framework was established to address that effort within a theoretical <u>100-year timeframe</u>. So various agencies and programs, like NFIP, FEMA, USACE, USGS, and everyone else focused on the question: what lands would the estimated 1% annual chance flood or so-called 'hundred-year-(risk-) flood' cover? That basic concept, also then scaled down to the risk over a 30-year mortgage span, was the basis for designing flood insurance policies and rates, and for identifying which borrowers would be required to purchase flood insurance.

This is where the 'X00-year storm' and 'X00-year flood' thinking took hold. It was a <u>financial risk</u> concept of weather, and not the only concept available, just a poor one for <u>general</u> use. Floods are the <u>only</u> natural disasters that are today principally defined by their estimated recurrence probabilities. I'll explain why this orientation is confusing, problematic and even dangerous.

So, what is confusing?

First, the '100-years' concept is more accurately described as follows:

- A once in 100 years [chance, or on average] event*;
- or better, a 'one chance in 100 years, on average' event*;
- or, more technically correct, an event* with an average annual probability of occurrence of 1/100, or 1%;
- and stated more professionally, an event* with an Annual Exceedance Probability (AEP) or Annual Chance of Exceedance (ACE) of 0.01, or 1%.

    [*Note that 'event' here refers to 'a thing that happens,' not to 'such and such a date and time.']

But many people have a very hard time grasping the idea that this probability-based concept does <u>not</u> mean that:

- Flood events will happen 100 years apart [nope!];
- or, that you will have one and only one flood in any, or every, 100-year period [nope!].

Other problems with this concept go deeper than such misunderstandings. Gamblers, who know what can happen whenever they throw a typical pair of fair dice ('boxcars,' or 12, comes up <u>on average</u> 1 time in 36 rolls), have a better sense of probability and uncertainty. And Congress tried to help financial gamblers hedge their bets by providing a systematic way of defining and limiting risk (by tasking professionals to use a standardized method to try to imagine the kinds of dice that centuries of weather systems would be rolling).

As an exercise, I recently started collecting headlines reporting '1000-year floods' in the USA and around the world. Frankly, this particular 'expert claim' is being made so often, even into 2023, I tabled the project after finding a few dozen stories from this decade. [Apparently I don't write and edit fast enough: after several in the USA in 2022, now more so-called '1000-year storms' in Florida (April, 2023), New England (July, 2023; breaking with tradition, the governor of New York called this one "the new normal"), and an "unimaginable" storm in the south Sierra, implied to be entirely off the scale (March, 2023).]

> "1-in-100-year floods happening so often, the term may change." —ABC News headline; see quote below

We, the public, have a growing sense that something is off-kilter in that whole concept. (The NWS meteorologist now being quoted as saying that today's [March 2023] actual storm weather in Kern County is "unimaginable" should raise multiple red flags.) Here's why.

A gambler knows the numbers and combinations on <u>any possible</u> pair of dice, and what odds to expect, <u>if</u> the actual dice are examined and found fair, particularly if they've been tested by being thrown hundreds or thousands of times. But who knows exactly how the weather behaves? And how many years, and which years, would make a fair 'test?' When NFIP and partner agencies rolled out flood risk estimates (calculating frequencies or return intervals for floods of different sizes) after 1968, they used what is called an 'observational approach,' relying upon small samples of observed weather records or streamflow data, usually from the middle part of the 20th century, to predict future weather patterns and to estimate probabilities for ranges of weather events. One official USGS flood-risk study I looked at (Chehalis River, WA, discussed below) initially used 30 years of data; FEMA has said that you can proceed with only 10 years of data (nine, in the design of our closest old state highway bridge here). Making predictions for 100 years or 1000 years of events based on 10 to 30 years of data is sketchy; some basic reasons are that small samples are too flimsy (not robust, possibly distorted) for making accurate predictions, and may even be unrepresentative if they did not capture a fair sample of the full range of actual weather variation (for more details see Chapter 20). There are also potential and known problems with methods for how such estimates are made from the data samples, but for starters, let's just consider sampling (and perhaps psychology).

So, **one assumption** in these probability estimates is that small samples of recent weather are adequately representative of longer spans of past, present and future weather… like if someone rolled some number of never-seen, hidden dice (maybe 3 dice, maybe 20-sided, maybe loaded, maybe with some repeating numbers…) three times, and you were told that the totals were 3, 7, and 6. Can you assign odds to a span of possible totals yet?

We know there was a wide-scale megastorm in 1861–62, and there is good evidence for another, earlier regional one in Northern California in 1805; working backward through lakebed deposits in the Sacramento Valley, even more megastorm events occurred here, averaging roughly every 100–120 (~200) years. <u>None</u> of these giant storms or anything like them—an entire category of known weather phenomena—are represented in any accepted weather data samples used for flood estimation.

Just now, in early March 2023, I saw an expert precipitation map of the USA showing vast areas where the recent (and still unfolding) 2022–2023 AR storm systems have delivered more precipitation than "anything on record." <u>The "record" only goes back to 1895</u>. Messaging is only the first problem here.

So, we know that important weather events are missing from the underlying basis of estimates now in official use. But, very oddly I think, I've never seen a formal, explicit acknowledgement by those making or using them—with one notable, retrospective exception (Jones, below), plus some hints—that the official, standardized flood estimation methods may be (or are) missing some important information, and are therefore unrepresentative (note that the USGS in 2011, and Huang and Swain in 2018–2022, using different approaches, put this 'heretical' conclusion between the lines in their study reports). The fact that such biases in the methods always lead to risk underestimates takes us toward the topic of psychology, including institutional outlooks, which is considered later in this book.

Lucy Jones, chief scientist for the USGS MHDP team that produced the ARkStorm report, later wrote, in 2018:

> "The standard method for estimating how bad a flood could be requires using recorded history. The length of that history—what the hydrologists call the "period of record" — rarely exceeds one hundred years in the United States, because the first stream gauge was invented only in the late 19th century. That means that old floods, such as those in 1861–62, aren't integrated into predictions, even when we know about them. Across the country, people build houses and businesses in floodplains based on insufficient data, creating greater risk with each new construction project."

The U.S. Army Corps of Engineers team, while perhaps not yet about to change their estimation approaches, hinted at an inkling of an aspect of essentially this problem in the 2015 Central Valley Hydrology Study:

> "The primary problem with this approach is the **scarcity of historic events that are truly representative of the type of storm that would be expected to stress the flood control system.**" [Note: 'Historic' here means 'within our data sample period.']

A second assumption of the standard storm and flood probability estimation methods has been the assumption of a stable climate (*i.e.*, stasis). While changing weather patterns are now accepted as fact by most government agencies, this follows decades of foot-dragging in which it seems that politics, technical complexity and perhaps the inertia of institutional traditions (this is speculation) may have played a role.

> "What is certain—given the global climate changes now underway and accelerating—is that **continuing to rely**

solely on historical data and the assumption of stasis as a basis for infrastructure-related decisions from now on would ignore empirical reality and the best science available to inform planning for the future." —Climate-Safe Infrastructure Working Group report to the California State Legislature, 2018 [Note: called 'Climate-Smart' in some state documents, avoiding an implication of anything 'unsafe.']

The problems arising from the assumption of an unchanging climate (or 'weather pattern,' if you prefer) are probably some of the easiest problems for people to understand. If the last hundred years is not like what the next hundred years will be like, then future estimates based only on past experiences are inaccurate, estimation becomes much more complex, and the 'hundred year' definitions of storm events become meaningless (and even more confusing). Consider these statements:

> "…imagine engineers designing infrastructure systems in a watershed in which **the historic 500-year flood is becoming more frequent.** … The first combination might meet those goals **if the historic 500-year flood occurred as frequently as once every century.** The second, more expensive than the first, would meet those goals **if the historic 500-year flood occurred as frequently as once a decade.** The engineers would then work with climate scientists to determine if there is any evidence that the historic 500-year flood could occur once a decade and, ideally, if there were any trends in climate indicators engineers could observe that would signal whether and when such storms are becoming more frequent in the future." —Climate-Safe Infrastructure Working Group report to the California State Legislature, 2018

> "What was once a 1-in-100 year event may now be a 1-in-20 year event where climate change velocities are high." —Kelsey Jensco, Montana State Climatologist, quoted in the Washington Post, 6 December 2022

Basically, those writers are referring to a volume (think 'bucket,' in very simplistic terms) of rain or floodwater; more technically, a volume of surface runoff floodwater represented in time and space by the parameters of a hydrograph, or, literally, a 'flow chart.' But the vocabulary is a problem. Trying to keep using the '100-year' labels for things is going to become even more confusing tomorrow than it is now. I predict that it will be abandoned; the question is when, and what naming system will replace it? Stay tuned. Even now, engineers and other experts are increasingly and awkwardly referring to the "<u>historic</u> 100-year flood" (that big bucket), meaning some old obsolete probability estimate (for that bucket) from decades ago, which might now actually be the '50-year flood' and which could become the '20-year flood' a few years from now (but really, still all exactly the same bucket). First Street Foundation (2023) has flagged a few U.S. counties in which they estimate that the stated FEMA 1% chance flood is now a 10-20% chance (once in five to ten years on average) event. I think you can probably see why this whole approach is becoming even more confusing (the word 'historic' is starting to get quite a workout… and: which history?).

According to reporting by ABC, the terminology issue is getting some attention from USGS.

> "Attempts to quantify a flooding event often involves the use of the term "a one in 100-year event." In terms of floods, it pertains to the flood flow rate that has a 1% chance of being equaled or exceeded in a given year, Robert Mason, extreme hydrologic events coordinator and Delaware River master for the U.S. Geological Survey, told ABC News.
>
> But this term is expected to change because it is only an estimate based on data, Mason said…" —Julia Jacobo, Daniel Manzo, and Ginger Zee, ABC News, August 5, 2021

A third assumption, not as obvious but very relevant to understanding megastorms, is the convenient assumption that all weather is the same, just in bigger and smaller versions, and that all storms can be represented by points on one single mathematical curve for all probability estimates. One might suggest that hurricanes and tornadoes should temper that simplistic assumption. It is possible that Pacific AR-megastorm conditions also differ categorically from more common weather conditions in most other years, and so cannot to be fit to, or lumped into, the same currently standard probability estimation curves. The coming centuries should clarify this. For now, just flag megastorm events as potentially likely to reflect estimation method errors.

Other issues exist in addition to those noted above. As an example of an overlooked subtlety in probability mapping: a flood zone with a 1% AEP may be describing an estimate for the outer <u>edge</u> of the zone (furthest from the stream), while paying only rough attention to flood depth. Here's another: across the USA, the data samples (including old data) used for estimates and maps not only have different starting years, but also different <u>ending</u> years (as climate changes), so the underpinnings of estimates and errors (uncertainties) are unequal from one map to another.

For a thorough, eye-opening discussion of several precipitation-related estimation issues, based on re-analysis using newer methods and data, I recommend "The 8th National Risk Assessment: The Precipitation Problem," released by the First Street Foundation (FSF) on June 26th, 2023. Maps of the USA show 20 counties in which the most recent federally estimated (collected in Atlas 14, by NOAA, 2013, and based largely on decades-old data) so-called '100-year' precipitation events are now expected by FSF to happen <u>every 5 to 10 years</u>; 21.3% of the U.S. population live in areas where the obsolete, benchmark '100-year storm' is expected to occur one or more times, on average, in a 25 year period (which will keep shortening in future). By their estimates, half the U.S. population is actually exposed to at least double the federally estimated flood risk. Many upland Northern California counties are shown by FSF to have now a roughly 10-fold increase in the recurrence of those extreme, benchmark storms. Numerous counties in California, the West, and elsewhere, are estimated to have 5 to 8 times more properties with flood risks than what are accounted for in FEMA's Special Flood Hazard Area (SFHA) maps. Consequences of risk underestimation for property owners are noted, as I also do below. Consequences for infrastructure, especially in view of pending federal investments in new infrastructure relying upon old flood maps and estimates, are also flagged in the FSF report. The release of NOAA's Atlas 15 is not expected until 2027.

Finally, with some thought, you'll see that a 2023 estimate for an actual 1-in-100-year storm (a moving target) must now involve a larger storm than what was previously imagined back in the 1970s; trends keep creeping upward toward the range of our basic concept of a megastorm. I recommend the FSF report highly to anyone wanting a deeper understanding of this situation. In tandem, the FSF FloodFactor product provides detailed online maps of <u>their estimate</u> of an actual 1% (or 'hundred-year') flood. Remember, all forecast estimation methods including the FSF methods must ultimately face the tests of time, as well as continuing adjustments for evolving climate trends.

Consequences

Many of the storm flow-frequency estimates (for magnitude and probability: how big, how often?) made in California during the 20th century dam-building era, the levee building eras, and the NFIP flood-zone mapping era have consistently proven to be underestimates. Not just inaccurate estimates, but too-small, too optimistic estimates. As one example, the USGS reviewed streamflow projections on the Chehalis River in Washington; the original estimate of what they called the "1-in-100 chance flood" was made in 1975 based on data from the preceding 30 years. When they reviewed this estimate 20 years later, with more data, they found that a '1-in-100' flood (estimated, again) actually would be 40% larger than what was predicted by the 1975 estimate. That's a big difference.

This issue began to surface in the mid-20th century, before much change in weather and climate patterns had emerged, which strongly suggests that sampling issues, methods, and perhaps outlooks (*e.g.*, in infrastructure planning guidelines) produced unreliable estimates (as noted above, these may have been after-the-fact estimates for federal dam projects). Now, as the decades roll on, and more data are added when each local flood-frequency estimate is recalculated, we can see that the original estimates are becoming more and more incorrect. Many readers will accept that weather patterns and climate trends have been changing, while some still resist this idea. But it's clear that the original '100-year-style' pronouncements either were too optimistic, for whatever reason, or have become obsolete, or both (I'm confident it's both). Again, if weather patterns are changing, then <u>there really is no such thing as a 100-year pattern</u> or a stable prediction at all. ['Normal' and 'average' are also very different concepts; both drought and flood are normal in the West.]

There are additional critiques of the US-standard flood mapping and estimation approaches, which I'll mention here only to alert you to problems with mapping accuracy (and insurance matters). For example, also missing from long-standard local flood risk estimates, particularly as they are mapped as 'probability zones' by FEMA, is another important element, strange as it might seem: local rainfall.

> "Today, the most recent Federal Emergency Management Agency (FEMA) flood hazard maps for Los Angeles County (Supplementary Fig. 1) show a very small '1% annual chance flood hazard' area with a population of only 23,169, or <0.3% of the population, where flood insurance is required under the National Flood Insurance Program. This exposure is reflective of fluvial and coastal flooding only, in line with FEMA directives for flood hazard mapping, so **pluvial flood hazards have not been addressed**." —Sanders *et al.*, 2022

Pluvial refers to <u>direct</u> rainfall effects, rather than 'fluvial' runoff from stream and river channels. Combinations of flat or low ground and insufficient storm drainage can cause flooding from rain even when river flooding is not an issue. Standard maps do not account for this risk contribution. If you think direct rainfall effects will always be minor, I'll borrow this megastorm prediction from the next chapter: maximum <u>daily</u> total precipitation would approach 27" in parts of Southern California and 11" in the Sierra; maximum sustained average hourly precipitation would be 1.6" (Sierra) to 2.0" (South). See also the Sanders *et al.*

analysis of Los Angeles vulnerabilities. As I edit this, on March 11, 2023, parts of California including coastal areas are reporting double-digit 24-hour rainfall (13.4" in Pacifica) from the AR 3 storm system that hit yesterday.

[Personal note: In 2011 I was caught in an intense pluvial flash flood while driving on a city street in Pittsburgh, PA. It was a genuinely alarming experience. About a week later, <u>in the same spot</u>, four people drowned in their cars when 'the same thing' happened again. Others were rescued by boats that floated over the submerged cars on nine feet of floodwater. The storm drains there were inadequate, due to design and/or maintenance issues. Later, I'll write about risk neglect.]

So, what is dangerous?

Systematic and methodological problems with flood risk estimation become public safety problems. A 2022 paper by Sanders *et al.* is a good first, general look at the related issues (although its benchmark event is limited to a traditional-concept '100-year flood') for the example of Los Angeles:

> "Flood risks in the United States have historically been underestimated, particularly with respect to human well-being and within low-wealth and marginalized communities." — Sanders *et al.*, 2022

> "We found that nearly 1 million people are living within areas [around Los Angeles] that could be threatened by a 100-year flood," said Brett Sanders, a professor of civil and environmental engineering. **That's roughly 30 times more people at risk than what the Federal Emergency Management Agency suggests.**" —Los Angeles Times, 31 October 2022

The FEMA website, and reporting in the Washington Post, indicate that some changes, including new maps, are underway. Details remain to be seen. Meanwhile, the First Street Foundation has funded development of an independent flood risk mapping application, using a new suite of methods developed independently, now online at www.riskfactor.com. Comparative examples (vs FEMA maps) are presented in the Washington Post article cited below. It is very interesting to use their FloodFactor product to see what their approach shows for the estimated 1% flood in 2023 (or 2038, or 2053) in any area. [This and other competing or emerging new estimation and mapping products have not yet 'stood the test of time,' as there has not yet been much time since their release. While the recent real-life comparisons with FEMA's estimates are encouraging with regard to improved predictions of flooding extent, I refer to them in this book only as an interesting and useable product providing an alternate (and arguably better) source of flood-map forecasting. Remember that, like other methods, these are <u>estimates</u>, at a given probability, used to produce flooding forecast maps.]

FEMA, for its part, had this to say to the Washington Post in December 2022, about FEMA's own maps:

> "FEMA stresses **the maps are not meant to be predictive** and that residents considering buying flood insurance should take into account other aspects of the overall risk to the property.
>
> **Maps do not forecast flooding. Maps only reflect past flooding conditions** and are a snapshot in time. **They do not represent all hazards and do not predict future conditions**," Michael Grimm, acting deputy associate administrator of FEMA's Federal Insurance and Mitigation Administration, told The Post [views that have that surely made an impression on the mortgage lending and insurance industry].

In fact, relying literally upon current, traditional or 'historic' flood zone probability estimates runs a distinct risk of misperceiving and mismanaging the actual risk. When you look at official flood zone maps for your area, you have permission to cross out the year-numbers or AEP % numbers, perhaps to indicate your sense of a greater risk than what the official methods, with all of their possible problems, limitations, and any deficiencies or omissions, have estimated. In 2021, FEMA/NFIP announced a policy shift (to recalculate risks and reset insurance premium rates) potentially more inclusive of this view; details are still emerging.

What are the problematic consequences of flood risk underestimation? People in mapped flood zones pay unrealistically low insurance premiums, with the difference in losses made up (so far) by the U.S. taxpayer. People who live outside of mapped flood zones, but who are actually at a 'higher-than-advertised' risk of being flooded, may be influenced by the maps to decline to purchase valuable (and also underpriced!) flood insurance, and thus suffer avoidable exposure to damage losses. This applies to public and private infrastructure vulnerabilities as well. Land-use planning will rely upon incomplete risk assessment. And hazard mitigation and disaster response and relief planning efforts may be underestimating the scope of future weather and flood events which are larger, more severe, and more frequent than what traditional methods have indicated. County 'Multi-Hazard Mitigation Plans' and other documents rely upon FEMA flood estimates.

If you live behind levees, there are additional sets of risk maps and additional types of vulnerabilities, but for now please be aware that (1) there are known issues in some areas with levee conditions, elevations, and subsidence, and (2) studies on levee adequacy emphasizing legal compliance (with federal and state standards directed toward avoiding overtopping events, but not other issues) may only consider the possibility of a so-called 'hundred-year storm' based on dusty old-school estimates from 50 years ago, while even the best study as of 2018 (which documented potential levee vulnerabilities) did not examine scenarios beyond what those same traditional methods would call a '200-year storm' (so, in other words, no clear megastorm scenarios have been evaluated yet). This book promotes awareness, even if the news might be unwelcome. I'll tackle levees and megastorms again later.

Also later, I'll quote a small sample of the very large numbers of politicians and officials who, for whatever reason, reassure their constituents after a disaster by calling it a once in 200-, or 500-, or 1000-years event. They, and the dutiful reporters who amplify their messaging, are big proponents of this calming 'psychological management' language, presented as technical perspective, while silencing mental alarms. This routine messaging is unhelpful (a carefully chosen word) if it is incorrect, and if it sells people on the implicit idea that they will not have to worry about such an event again in their lifetimes. Keep track also of how often you hear the word 'unprecedented,' implying that 'no-one could ever have conceived of such a thing…' See Chapter 18.

All forms of hazard-related miscommunication can be problematic. If authoritative information is not expressed carefully and clearly, then threats and risks can easily be misunderstood and misperceived. Even good reports sometimes take unfortunate verbal shortcuts. This is a topic I'll return to later.

Last but not least, a final, insidious problem

Since flood concepts are entangled with financial risk, consider this aspect of flood risk estimation. You will notice, if you look at the NFIP, its X% AEP flood zone definitions, its maps, and most related documents including hazard mitigation plans, that US flood impact and risk estimation—our national system—is focused on <u>risks to property and dollars</u>. (Pause here to think for just a moment.) And you will find this framework prevalent just about everywhere, from the costs detailed in the USGS ARkStorm study to (perhaps) your own county's Multi-Hazard Mitigation Plan and community development work in flood zones. It's not an exaggeration to say that the human costs of suffering and mortality have been absent from (or obscured in) our formal national flood risk estimation program and its calculations. Those are 'intangible' considerations that are generally kept somewhere in the portfolios of various agencies, while those same agencies' hazard mitigation initiatives may well remain within the framework of… property value protection. Noted: some early signs of change have appeared.

One aspect of this issue might be an assumption that at-risk property is typically immobile, whereas people are considered to be mobile and able (and even duty-bound, in the eyes of authorities) to move out of harm's way. While that distinction might seem to make sense, up to a point (if dislocation costs and other burdens are ignored), that simplification may be far from true in a large or abrupt disaster event (megastorm flooding, levee break, dam failure, especially with loss of roads, or… delayed evacuation orders), or among certain less-mobile populations and communities, when evacuations become complicated or difficult.

> "Research has shown that the majority of deaths during emergencies occur in people older than 65. … Also, in most cases when a large-scale evacuation is taking place, the senior population suffers the majority of the consequences." —USGS, 2011

A working estimate among emergency planners in California is that 20% of the affected Valley floodplains population would be unable to relocate without transportation assistance; this percentage will be higher in less affluent communities, which also tend to be at greater risk of flooding.

Furthermore, property is tangible and will have an appraised or market value, whereas life and experiences are intangibles that elude formal cost-benefit analysis. This might seem cynical; it's actually a clash arising from the distinctly different natures of the things being valued, and of the value systems themselves. (There are relevant concepts for quantifying financial liability in wrongful death, for example 'lifetime earnings potential,' which lowballs the value of the lives of low-income people and those outside the workforce.) You may also find echoes of this in the priorities and rationales adhered to in the USACE's mid-20th century engineering manuals for dam design and cost / benefit expenditure justification (which, however, did allow for special non-monetary considerations when mass casualties might be an issue).

For a good introduction to this paradigm, I cite below a March 2023 Los Angeles Times article:

> "WATSONVILLE, Calif.—Officials have known for decades that the Pajaro River levee that failed this weekend—flooding an entire migrant town and trapping scores of residents—was vulnerable but never prioritized repairs in part because they believed it did not make financial sense to protect

the low-income area, interviews and records show." [This is embedded in our public flood control investment structure and cost / benefit analyses; it is not an isolated incident.]

...

"...the [USACE] Corps initiated a study that resulted in a report demonstrating **"there would be some value for life safety, even though the project benefit-cost ratio was pretty close to unity for the costs to equal the benefits**," he said." —Los Angeles Times, March 12, 2023 [In case you wondered why this book advocates for taking personal responsibility...]

You may want some straight talk from levee owners and others on whether you and your community are deemed worthy of adequate protection.

[One might wonder whether this sort of accounting is applied elsewhere. Electric utilities are beginning to underground some existing overhead lines in response to reappraisal of (meaning, painful lessons from) ignition hazards and potential property damage and safety risks in forested or vegetated areas. While undergrounding does improve public safety, as advertised, would an attractive business strategy aim to rapidly minimize the companies' liability exposure to potential wildfire related property-loss costs? One could examine maps of planned undergrounding activity to infer whether implementation of the programs was giving priority to more affluent areas in threatened rural districts.]

The federal program of monetary awards to victims of the 9/11 attack, and their families, provides some perspective on 'value of life;' I provide some details in Chapter 11.

In future, as court rulings have recently placed liability for levee failures in California squarely on levee owners, any failure of any flood-control infrastructure leading to a mass-casualty event might be a turning point, to put human costs and property costs on an equal footing within risk assessments. Or, better yet, the point could turn sooner, and formally adopt life-value accounting without a mass-casualty event. Just imagine now: what would be the effect of preparing flood maps showing a 1% annual-chance-of-drowning zone? It would be macabre, but sobering, to re-label storms and floods as 'X00-casualty' events.

The 22-day AR sequence from December 26, 2022 in California was generally reported (in January 2023) as having caused a billion dollars of immediate damage... and 18 fatalities. It may take a while to wrap your mind around what exactly this structured messaging means, but if your life is more important to you than your bungalow, it's worth absorbing. It provides a valuable lens through which to see things.

To summarize

If you read about a 100-year level, or a 1000-year event, the writer is using an old, arguably obsolete, and often inaccurate (in my view) but universally popular calendar-based way of thinking to describe what is essentially that giant bucket of water, pouring onto the land with a certain rhythm, intensity and duration (and average recurrence interval, which remains a murky estimate), running down the rivers, and spreading across the floodplains. We can talk about the event and the various levels expected or measured: how big the bucket is, where and how fast it is pouring, how high the rivers are, and how broad the flooded areas are or will be. But unless you are an insurance analyst, or a gambler trying to decide how little to pay for a house on the floodplain, or a legislator being sold on the cumulative benefits of a massive flood control project, or a state or county planner trying to make prudent infrastructure lifecycle investment or reserve fund decisions, there is simply no fundamental need to try to stick years of risk forecasting onto your basic assessment of storm or flood <u>magnitude</u>. And there are ample reasons to have less than complete confidence in such traditional estimates. Unfortunately, in my view, for public officials, the handy 'hundred-year' or 'thousand-year' framing of natural hazard events provides an accepted way to conveniently soothe an alarmed public, but may well spread inaccurate misinformation, and misperceptions, and unfortunately tends to undermine our preparedness orientation at every level.

Next, I'll begin a series of chapters describing what a megastorm could do to present-day California.

* * *

Further reading

https://www.usgs.gov/mission-areas/water-resources/science/flood-frequency-reports

U.S. Army Corps of Engineers, 1 March 1965. Standard Project Flood Determination. https://www.publications.usace.army.mil/Portals/76/Publications/EngineerManuals/EM_1110-2-1411.pdf [If this link no longer works, a search will be necessary]

https://abcnews.go.com/US/100-year-floods-happening-term-change/story?id=78969683

https://pubs.usgs.gov/fs/FS-229-96/pdf/FS_229-96.pdf

The 100 Year Flood Is Not What You Think It Is (Maybe) - YouTube; https://www.youtube.com/watch?v=EACkiMRT0pc

Jones, Lucy. 2018. The Big Ones: How natural disasters have shaped us (and what we can do about them). Doubleday, New York. 242 pp.

Sanders, B.F., Schubert, J.E., Kahl, D.T. *et al.* Large and inequitable flood risks in Los Angeles, California. Nat Sustain (2022). https:// doi.org/10.1038/s41893-022-00977-7 [paywalled article]

Rust, Susanne. Before disastrous flood, officials knew Pajaro River levee could fail but took no action. Los Angeles Times, March 12, 2023. https://www.latimes. com/california/story/2023-03-12/authorities-knew-the-levee-could-fail

Overview of National Flood Insurance Program: https://en.wikipedia. org/wiki/National_Flood_Insurance_Program

Oakford, Samuel, John Muyskens, Sarah Cahlan and Joyce Sohyun Lee. America underwater. Extreme floods expose the flaws in FEMA's risk maps. Washington Post, 6 December 6, 2022. https://www.washingtonpost.com/ climate-environment/interactive/2022/fema-flood-risk-maps-failures/

Harris, Lee. Rise of the Climate Rating Agencies. The American Prospect, April 12, 2023. https://prospect.org/environment/2023-04-12-rise-climate-rating-agencies/

https://www.cnn.com/2023/04/12/weather/florida-flash-flood-fort-lauderdale/index.html

First Street Foundation, June 26th, 2023. The 8th National Risk Assessment: The Precipitation Problem. [The highlights page linked below includes a further link for downloading the complete report.] https://firststreet.org/research-lab/ published-research/article-highlights-from-the-precipitation-problem/

Note: new techniques, future weather

Computer technologies and models have improved greatly since 1968. It is now possible to go beyond the use of only 'observed weather records' and instead use 'simulation approaches' to create hundreds of years' worth of realistic 'simulated weather'—which can be produced for past, present, and predicted future climates—to estimate how often megastorms might arrive by chance and how big they might be. This approach can be, and has been, tested by simulating 20th century climate and comparing those simulated years of weather with historical records. We may be on the verge of formally comparing or even reconciling the dual observational and simulation approaches to obtain more realistic estimates of present and future storm and flood risks. This would be a major improvement.

Note: Cherry-picking weather data for 'preferred' water infrastructure design

Although I earlier mentioned some issues with standard 'modern' flood-frequency estimation, I saved this special topic for last. Here is a paragraph from the official USACE manual (EM 1110-2-1411, from 1965) of standard methods and practices used in the design and construction of many 20th-century American dams and water projects, predating the widespread adoption of 'X00-year' recurrence interval estimation. These earlier official methods used formal weather data analysis, followed by one or more rounds of 'picking and choosing' [!] to arrive at a comfortable storm (for lack of a better term) to design for. They reflect the mid-century federal institutional goals, values and outlook, cost/benefit driven, within congressional authorizations, discussed above and elsewhere in this book. Their fundamental impact on 20th-century flood control infrastructure design and capacity interferes with my sleep:

> "A general comparison of maximum storms of record in the region, supplemented [by] meteorological investigations, serve[s] as a basis in **selecting rainfall criteria to represent the most severe storm that is considered "reasonably characteristic" of a region. Certain storms of extraordinary severity may be eliminated as too unusual and extreme** to warrant adoption as the standard project storm." —USACE, 1965

4

Physical Impacts of California's Next Megastorm

An overview

"Look on my Works, ye Mighty, and despair!" —Percy Bysshe Shelly, Ozymandius

This chapter will cover general and some regional impacts of an ARkStorm-scale megastorm based on the USGS study scenario and other information. Mountains, foothills, valleys and floodplains, inland waterways, coastline and coastal plains, desert basins… different regions and terrains will experience storm effects differently.

Megastorm impacts as determined in the 2011 USGS ARkStorm simulation

The United States Geological Survey (USGS) Multi Hazard Demonstration Project (MHDP) carried out a first in-depth study on western AR-megastorms—considered to be recurring and inevitable events—and their impacts. In 2011, USGS MHDP released a 201-page report, *Overview of the ARkStorm Scenario* (Porter *et al.*, 2011; see citation above for free report available online), summarizing the results of this novel study on the possible 'shape' and likely impacts of a near-future megastorm in California. More than 100 experts, including scientists, infrastructure owners and operators, and industry and emergency professionals, worked through various details of a disaster scenario called the ARkStorm, a simulated (but reality-based) 23-day-long severe winter storm event set in the present time period, approaching the magnitude of the actual 43–45-day storm sequence and Great Flood that hit California and western North America in 1861–62. The agency felt so strongly about the hazards of a megastorm that they also made and released a three-minute video warning, posted online, https://www.youtube.com/watch?v=8P-

N-HA9iS8, to raise awareness and promote planning and preparation. Note that only the impacts to California were considered in this study.

[If I write here that something 'will' happen, I'm describing the assessments from the ARkStorm study (based on that particular storm scenario) or other studies, but remember, we also have many records of actual comparable (or more severe) events in 1861–62 to use as bedrock truth, plus a longer geological record. Some differences exist: the 2011 ARkStorm study predicts flooding up to 20' depth for large areas, including a 4000 square mile lake in the Central Valley, whereas in 1862 flood depths of 30' were reported at places in an estimated 6000 square mile Lake Sacramento.]

General Impacts

In the ARkStorm model, maximum wind speeds would reach or exceed 78 mph in coastal and inland areas, and up to 112 mph eastward around the Mojave Desert [note that smaller AR storms have produced wind speeds over 100 mph along the coast]. Although high winds and some coastal storm surge flooding will cause serious problems in a megastorm, based on the ARkStorm simulation, it is precipitation, mostly rainfall becoming runoff, that will have the greatest impact on populations, property and infrastructure. Here are a few details.

> **"These ARkStorm precipitation totals greatly exceed** the National Weather Service's [traditional estimates of 1% Annual Exceedance Probability (AEP) events]." In rough terms, this means 'way above the size of traditionally so-called 'once-in-one-hundred-years' events.' Note, again, that <u>levels</u> are being compared here, not probabilities or timetables.

> **"Total runoff from the central and southern Sierra Nevada is particularly enhanced (>10 times larger than their historical counterparts),** as are daily peak runoff rates in the Sierra Nevada and in Southern California mountains. More broadly, daily peak runoff rates are 3–5 times greater than historical in much of the coastal plains of Southern California and the Central Valley." —Dettinger *et al.*, 2012 ['Historical' here means 20th–21st century data.] Details from this study:

- Maximum 23-day storm / event precipitation amounts of 125", almost 10 and a half feet, in the Northern Sierra, 134", or 11 feet, in the Southern Sierra, and 91", or 7 and a half feet, in the mountains between Los Angeles and the Mojave Desert; around 18–19" of rain in Sacramento and Los Angeles.

- Maximum <u>daily</u> total precipitation would approach 27" in parts of Southern California and 11" in the Sierra; maximum sustained average hourly precipitation would be 1.6" (Sierra) to 2.0" (South).
- Storm runoff would reach more than 10 times greater* than what was experienced in post-1862 storms including the big AR storms of 1969 and 1986 (*in some areas including the High Sierra; perhaps less at lower elevations.)
- A more recent study indicated that in megastorms currently considered to be likely in the 21st century, statewide volumes of precipitation could be around 45 cubic miles, and possibly up to 60 cubic miles in some even larger storms, the latter causing runoff 200–400% greater than anything seen since 1862.

Remember, the 'ARkStorm' and later estimates are for <u>one</u> storm sequence, which in these simulations lasted about three to four weeks, not for the entire rainy season, which was very wet in 1862 and is also wet in many of the new computer weather simulations that 'randomly' produced occasional megastorm events. The 1862 megastorm runoff descriptions are incomplete, but in one estimate they reached flow levels at the Fair Oaks gage on the Lower American River that (at 317,700 cfs) were twice as great as anything ever seen since (based on a true high water mark for the 1862 peak flow near Folsom Prison). Above that gage, at Auburn, the North Fork of the American River was reported by the New York Times and others to have risen to a 35-foot level on January 9th, 1862. River rise then in the Lower American River at Sacramento is not stated in the articles I've found, but a bit of math applied to other facts in the NYT article, regarding levees, and events, *implies that the river might have risen at least 30 feet there* (but, grain of salt, note that the river channel in 1862 was different from today's channel, not to mention flood control that now exists at Folsom Lake). A bit south, the Mokelumne reached a 44' stage near Jackson (~4' above the height of the current SR 49 crossing there) and perhaps 60' or more elsewhere, per 1862 news reports.

It's accepted that one effect of warm atmospheric river storms can be to cause rapid melting of the snowpack, and careful research established that this effect occurred in the 1862 floods (see "Lake Sacramento" in Sources), in 1996–97 (NOAA report), and in other floods. Possible 'rain-on-snow' effects make flood levels less predictable and potentially greater than what rain alone would produce.

I'll briefly describe some impacts from the ARkStorm scenario below, and then in more detail in the coming chapters. Remember, the actual 1861–62 megastorm is believed to have been bigger than the ARkStorm simulation.

In the interior of California alone ("Inland Region" of mostly Central Valley and Delta areas: Butte, Colusa, Fresno, Glenn, Kern, Kings, Lassen, Madera, Merced, Modoc, Sacramento, San Joaquin, Shasta, Stanislaus, Sutter, Tehama, Tulare, Yolo, and Yuba counties, plus Contra Costa and Solano counties), after prolonged heavy to torrential rainfall in the ARkStorm Scenario, 4000 square miles will be underwater, to depths reaching 20', lasting for one or more months in places.

Using adjusted data from the 2000 census, USGS estimated in 2011 that 6.5 million people lived in that region; an estimated 1.538 million of those residents would be forced by residential flooding to relocate to higher ground (presumably including the Sierra Foothills), with more than 220,000 people needing emergency shelter. California's Office of Emergency Services, or Cal OES, in 2018 made a similar estimate for a smaller area of 10 Valley counties north of the Stanislaus River: 1.4 million people may need to evacuate, with 20% lacking transportation or mobility, and 25% (up to 350,000 people) likely needing emergency shelter from a big storm. Remember, population numbers are increasing. There will be additional significant impacts on populations in other parts of the state, and beyond. Large numbers of pets and livestock will also be at risk.

In some valley areas, roads including major highways, and rail lines and yards, docks, and even some airport runways could or will be underwater, complicating evacuations (if delayed) and restricting overland movement of goods, equipment, and personnel around the region. Highways across the Sierra (like many smaller roads in steep terrain) are likely to be closed by landslides in addition to experiencing heavy winter storm / snow conditions. Tens of thousands of landslides are predicted statewide, a reminder that mountain road networks, for example east of Highway 49, where landslides are already familiar, are vulnerable to closures; some communities could become isolated as happened in 1862. It follows that roads at moderate elevations through rolling or gently sloping terrain with good drainage and bridges may become critical transportation routes above the Valley. *Vulnerabilities of road bridges were noted but not evaluated in the 2011 USGS study.*

Flood control infrastructure will be subjected to the most extreme conditions it has ever faced. Dozens of urban and Delta levee breaks are predicted. USGS panelists had at least some reservations about how dams and spillways may react (this was six years before the Oroville Dam spillway failures in 2017). One large dam in Southern California, upstream of 1.2 million people, is considered at risk for problems under severe storm conditions, until repairs are carried out (funding to start repairs was recently approved and reconstruction is slated to run from 2025 into 2030). "It is entirely possible that **flood-control infrastructure and mitigation efforts could be overwhelmed** by the USGS ARkStorm scenario, and the report suggests ways forward to limit **the damage that is sure to result,**" said (then) FEMA Region IX Director Nancy Ward. [As of December 31, 2022, Ward has been the appointed Director of Cal OES.]

The electrical grid will be faced with storm conditions at least as severe as anything yet experienced here; unfortunately the USGS report was unable to provide much detail about overall grid reliability (except for likely failure due to <u>direct</u> effects of wind in some areas where winds will reach 100–125 mph; however, extended outages lasting weeks were projected to be widespread). Furthermore, electrical power generation will presumably be curtailed at some plants due to flooding. *The production, distribution and availability of hydrocarbon fuels was not discussed,* but known vulnerabilities exist at all levels for all of the liquified and gaseous hydrocarbon ('fossil') fuels. As one example, trucked fuels, including gasoline and propane, to local distributors and end-users would also face any general vehicle transport disruption issues. An outline of vulnerabilities in California's energy infrastructure is provided in a later chapter.

Damage to, or failure of, water systems, wastewater treatment, and telecommunications networks will also be substantial in some areas due primarily to flooding or to a lack of power or fuels. All of this means that even some people and communities who 'shelter in place' will not always be able to rely upon the customary services, nor will they find it easy to obtain supplies or equipment, nor easily travel to places where things they need will be readily available, which in any case may a long distance away for some.

The USGS report avoids predictions about loss of life or details of hardships people will experience. We are left to imagine the effects of floods, evacuations, life in emergency shelters, interrupted road networks, restricted travel and transportation, and shortages, as well as losses of power, clean water, functioning sewers, and telecommunications that some communities will experience. Instead, the report details some dollar costs and loss estimates that provide perspective. I think the report has gaps, and their estimates seem to be on the conservative side. The most commonly heard megastorm damage estimate in 2022 is one trillion dollars; however, as I've gone through the ARkStorm report and considered trends over the past 12 years, I've concluded that costs and losses could be considerably higher. Total, in my tabulations: between one and two trillion dollars, more than the traditional annual federal deficit in peacetime. In comparison, California expects to collect $231.9 billion in state taxes in 2022, and at the start of 2022 had a General Fund surplus [reserve] of $20.6 billion; news reports from early 2023 suggest a possible $22.5 billion budget deficit for this year. Potential megastorm losses far exceed ready cash.

Lost wealth and income will be a serious problem for many; so will lost tax revenues needed for reconstruction. Compare that to around $100 billion, very roughly, estimated for a major earthquake or a hurricane like Katrina. The challenge of rebooting California will be massive, as it was in 1862, physically, fiscally, organizationally, and psychologically.

Regional impacts

Although this book, like the 2011 USGS ARkStorm study, is focused on California, remember that the 1861–62 storm sequence affected a region several times larger than California. Imagine if you are a FEMA manager trying to respond to a disaster affecting much of the western United States (and neighboring countries). Imagine if you are someone waiting for organized emergency assistance of any kind.

If you are anywhere on or near the West Coast but outside of California, the basic story here is also relevant to you. The 1861–62 megastorm affected a vast area extending into Canada and Mexico, and inland. You can use maps, including floodplain maps, USGS topographic maps, Google Earth, etc. to look at the terrain and geography of the places I refer to, and make comparisons to the area where you live. The same approach may apply to reviewing your road network and other infrastructure, and your state agencies, plans and policies.

Specific impacts: mountain, foothill, and isolated communities

AR storms including megastorms are winter storm systems, most often making landfall from December through February, sometimes occurring earlier or later. Those people in residence at high elevations are likely to experience heavy snowpacks, or heavy rains, or both, depending on air temperatures of the incoming storms. It may be difficult to keep mountain roads open, even the major highways, if there is heavy continuing snow. Another problem is that mountain highways are vulnerable to landslides and erosion when liquid water is on the move, or in avalanches. The major highways over the Sierra are projected to be closed or restricted by these conditions. Availability of goods and services including emergency aid will be impacted by local and general transportation disruption. <u>In 1862, starvation was a risk or a problem for some isolated / mountain communities; food rationing was widespread.</u>

Communities at upper Foothills elevations (from about 1500' to about 3500') have terrain that can be as steep as in higher mountains. However, granite and other rock may be more weathered at lower elevations, leading to increased landslide and erosion risk, and roads and structures may be vulnerable. Also, river forks come together and drain increasingly large watersheds as one travels downslope and, in the Sierra, westward. At these elevations, under high precipitation and/or snowmelt conditions, stream banks and road crossings can be subjected to very high volumes of fast-moving water. Bridges, and roads running along the lower areas of valleys, can be at risk from stream flows several times greater than anything seen since 1862. As most of our surviving bridges were built in the 20th century (and apparently almost none that existed in 1862 survived; the exceptions were high suspension bridges), no standing bridge in California has been subjected to (a potential flow of) multiple times the peak runoff of our biggest 20th century storms. It is not hard to imagine some bridge failures in a megastorm (it is harder <u>not</u> to). Consequently, areas served by few roads and bridges may be at significant risk of prolonged isolation. The 1862 report of a native bridge 60 feet above the Mokelumne River being swept away in the flood does not seem so improbable, considering that the Great Flood was apparently larger than the ARkStorm simulation that generated the peak flow predictions above.

Communities in the gentler terrain of the lower Foothills of the Sierra and other ranges, from 100-plus feet above sea level (= ASL) to about 1000– 1500', may have an easier time of it. Lots of water will be flowing in familiar and unfamiliar channels, and many low-lying areas will become impassable or inaccessible (by land) due to standing water; infrastructure and services located in those low areas (for example, sewage pumping or treatment) could go offline. Other than that, the road network there may suffer the least interruption of almost any area, and most land above low places should fare well. Landslides are not as great a problem in gentler-sloping terrain, though erosion and loss of bridges and structures is possible. Debris being washed down from higher ground may start to accumulate as water loses velocity if not volume; debris is a major concern of state emergency planners.

The most significant aspect of the lower Foothills may be that (1) it is an obvious destination for displaced evacuees from the eastern Valley, and (2) it may retain the most functional road networks east of the Coast Range; if so it could become a primary corridor for the movement of goods, relief supplies, equipment, and personnel. If you spend enough time with maps and other tools, you can make corresponding predictions for other regions that are relevant to you, for example from the western Central Valley westward across the Coast Ranges.

The reason I treat that relocation / relief effort as an impact is that potential upland 'destination' counties, for example those like Amador, Calaveras and Tuolumne, each have resident populations much smaller than the potential number of 'lowland' displaced persons that may seek (or be directed to seek) to shelter there. The USGS 2011 estimate is that around 1.5 million people would flee their homes in the Central Valley for higher ground, including hundreds of thousands of refugees that would need emergency shelter and services. Those east of the Sacramento and San Joaquin Rivers would presumably relocate further eastward to several different Foothills counties (especially if the High Sierra is impassable), in numbers that could dwarf the established Foothills communities' populations. Those kinds of possible numbers are overwhelming in all regards, starting with traffic and parking and progressing from there.

This alone is a strong argument for all of us who live on high ground to be making preparations to shelter in place, if we / you are not flooded and are otherwise able. Isolated communities that don't precisely fit into the categories above will experience many of the same issues, depending upon terrain. The northwest of California, from around the 'wine country' northwest of San Pablo Bay into Oregon, is a prime example of this type of settlement. It's also a region of fractured rock, paralleling the San Andreas Fault, and it's at a higher risk of landslides. Isolation in place is a probable outcome for people trying to ride out a megastorm in such areas with extensive steep terrain, or with road networks that follow river valleys.

The Valley and the Delta

California's Central Valley will be one of the hardest-hit regions, especially in the large subregion where the Sacramento and San Joaquin Rivers approach or reach single-digit elevations, flow into the complex waterways of the Delta estuary, and comingle. (It's in areas like the Valley floodplain that the term 'megaflood' is most likely to be used; when you hear it, it's worth pointing out that a megastorm is actually a more comprehensive catastrophe also impacting higher ground.) Large areas of several counties there, within about 50 miles of Sacramento, are close to, or at (or below), sea level, and these areas are projected to flood at depths from 10' to 20' under ARkStorm scenario conditions (levees are a wild card in these areas). Much more of the Valley could or will flood to lesser depths. Low-lying areas around Manteca, for one example, are 55 crow-fly miles from the narrows of the Carquinez Strait, through which they must drain. Floodwaters will remain in place for months.

Both urban areas of the Valley and agricultural areas, especially the islands of the Delta, are protected from floodwaters by many thousands of miles of levees. Experts on the USGS study team predicted that several levees will fail under these conditions. The Delta area has received particular attention, for example in sub-reports of the California Fourth Climate Change Assessment (2018).

The Coast, the Bays and the Delta

Even 'ordinary' strong-wind storms can push ocean water against the coast and into the Bay. Winds from a megastorm will potentially exceed 'ordinary' effects, and coastal storm surge is predicted to be a problem, especially in Southern California (per USGS). I think there is some uncertainty about what to expect at the coast; studies of storm surge here are continuing. In the references provided below are more recent studies (which used various methods); they tend to be complex in all regards but are very interesting to tease apart; they are also quite valuable but even

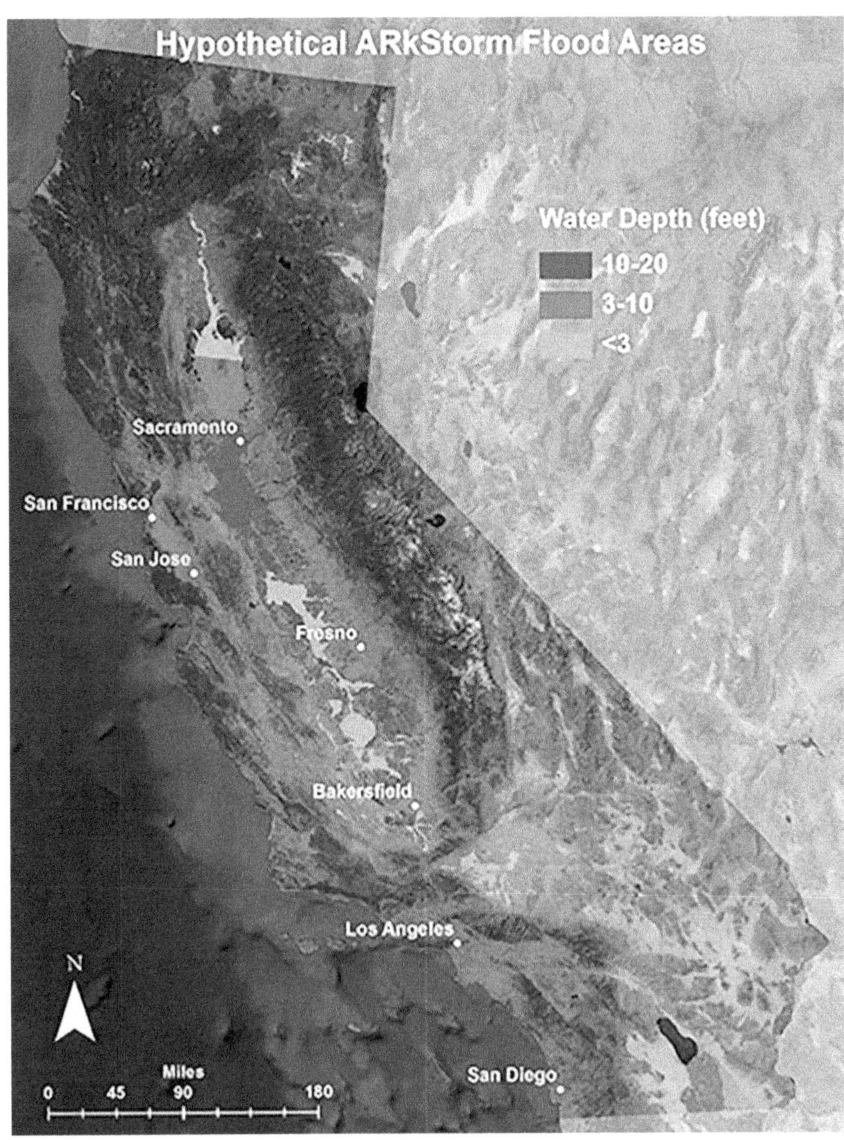

The flood depth and extent map shown here was not included in the ARkStorm Scenario Overview, but was prepared from those data by Jeff Peters, and appears here courtesy of Jeff Peters and Anne Wein, U.S. Geological Survey. 10-20' flood depth estimate extends from Yuba City through Sacramento to Modesto. The related graphic on page 10 of the online ARkStorm 'Overview' also provides coarse flood duration estimates. Brightness and contrast have been adjusted here. Original color image source is linked below.

those studies have limitations. Here I'll just say that records of 'typical' high storm tide studies show that they can incorporate <u>coastal</u> 'surge' of from several inches to around two feet at different points along the West Coast. When all elements (surge, tides, waves, etc.) are considered, seawater in a big storm can at times reach up to 20' above sea level (see Barnard references below). One estimate of an <u>inland</u> surge of six to ten feet (combining all influences including runoff) at the lower reaches of the Napa River under somewhat strong storm conditions is noted below.

The bays and waterways from the Golden Gate (at San Francisco) throughout the Delta are arguably the most complex and dynamic system for hydrological analysis anywhere in California. Tidal effects extend far into the Central Valley. To make a long story short, here are some bullet point takeaways:

- Sea Level Rise (SLR)
  - Any storm / megastorm, tidal and wave effects will combine with any SLR
  - By A.D. 2100, mean sea level is expected to rise by 1' to 3.4' (CA DWR)
  - Sea level has recently been rising at a measured rate of (3.1-) 3.7 mm or ~0.14"/year, meaning *ca.* 1" every 7 years, and SLR is expected to accelerate to more than double that rate within the next 30 years (NOAA, 2022)
  - Future ice sheet behavior adds uncertainty
  - Mean sea level has risen 8" since the California Gold Rush; sea level has risen another inch and a half since 2011
  - Sacramento and Stockton experience tidal effects

- Coastline Storm Surge
  - There are varied estimates obtained by different methods and studies
  - 36 years of records on <u>only ARs 'at their peaks'</u> (at landfall) indicated surge maxima of
    - 2–6" in Southern California
    - 20–28" in Northern Washington
  - A different study of <u>all</u> records at the Golden Gate found peak surge <u>including runoff flow</u> of 24" on 3 recent occasions
  - We have no records from prolonged megastorm-scale conditions
  - USGS estimates from after the ARkStorm study project 0.1–0.7 m of atmospheric storm surge plus 0–0.2 m of fluvial water level increase on the coast: up to 3' total

- Effects on waterways from the Golden Gate to the Central Valley
  - In the 1862 flood, steamers traveled between San Francisco and

Sacramento (and for miles away from the rivers, across the flooded Valley)
- ° U.S. Coast Guard may restrict ship travel during high flows
- ° The bed of the Sacramento River in Old Town Sacramento is at about sea level
- ° One CA DWR 2018 study (by Maendly) predicts that in a [so-called] '200-year-flood in 2067,' compared to a '10-year flood' today, water levels would increase at the <u>western edge</u> of the Delta by about an additional 1–2' [Note that the so-called 200-year flood magnitude of 2067 (using traditional estimation plus rough extrapolation) may fall short of the magnitude range of past and future megastorms.]
  - ▪ Stage increases at Sacramento would be about +5' to +6' in the same comparison
  - ▪ Stage increases at Stockton would be about +8' to +9' in that comparison
  - ▪ Some levees as they currently exist would be overtopped by such a flood
- ° The level of the San Francisco Bay might increase at least 24" (already observed)
- ° Graphical indications from USGS (2011) of a 3–10' megastorm water level increase in the Bay-Delta system are too vague

One excellent (but sub-megastorm scale, and using only mild tidal influences) study by Maendly (2018) looks at multiple waterway scenarios in present and late 20th century climate, and provides a wealth of detail. Here is one brief example from my own synopsis of that report; we can use the flood "B" below as a stand-in for what a smaller megastorm might do.

Comparing only what was called a present-day '10-year-flood'—call that (A)—and (B) a late 20th century '200-year-flood' [these are actually data from (for A) the 1986 flood scaled down to 60% and (for B) the 1997 flood scaled up to 140% plus SLR, and approaching possible megastorm magnitude], Maendly calculated estimated water level increases (meaning B <u>above</u> A) of 2–3' at Collinsville (at the mouth of the Sacramento River) to about 6+' at the confluence of the American River. Similarly, on the San Joaquin River, estimated (B) water level increases <u>above</u> (A) were about 3' at the mouth of the river, rising to a maximum increase of about 11' at French Camp Slough, and staying at an average of about plus 10' up beyond Paradise Cut, 110,000' upriver. Finally, the graphs of water elevation profiles along these two rivers also show a line indicating the heights of levees along the rivers, with specific examples of existing levee heights that would be <u>below</u> the level of **any** ~200-year floodwaters (of flood B in particular; figures 37 and 38 if you want to look at the online Maendly 2018 report and see for yourself). [Note: My quibbles with this valuable study are about some approaches: 'climate adjusted traditional observational methods' were used for estimating these so-called '10-year' and '200-year' floods; the '200-year' flow levels may be much less than what a mid-sized megastorm could produce more often than the '200-year' guesstimate; some of the tidal, surge, and sea level rise effects and interactions may have been treated very conservatively (which makes for restrained speculation but unfortunately could cause hazard mitigation and planning to fall short of many bad-to-worst-case scenarios).]

Coast Ranges and valleys

Ranges like the Santa Cruz Mountains are not as high as the Sierra, and rainfall may tend to be less, though that is not an unbreakable rule (extreme rainfall has been experienced in many storm events in the Coast Range in recent decades, most recently, for example, 36" in 21 days ending in January 2023, in Ben Lomond; on occasion more than 10" has fallen in that area in a 24-hour period). Much of what happens in the hills of the Coast Ranges will depend on terrain; the area is prone to landslides, and valleys will be carrying a lot of water, affecting adjacent roads and infrastructure.

In the larger, lower elevation coastal valleys, a lot of water will be moving, either toward the San Francisco Bay or directly to the ocean. Substantial flooding around the valleys near rivers of the Coast Ranges is expected to occur.

Southern California

Here are some things to remember:
- Dettinger *et al.* in 2012 predicted that the ARkStorm would bring truly intense rainfall to Southern California (see numbers above; more recent data below).
- That also happened in 1861–62, and caused widespread flooding and destruction, both west and east of the mountains.
- 6.4" of rain on average across the L. A. Basin adds 1 cubic mile of water to the system.

- The large rivers in this area have extensive floodplains, especially the Los Angeles River (maps are online). The estimated '1%-annual-chance' (so-called '100-year') floodplain would, I think, provide a minimum estimate of flooding; detailed maps in USGS 2011 are limited, but their coarse-scale map suggests megastorm flooding there out to the so-called '500-year zone' boundaries, at least briefly.
- If you want to do more than just read about this, do some map research and find out how many emergency services facilities and critical infrastructure sites are located in the SoCal floodplains. You might start with a look at the petroleum terminal facilities in Long Beach. Environmental hazards arising from storm and flood conditions have been noted elsewhere but are beyond the scope of the present book.
- USGS considers much of the coastline to be at risk from inundation during a megastorm.
- The highest megastorm winds in the state are expected to hit east of the 'southern' mountains. Winds at the coast are also often very strong in AR storms.

It's worthwhile to learn more about historical storms and floods in Southern California, and this should include events of the 1930s. Following the major flood of 1934, and then "a severe dry spell," better known as the American Dust Bowl era,

> "The flood of March 1938 inundated parts of Los Angeles, Orange and Riverside counties with water due to storms that pounded the area from Sunday Feb. 27 to Friday March 4. The storms began with light rain, hardly anything remarkable during the height of California's wet season. The 1938 showers were likely welcomed after a string of dry years, but the rainfall intensified the next day." —KNBC, February 28, 2017

To give an idea of the amounts of rainfall that can cause damaging floods in Southern California, here are some five-day rainfall totals from the 1938 storms:

> Los Angeles (USC): 11.06"
> Burbank Fire Department: 12.77"
> Pasadena: 14.81"
> Pomona Fairplex: 10.25"
> Santa Ana Fire Station: 7.73"
> Oxnard: 7.55"
> In the 'headwaters' mountains surrounding Los Angeles: 32"

The 5.88" of rain in downtown Los Angeles on March 2 was extreme, but so were the five-day totals, for example in the mountains (32"!). To give you an idea of the severe flooding impacts, more than 100 people died, and about 5,600 homes were destroyed, as were bridges in Downtown Riverside and Universal City. The experience led to acceleration of the complete concrete canalization of the Los Angeles River and its tributaries.

A year later, Southern California experienced the only hurricane or tropical storm to hit the U.S. West Coast in the 20th century. Some quotes from a Wikipedia article: "The tropical storm made landfall near San Pedro, California, early on September 25 [1939], with winds of severe gale strength." Weather records are more detailed than in 1862:

"The storm dropped heavy rain in California, with 5.66 inches (144 mm) falling in Los Angeles (5.24 inches or 133 millimetres [sic] in 24 hours) and 11.60 inches (295 mm) recorded at Mount Wilson, both September records. Over three hours, one thunderstorm dropped nearly 7 inches (180 mm) of rain on Indio. 9.65 inches (245 mm) fell on Raywood Flat, and 1.51 inches (38 mm) on Palm Springs. 4.83 inches (123 mm) fell on Pasadena, a September record at the time. At the Citrus Belt near Anaheim, at least 4.63 inches (118 mm) of rain fell. The 11.60 inches (295 mm) at Mount Wilson is one of California's highest rainfall amounts from a tropical cyclone, although at least one system has a higher point maximum. The rains caused a flood 2 to 4 feet (0.6 to 1.2 m) deep in the Coachella Valley with heavy rain immediately preceding the tropical storm dropping 6.45 inches (164 mm) the day before the storm hit. The Los Angeles River, which was usually low during September, became a raging torrent…

"Many low-lying areas were flooded. The Hamilton Bowl overflowed, flooding the Signal Hill area. Along the shore from Malibu to Huntington Beach houses were flooded. Throughout the area, thousands of people were stranded in their homes. Streets in Los Angeles proper were covered with water, flooding buildings and stalling cars. Flooding in Inglewood and Los Angeles reached a depth of 2 to 3 feet (0.61 to 0.91 m). Construction on a flood control project in the Los Angeles River's channel by the Army Corps of Engineers was stopped by the flooding. Windows throughout Long Beach were smashed by the wind. At Belmont Shore, waves undermined ten homes before washing them away. Debris was scattered throughout the coast. Agriculture was disrupted. Crop damage in the Coachella Valley reached 75%."

Flood risks have recently been reassessed in detail for the Los Angeles region. Reporting on a new study led by Dr. Brett Sanders at U. C. Irvine, the Los Angeles Times wrote on October 31, 2022, that

> "… **a 100-year flood** could rapidly overwhelm the area's principal waterways—the Los Angeles River, the Dominguez Channel, Compton Creek and the San Gabriel River—as well as storm drainage systems that were originally built seven decades ago to make the region habitable, researchers say… If the study's worst-case projections come true, many low-lying impoverished communities in the vicinity of the region's aging system of dams, debris basins, storm drains, levees, and sculpted river channels—and **outside of federally designated inundation zones**—could be under six feet of water… More than 10,000 buildings in the city [of Long Beach] could be hit by flood heights greater than six feet." [Note: A so-called '100-year flood,' however estimated, is by far not the worst storm threat this or any area could plausibly face.]

* * *

These have been general descriptions of impacts, with some indications of differences between regions. For now, just as USGS did, I'll leave the human dimension of these impacts to your imagination (until a later chapter). I'll take up some of these topics in more detail in the following chapters.

* * *

Further reading

Maendly, Romain. (California Department of Water Resources). 2018. Development of Stage-Frequency Curves in the Sacramento-San Joaquin Delta for Climate Change and Sea Level Rise. California's Fourth Climate Change Assessment. Publication number: CCCA4-EXT-2018-011. https://www.energy. ca.gov/sites/default/files/2019-12/Water_CCCA4-EXT-2018-011_ada.pdf

Piecuch, Christopher G., Sloan Coats, Sönke Dangendorf, Felix W. Landerer, J. T. Reager, Philip R. Thompson, & Thomas Wahl. 2022. High-Tide Floods and Storm Surges During Atmospheric Rivers on the US West Coast. Geophysical Research Letters 49(2). https://agupubs.onlinelibrary.wiley.com/doi/10.1029/2021GL096820

Barnard, P. 2016. Sea Level Rise, Storms, Waves, and Climate Change http://climate.calcommons.org/aux/2016OceanClimateSummit/ Web%20Update/Presentations/2_1_Barnard.pdf

Herdman, L. M., Erikson, L. H., and Barnard, P. L. 2018. Storm surge propagation and flooding in small tidal rivers during events of mixed coastal and fluvial influence. Journal of Marine Science and Engineering pp. 1–26. https://pubs.er.usgs.gov/publication/70201673

Sahagún, Louis, & Sean Greene. [Study says L.A. flood risk is far greater than expected] - Los Angeles Times October 31, 2022. https://www.latimes.com/environment/ story/2022-10-31/study-says-l-a-flood-risk-is-far-greater-than-anticipated

Sanders, B.F., Schubert, J.E., Kahl, D.T. *et al.* Large and inequitable flood risks in Los Angeles, California. Nat Sustain (2022). https:// doi.org/10.1038/s41893-022-00977-7 [paywalled article]

Lloyd, Jonathan, and David Biggar. In March 1938, the Catastrophic LA River Flood Devastated Los Angeles. KCRA, February 28, 2017, updated on March 4, 2021. https://www.nbclosangeles.com/weather-news/disaster-storm-1938-los-angeles-santa-ana-la-river-flood-california/31771/

Taylor, W. Leonard, and Robert W. Taylor. The Great California Flood of 1862. Report to the Fortnightly Club, Redlands, California. http://www.redlandsfortnightly.org/papers/Taylor06.htm

For impact assessments including maps of highways running through Central Valley basins with flooding frequencies estimated by traditional methods for 2015 and 2060: CVIFMS draft plan 2015 (see in particular Attachment E Figures 1, 7 & 8): https://www.spk.usace.army.mil/Portals/12/documents/civil_works/ CVIFMS/CVIFMS_Draft_Watershed_Plan_Public_Release_DEC2015.pdf

Supplemental ARkStorm study overview and materials from Anne M. Wein, a study coordinator: https://www.usgs.gov/centers/ western-geographic-science-center/science/arkstorm

NOAA. 2022 Sea Level Rise Technical Report: https://oceanservice. noaa.gov/hazards/sealevelrise/sealevelrise-tech-report.html

5

Infrastructure Impacts of California's Next Megastorm

Loss of capabilities and services

"For Want of a Nail…" —*13ᵗʰ century (or older) proverb*

What is 'Lifeline Infrastructure?'

The overview in the preceding chapter includes megastorm weather impacts (precipitation, wind) on the environment (runoff, flood), on communities, and, briefly, on 'lifelines.' The USGS ARkStorm study looked at several infrastructure lifelines. Lifelines are an important concept in modern society, and a critical part of it, and they will receive much more attention in the coming chapters of this book. First, here is a brief introduction, in five important paragraphs, to our lifelines <u>and their interdependencies</u>. The complicated ways in which many things we depend upon also depend upon each other are increasingly being appreciated by emergency managers, and we—you and I—also need to understand how interconnected our support systems are, and how any weak links can cause multiple systems to begin to unravel. The following introduction is provided by the 2018 Cal OES State Hazard Mitigation Plan, Annex 3:

> "A functioning society requires basic essentials (such as water, electricity, etc.) that are delivered through systems often referred to as lifeline infrastructure. California has vast networks of vital lifeline infrastructure upon which normal daily human activities depend.
>
> A lifeline is defined here as any spatially continuous engineered system that delivers essential services. The main categories of lifeline infrastructure systems can include transportation, communication, power, gas, water, and

wastewater ... Other services and facilities interact with lifelines, such as; responders (*e.g.*, police, fire, ambulance), distribution services (*e.g.*, food), collection services (*e.g.*, solid waste), and emergency operations centers used to support disaster response.

These systems are often interdependent so that a service interruption in one may lead to failure of another. They are also interdependent with service sites and facilities such as city halls, schools, hospitals, and parks. While separate service sites are important, this discussion will focus on lifeline systems and the special considerations they require due to their system structure."

...

"Lifelines must be seen as systems where the failure of a single component has the potential to affect the whole system, well beyond the failed single component"

"Similarly, restoration of each lifeline following a disaster is largely interdependent with restoration of all other lifeline services. Communication systems and transportation networks are needed by repair crews to restore services. Those same lifelines often require electricity or other lifelines to operate. **The interdependence of lifelines is often not fully realized until a cascading failure has occurred.**"

California's Fourth Climate Change Assessment authors (2018) described that understanding in a more proactive way:

"A study prepared for the Fourth Assessment demonstrates that managers also need maps of interconnected lifeline systems, particularly in metropolitan areas (Moser & Finzi-Hart, 2018). These integrated maps can help practitioners be **more aware of the importance of cascading events** and geographically-connected impacts (teleconnections), as well as effective efforts to prevent or otherwise mitigate them. This study highlights that **some interconnections may be beyond the traditional jurisdiction scope of local emergency managers and may occur far outside their territory.** Emergency managers and other planners need the tools and knowledge to assess, internalize, and capitalize on the understanding of how electricity infrastructure, economic sectors, and other systems are interconnected. This information must be used not only by emergency managers, but also by control room operators for those who oversee the state's critical infrastructure systems

... This is vital because **the full spectrum of emergency management must start with the emergency prevention activities taken for key critical infrastructures.**
Further research to develop and test methods for more inclusive risk and vulnerability assessments is needed."

Here is an example of systems failure cascades from Radke *et al.*, 2018, within the larger CA4_CCA report (see Sources), specific to the Transportation Fuels sector (TFS) 'lifeline' in CA, which, if it failed, would soon prevent vehicles from moving and transporting goods and materials... including fuels:

"Not knowing the vulnerability of interconnected assets, on which pipeline managers, for example, are dependent, increases uncertainty and is a very real threat to the resilience of the TFS pipeline system. For example, **if electricity is interrupted, the pipeline pumps fail to operate, fuel is not transported, the intermediate transshipment nodes fail, and that section of the TFS is broken.**"

...with repercussions far beyond the pipeline and its fuels. Failure of natural gas pipelines would also have large cascading impacts, beginning with reduced electrical energy production. Again, from Radke *et al.*:

"...it is beyond the scope of this study to model flooding and wildfire impacts on sectors that are interconnected with the TFS and critical to its performance and operations. **Interconnected sectors are those on which the process of producing, transporting, refining, and distributing the transportation fuels depends. They include the electrical power, water, data- and telecommunication, process inputs, and waste removal sectors needed by the TFS to sustain operations.** More details of the links between the TFS and these sectors are discussed [elsewhere]."

The vulnerabilities of the energy sector in California have been studied in considerable detail, and I'll return to that shortly. But here I'd like to highlight examples of a very common lifeline infrastructure interdependency that leads to a common cascade of lifeline failures. Electrical pumps that remove floodwater often fail when most needed, either due to electrical grid failures, or—astonishingly enough—due to flooding. Flooding then disrupts other infrastructure lifelines, including the road network. Pumps failed in New Orleans in 2005, in British Columbia and in downtown Sacramento in October-November 2021, and in the

Natomas area of Sacramento in 2023 (for a few examples). Remarkably, of the seven pumping stations protecting the Natomas community behind its levees, only one had a backup electrical generator. The losses from damages to a few private homes there could probably be comparable to the cost of having provided each pumping station with a backup generator. They can even be rented! Some instances of risk neglect—discussed later in this book—challenge our notion of living in a rationally managed society. On the bright side, we are free to exercise personal responsibility.

Coming up next: assessments of some of California's infrastructure lifelines, beginning with California's transportation infrastructure—roads, highways, and their structural elements, rails, airfields and ports—things that may be more familiar to most readers. I'll start with a summary of expected megastorm and flood impacts to those lifeline infrastructure systems. Then, in following chapters, I'll provide a look at energy sector vulnerabilities, water systems, and communications infrastructure. Remember, a vulnerability in one lifeline system would often affect other systems.

* * *

Further reading

2018 California State Hazard Mitigation Plan (SHMP) [1088 pages]: https://www.caloes.ca.gov/wp-content/uploads/002-2018-SHMP_FINAL_ENTIRE-PLAN.pdf

CA CSIWG Report (2018):
Paying it Forward: The Path Toward Climate-Safe Infrastructure in California: A Report of the Climate-Safe Infrastructure Working Group to the California State Legislature and the Strategic Growth Council. https://files.resources.ca.gov/docs/climate/ab2800/AB2800_Climate-SafeInfrastructure_FinalWithAppendices.pdf

6

Impacts on California Transportation and Travel

"All the roads in the middle of the state are impassable..." —
William H. Brewer, Journal entry for January 31, 1862, writing
from San Francisco

The bigger picture: the road network

There are 394,383 miles of road in California, including more than 50,000 miles of state-maintained highway and 23,000 bridges. Roads in low-lying, very flat, or poorly drained areas are prone to occasional flooding. Roads in steep terrain, especially in some of the more active geological areas of the state, are vulnerable to landslides that can block or destroy them. Roads deep in canyons are vulnerable to both. What terrain do you live on? Keep in mind that the rail network faces similar vulnerabilities.

Elevation above sea level (ASL) is easy to check while driving using a (properly calibrated) GPS device, including newer smartphones. Try it when you're crossing low ground. I recently travelled U.S. 99 in San Joaquin County and made note of when I was driving at very low elevations, or below grade (lower than the surrounding area). Only short stretches need to flood, slide, or be washed out, to sever a transportation artery and interrupt travel. You can also check land (and some structure) elevations on a computer by using an app like Google Earth Pro, while less detailed topographic elevations are available by using the USGS National Map Viewer online (with the topographic data layer selected, and zooming in), or other USGS map products. [Note: Technical reports specify which official 'datum,' out of several available, is used to calculate elevation above sea level; in this book, data from maps and instruments are accepted at face value.]

Elevation alone doesn't predict flooding, which depends upon several factors, but elevations near sea level, and height of the land above local streams or rivers, and slope across the land, give a reasonable indication of how easily and rapidly standing surface water might either accumulate or flow off toward the sea.

So, for your consideration, here are some notes on the approximate elevations above sea level (as reported by Google Earth Pro and/or USGS) of some highways and other transportation infrastructure in heavily travelled, and flat, parts of the Central Valley. All of these points are ~45-55 miles 'as the crow flies' from the Carquinez Strait at Benicia, where all runoff water from the Central Valley drains; the overall slope of the land that floodwaters will pass over is much less than one foot per mile over a large area:

- I-205 near Coral Hollow Rd., Tracy: 19–20'
- U.S. 99 at the Stockton Municipal Airport runway: 25–32' (runways: 20–25')
- I-5 near Walker Slough, Stockton: 20–24'
- Rail freight yard, Stockton: 17–30'
- U.S. 50 at 48th Street, Sacramento: 12–15'
- I-5 at the Capitol Mall, Sacramento: 5' (structures block full view)
- I-5 ramp at U.S. 50: 4–10' (structures block full view; GPS reported <u>minus</u> 6')
- Amtrak Sacramento station: 34'
- I-80 near Levee Road, Davis: 12–16'
- Sacramento International Airport runways: 18–21'

Particularly on I-5, our primary north-south highway artery, in Sacramento, you can appreciate the importance of having functioning pumps in service. Remember, the elevations given above are reasonably accurate numbers obtained from mapping applications. The areas noted above and many others would generally be likely or expected (per USGS in 2011, and depending upon levee adequacy, which is uncertain) to flood to a depth of 10'–20' over the general land surface ('above grade') during a megastorm like the one in the ARkStorm simulation (thought to be a smaller storm than the actual one in 1862). Under those conditions, overland travel through the Central Valley in any direction over road or rail, especially in San Joaquin and Sacramento counties but also in many other areas, would generally be impossible due to interruptions at key lower-lying points until much of the valley had drained and various repairs could be completed. Keep in mind, also, that levees (and other water infrastructure) could either do their job, or could fail or be overtopped. In that regard, note that on the huge, newly formed Lake Sacramento in 1862 "…the winds made high waves which beat the farm homes in pieces." (—Brewer); all structures and infrastructure including levees would feel the potentially destructive action of waves, which they are not designed for. Each levee failure could increase the extent of the expanding new lake, and possibly amplify the reach and force of waves being driven downwind to beat upon more (and more) levees: a possible cascade of failures.

Levees and raised roadbeds will have effects on water movement, drainage, and depth. Any infrastructure situated at elevations in the low double digits might become undependable. In addition to water, debris is a related and potentially widespread 'travel complication.' (For watercraft, including rescue craft, many obstacles will be present).

The USGS ARkStorm study in 2011 provided maps of which state highways would become unusable during and after a megastorm, and for how long they would be out of service. Many and perhaps most major highways would have sections that were flooded or were damaged or destroyed by landslides. Any section of a highway that is impassable makes ground travel and transport in that area impossible or much more difficult. If there are no passable detours, then ground travel and transport from one area or region to another is halted. The expert review presented by the USGS predicted that multiple blockages on most major highways in California would be extensive, with some closures or restrictions persisting for up to a year. One brief take from USGS on the highway failure mapping and impacts:

> "Note that the figures show that the storm largely cuts off traffic from Los Angeles to the north and east for 1-2 weeks, with gradual recovery. The same is true of Sacramento: traffic to the north, south, and west is largely cut off for 1 week or so, with gradual recovery thereafter." [Note: to the east of Sacramento also, per USGS maps.] …
>
> "Three important limitations of this scenario were recognized during the initial panel discussions. First, **these restoration times may underestimate competition for limited resources**. Second, these restoration timelines were laid out **without full consideration of the needs for evacuation**. Third, the landslide assessment for northern California was not available at the time of the panel discussions. **New landslide information might affect the assessment of both damage and restoration. Other considerations that were overlooked during the panel discussions also may affect restoration.**"

California's Fourth Climate Change Assessment (CA4_CCA, 2018) summary report attributes the following paraphrase to the sub-report prepared by Radke *et al.* (2018), but this passage did not appear in the final version:

> "Recent modeling of flood events indicates that ~225 km (~140 miles) of highways are susceptible to flooding in a 100 year storm event by 2020, and ~595 km (~370 miles) by the year 2100 (Radke *et al.*, 2018). The amount of temporary road inundation is estimated to be approximately 2,460 km (1,540

miles) in the 2020-2040 simulation window, and 6,085 km in 2080-2100, but Radke *et al.* (2018) show that the impacts of this flooding remain localized and will not increase the probability of failures for regional accessibility." [I'm not sure how ~3650 flooded miles of our best highways will not seriously compromise regional accessibility; also bear in mind the '100-year' scenario limits built into the assessments in this report.]

This statewide highway assessment is a grave red flag for emergency operations and relief efforts, but I think it doesn't paint the full picture. 340,000 miles of smaller highways and county roads not assessed by USGS, *i.e.*, potential detours, are also vulnerable, often more so; they usually are not engineered or maintained to the standards of the major highways, so may experience even more damage. Furthermore, the USGS noted the <u>potential</u> for damage to, or the loss of, bridges, on the road network, but did not flag specific vulnerabilities in their assessment, or include bridges in their failure projection. Similarly, they noted the possibility but did not factor culvert failures into their detailed assessment of highway vulnerabilities; culverts are often unnoticed but can destroy roads when they fail or are overwhelmed by surface runoff. Taken together, not only major highways, but smaller state and local roads—the potential detours—are likely in many areas to become unusable for an extended time, including the critical period when evacuations are transitioning to shelter and relief operations.

When the state becomes involved, after the counties and their sheriffs, vital transportation routes for evacuation will be established by or with Caltrans (the state 'highway department') and controlled by CHP (California Highway Patrol), per the State Emergency Plan (SEP). I'll speculate here beyond what the SEP states: *General transport traffic will likely also need to be controlled by a designated emergency authority like CHP, or Cal Guard, in order to prioritize the movement of essential materiel and personnel in the entire region under such extreme emergency conditions, potentially limiting civilian travel. For all these reasons, travel, especially civilian travel, during a megastorm, and for some time afterward, could be restricted or otherwise very difficult. Equally, even with priority, transportation of goods and materials toward the Foothills (and other areas) from various directions could become sporadic or be interrupted altogether for some time. Anyone riding it out on high ground, for example in a place like the Sierra Foothills, will possibly be stationary there, at or near home, for a while, and will benefit from having made adequate preparations. This is likely to apply to several areas in California and the West, depending on road networks, terrain, and storm impacts.*

The map below is the first of a series in the 2011 USGS ARkStorm scenario report, focusing on highway closures due to megastorm impacts, primarily flooding and landslides (plus debris flow and 'erosion'). As noted above, road closures on smaller roads, and due to bridge failures and culvert failures, are expected to occur but are not included on these USGS closure forecast maps. But the anticipated closure of the Sierra passes, and of sections of the major highways in the Central Valley, indicates that there could or will be regional isolation and extreme impairment of movement of supplies in much of California. The original map figures are in color and are much easier to see (the ARkStorm Scenario Overview is online, and free). The complete series of maps indicates how long closures and constrictions are expected to persist (in some cases, up to a year). Repairs will be a massive undertaking, equally so for counties, which do not have the same resources and capabilities as state and federal agencies do. Bridge replacements would take years.

Figure 20. Causes of ARkStorm cumulative highway damages. Red indicates debris flow, blue indicates flooding, green indicates flooding and erosion, yellow indicates landslide other than debris flow.

Figure from USGS: Overview of the ARkStorm Scenario, 2011. Original and related figures online are in color.

Railroads may use different construction techniques and different approaches to grades and crossing terrain, but in general they are exposed to the same flooding, landslide, and other risks. In the severe 1986 storm some California rail lines were damaged and put out of service. That can prevent cargo, including critical and relief supplies, from reaching their destinations. I'm going to include this topic under the related umbrella of road closures; if you want to take it further, or if you are a railroad buff, you can trace where rail lines run and where they are located in terrain vulnerable to extreme weather impacts including flooding.

Airports

> "The Reno-Tahoe International Airport (RNO) was completely shut down to air traffic as flood waters submerged runways and portions of the terminal building." —NOAA report on the 1997 'New Year's Day' storm.

> "Another piece of critical infrastructure located in the Natomas Basin is the Sacramento International Airport, a major transportation hub for Sacramento and all of northern California. The airport can handle up to 29 flights per hour; in a typical month 800,000 passengers arrive or depart the airport. If a flood were to occur, passenger travel would be disrupted and those stranded at the airport would have to be evacuated to higher ground." U.S. Army Corps of Engineers report, 2015

Several California airports are already experiencing flooding or are expected to do so in the near future. Here are details from a recent report:

> "The need to address this growing flooding risk varies from airport to airport and what types of infrastructure are impacted first. While San Francisco and Oakland are already experiencing occasional flooding, Santa Barbara airport is expected to see flooding in the 2020–2040 period, San Diego not until 2060–2080. … Meanwhile sea-level rise (SLR) is impacting segments of coastal highways (SR-1, SR-37, etc.) as well as airports (San Francisco International, Oakland and San Jose), seaports and docks." —CA CSIWG report, 2018.

Note that SLR 'exposure' is actually a combination of sea level rise, high tide, storm surge, and includes some inland surface runoff. Storm calculations, for these flooding predictions, are usually 'capped' at some (old, obsolete?) estimate of a so-called '100-year-storm.' A bigger storm, whether a so-called '200-year-storm' or a genuine megastorm, would have even greater impacts (surge, waves, runoff) on coastal flooding and coastal transportation infrastructure. Unfortunately for us,

> "…the Airport Perimeter Dike FEMA and Seismic

Improvements Project is underway at Oakland Airport in response to sea level rise and includes FEMA certification requirements **for 100-year flood protection**." —Radke *et al.*, 2018 [But, which 100 years?]

Los Angeles, Salinas and Monterey airports are among those which are on higher, if often extensively flat, ground. Some military airfields appear to be out of flood areas, some are not. Moffett Federal Airfield in Santa Clara County, with important disaster relief responsibilities and materiel, is, like San Francisco and Oakland airports, located directly on the San Francisco Bay, with runways starting at 5' ASL.

Ports and shipping

Port facilities could be difficult or impossible to use if Bay, Delta, or Ocean waters were to rise substantially in relation to fixed infrastructure, or if storm weather conditions, winds, or channel currents became too strong. These particular impacts are not well quantified, based on various study results, and can't be assessed with precision at this time. Lucy Jones, chief scientist for the USGS MHDP team that carried out the ARkStorm study, wrote in 2018, about San Francisco in 1862, that "The narrow outlet of the bay at the Golden Gate had such a strong outflow that ships couldn't enter." Steamships were in common service at the time. Today, the U.S. Coast Guard may halt ship travel in waterways like the Delta under extreme conditions.

NOAA in 2002 quoted reports from 1862: "Reports from journals of the time state that for at least ten days 'water flowed through the Golden Gate in a steady torrent, blocking tide reversal.'" Their analysis appears to indicate this effect as a storm surge component sometimes exceeding one foot, mostly influencing low tides.

* * *

Concerns about the road network in (and into) East-Central California

Consider the following paragraphs as an example of an assessment of regional vulnerability to an extreme storm and flood disruption. You can apply the same process to evaluate the road connections into your own large or small area. It's not clear that any part of California's road network, including routes into the state, could absolutely dodge the full impacts of an ARkStorm-scale megastorm. A theme developed later in this book emphasizes preparedness; reading below you may begin to appreciate why.

Much of U.S. 99 lies on the floodplain of the San Joaquin Valley. In places the roadbed may be less that ten, or even five, feet above the surrounding terrain. One example of this is at the junction of SR 88, in Stockton. Two online maps put the roadbed at less than 10' above the floodplain, and not more than 15' above the Stockton Diversion Canal which crosses 99 at that point. On a recent Friday morning there I observed an average of 12 cargo and transport trucks passing southbound, and six heading northbound, every minute. Those brief estimates of potential cargo traffic through the area are indicative, not representative, but that's a lot of cargo (thousands of truckloads per day). Much of that cargo is 'necessities.' The ARkStorm projection is for that area to be flooded for 14–28 days, reaching depths of 10–20'. USGS maps show many other problem areas. For that general, basic reason I would give a high priority to (1) developing alternative north-south routing, possibly followed by (2) raising the existing road(s) where needed (these and other suggestions are collected in a later chapter).

Another issue with elevated roadways is that if there are not sufficient openings, as below overpasses, to allow floodwater (including local pluvial floodwater) to flow freely, then roadways can act to some extent as mini-dams, increasing flood depth on one side or the other of the roadway, potentially even overtopping the roadway in an extreme case. The volume or velocity of flood flows through openings not designed to handle them might in some cases raise the possibility of further impacts, for example scour of earth around concrete structures, weakening or damaging them. It is also instructive to note that in March 2023, pressure from storm-caused floodwaters accumulating on the uphill side of the Los Angeles Aqueduct caused it to rupture and fail near Bishop, California.

While the Tehachapi Pass (SR 58) and SR 155 and/or SR 178 past Lake Isabella may remain open for transport into south-central California from points east, the usability of U.S. 99 to Merced is less certain (and north of there, appears unlikely, per USGS). Although USGS mapping indicates only an average of up to 3 feet of flooding in some parts of the upper San Joaquin Valley, lasting 3–7 days, a concern remains that even small areas of deeper flooding could impact travel on U.S. 99. One area of concern might be in the flood-prone area northwest of Fresno. Road (and rail) crossings over the San Joaquin River, including U.S. 99 near the Fresno city limit, might deserve special (expert) attention in view of forecasts of more extreme flows in that river in the coming decades (Maendly, 2018). More detailed 2011 USGS mapping identified a series of flood vulnerabilities on SR 155 and 65, and U.S. 99, in and around Bakersfield, and some further expected interruptions on U.S. 99 south of Merced. Much of the land along the route between Bakersfield and Fresno is flood-prone at up-to-three-foot depth, per USGS in the ARkStorm report. So, is there a workable alternative routing from near Bakersfield east of U.S. 99, with continuity, to Coulterville or Sonora (assuming SR 49 would serve several areas north from there as a best route)? Some interruptions are also predicted for the corresponding stretch of I-5.

To the north, sections of I-5 south of the Oregon border are also projected by USGS to become flooded in a megastorm.

The east-west highways that are usually kept open (when possible) across the Sierra during winter are not flood-prone, at least east of the Central Valley and west of the Reno-Carson area, but instead have a fairly high risk of landslide closures in various places. The 2011 USGS projections indicate that I-80, U.S. 50, SR 88 and SR 4 are among the many routes that (if not also closed by snow conditions at the high passes, which is normal for Highway 4) will likely be closed by flooding, erosion and landslides. In USGS projections, none of those damaged highways would reopen in less than 30 days, and after 90 days only 1, 2, or 3 lanes would be open (presumably to priority traffic at first). Full restoration of highway transport across the Sierra, and statewide generally, would take at least several months, and more in extreme local situations. Limited availability of fuels and materiel could complicate repair activities and schedules. See also the USGS caveats to estimated restoration times, quoted above.

Avalanches are another likely problem, for example closing U.S. 395 as in 2023.

In conclusion, without a secure route for transport, with a best option (in my view) being an all-weather highway running from interstate highway connections out of the southeast, westward over the low Southern California passes and then northward above the floodplains and along the east side of the Central Valley, east-central California could be without overland access during a period of great need. Similar concerns and requirements exist elsewhere. Those who will shelter in place and who have made ample preparations will be well served by them.

I'm only scratching the surface here, but I <u>am</u> trying to flag up a couple of good scratches for some expert attention.

Getting around in, or out of, the Sierra: a regional example of a general problem

Try to visualize a similar driving experience in your own home terrain…

Imagine a modern drive out of the Central Sierra Foothills, but under storm conditions like those experienced here in January 1862, during the peak of the last megastorm to hit the West Coast. Starting out somewhere up the slope, through heavy rain or snow or 'mix,' the driver needs to find a westerly route around (or through) fallen trees, structural debris, mudflows, rockfalls, downed power poles and lines, roadway washouts, and any bridges that have become unusable (going, going…), until reaching the vicinity of Highway 49, where (south of I-80 at least) the river canyons start to widen out. How far out of their banks will any creeks and streams near the 1000' elevation be? Will debris (trees, structures, vehicles, rock, mud) be blocking the roads? Will culverts fail; have new water channels cut through the roads? Are any bridges out of service?

A new physical constraint, at this point and beyond, may be large numbers of displaced people and emergency and relief operations, vehicles and equipment; where evacuees will go, and park, and how they will be accommodated is unclear.

If a way can be found to continue west of SR 49, you might be the only one heading that way. In fact, at some point law enforcement or the Cal Guard might prevent you from entering the lower elevations while evacuation orders are in force. The route itself will begin to pass through more low-lying areas where water and possibly debris has accumulated but not yet drained. Will it be possible to find a route, say for rescue operations, that is passable down into the Central Valley and the major highways?

That will become harder and harder, the further west you travel, until (if you can) you reach some elevation—say, 50' ASL? 40'? 30'?—you will likely begin to see water stretching ahead to the west as far as you can see (standing at water level, the horizon is just over three miles away). For instance, on highways SR 16 or U.S. 50, from areas somewhere around Rancho Cordova and Rosemont, stretching west to Woodland and Davis and Antioch, and along large portions of the valley from Chico to Bakersfield, much of the land, where not protected by any intact levees, will become covered with water, in some areas up to 20' deep, according to the USGS (levees failed in several California counties in the 2023 storms). Low-lying roads, major highways included, and other infrastructure could be affected in many places.

Dry country

Desert landscapes might seem to be less prone to storms and floods, but the opposite is true; some areas can be severely vulnerable to the bigger West Coast (and other) storms. When you see "dry lakebed" on a map, cross out the word "dry." Recall the extreme Death Valley floods of 2022. I note some specific relocation routes through dry country that might be vulnerable and of concern, in the chapter on personal preparedness. What might it be like, driving through dry country well to the east of the Pacific Coast, in a strong AR storm? Here's a glimpse: the recent experience of Constable Brett Schmidt, on November 15,

2021, driving west from Kamloops, B.C., when all the highway passes to the coast became blocked by landslides, and he was forced to turn around and head back east through normally dry terrain along the Nicola River:

> "He carried on. The valley is normally a lovely one, the narrow river swaying between steep walls of rock or clay interspersed with terraces of sagebrush and bunchgrass…
>
> Schmidt was on a stretch of road running low along the river when he felt the ground shake under the wheels of his truck. Glancing into his rear-view mirror, he saw that the asphalt he had just passed over had caved in and fallen into the churning water…" —J. B. MacKinnon, November 15, 2022; www.hakai.org

* * *

Side Note: a few observations on overland travel difficulties:

Bridges:

If you want to find any detailed information on a specific bridge, including its rated condition, you need to consult the National Bridge Inventory maintained by the U.S. Department of Transportation. The online tool provided by DOT is called Infobridge and I'll recommend that you use the map-based selection option with the graphical inclusion tools for your area of interest. You can also filter the results to show, for example, only local bridges in 'poor' condition.

As an example, focusing on one region important in a flooding catastrophe: Infobridge unfortunately reports the percentage of bridges in poor condition on or near SR 49 in a three-county part of the Central Sierra Foothills to be around 15%, about four times the State Highway System's (SHS) average; at least some of the difference is related to county, rather than state, responsibility for many of these bridges, which might provide access or detour options. That's in sharp contrast to the potential importance of hill-country road networks, including in the Sierra Foothills, under extreme flood evacuation and relief conditions. A 'poor' rating does not strictly imply an increased probability of failure during flood conditions or extremely heavy transport use, but it might, depending on the details of the assessment (for example, the substructure vs the pavement). I would argue for Caltrans, now, to designate area routes, plus their main connectors, that will play a crucial role in future evacuations and relief efforts; as strategic transportation corridors under extreme storm and flood conditions, such designated roads and their bridges, both state and county owned, should receive a higher re-engineering, improvement, repair and replacement priority.

For information on California's transportation infrastructure and its condition, consult the online TAMP reports from Caltrans. The 2022 report addresses issues with four particularly important and vulnerable elements of the highway system: culverts, pavement, bridges, and 'traffic management systems.' Comparing the 2018 and 2022 Caltrans TAMP bridge assessments, the number of bridges in 'good' condition is dropping rapidly.

Beyond physical condition, bridge design, and suitability to site and environment should also be considered, especially for old bridges. USGS notes that:

> "…the primary causes of bridge damage in severe winter storms are scour undermining the foundations of bridge piers or abutments and hydrodynamic pressure at the upstream edge of the bridge superstructure."

Landslides:

Landslides have several possible causes; two transportation infrastructure influences are discussed below. Generally, regarding ARkStorm-related landslides and the road network in California, according to USGS (2011),

> "…the ARkStorm could cause **tens of thousands of landslides**, the vast majority of them debris flows, and [road repairs would] cost on the order of $3 billion [in 2010 dollars], " with indirect damages multiplying that number. Now, compare that number to the culvert situation described below in the 2022 Caltrans TAMP.

Culverts:

Below, in this note, is some information from the State of California about culverts in the road network (limited to the State Highway System, and excluding local roads). Seldom noticed or given much thought by residents, culverts potentially have a profound impact on how roads will behave in storms. Failure of an ancient culvert a mile from my place took out our lifeline state highway here during AR storms in 2017, leading to a massive, difficult, expensive, two-months-long repair, and an additional large 'detouring' expense (assuming an average of 30 extra miles one-way, the out-of-pocket driving cost to residents and transporters, at the federal mileage rate, was over $2 million) borne by residents and commercial vehicle operators, even before considering lost time.

Per Caltrans, in the 2022 TAMP report, it typically costs $2,000 per linear foot (elsewhere stated as $20,000 total) to install a new culvert or fix one in poor condition. Rehabilitative maintenance and reconstruction costs for a 30–50-year-old culvert (with a 50-year service life) are considerably higher, but still far less than the typical $1,000,000 cost to repair a road after a culvert failure, hypothetically occurring at around 60 years. An incomplete 2019 Caltrans inventory puts 10% of the state's ~205,000 SHS culverts as being in poor condition (that's more than 20,000… implying that a systemwide event that overwhelmed road drainage systems could result in a multi-billion-dollar potential damage repair cost plus extensive and prolonged transportation impacts and driver costs). This excludes damage and costs on additional county-maintained and other culverts, for which there is no ready information, but some unknown further amount of potential road destruction, travel impairment, and repair costs.

If you suspect a problem, including actual or potential blockage, of a county-maintained culvert, on a county road, bring it to the attention of your county Public Works department chief. That office can probably also guide you through the Caltrans bureaucracy if you want to report issues with state-maintained (SR) roads.

Roadcuts (& erosion, and landslides):

Roadcuts and other development that modifies the land surface or the flow of surface water often increases the frequency or likelihood of landslides or erosion. Exposure of subsurface layers increases weathering and the penetration of water, leading to increased weakness. Roadcuts can be steeper than adjacent slopes, and less stable. Removal of a 'slice' of the slope structure to create a roadbed means that material that anchored the upper slope in place is now gone. Surface water flows that become concentrated in new places, in culverts or not, can accelerate erosion at or under the roadway or on the downslope side. For these reasons, roadcuts and other development have often made hillsides and canyon walls more landslide prone, even more than in 1862 when many deadly landslides occurred. USGS in the 2011 ARkStorm report predicts "tens of thousands of landslides" statewide in a megastorm.

A 2018 research paper by Ersoz and Topal states:

> "Cut slopes are very sensitive to weathering because of disturbed rock mass and topographical condition by excavation. During and right after an excavation process of a cut slope, weathering and erosion may act on this newly exposed rock material and mass. These acting on the rock may degrade and change its engineering properties and the stability of the cut slope in its engineering lifetime."

A 2018 sub-report by AghaKouchak *et al.*, a part of the state's Fourth Climate Change Assessment, states:

> "Increase in intensity, duration, and frequency of extreme precipitation can adversely impact the integrity of infrastructure and natural and engineered slopes. Severe rainfall causes flooding, landslides, and soil erosion and jeopardizes functionality or integrity of infrastructure systems. Infrastructure built with soil (such as earthen dams, levees, or embankments), or the ones that interface with soil (for example roads, bridge, pipelines, and foundations) are often more vulnerable.
>
> In addition, recent studies have shown that, given the expected increase in future precipitation, there is a high chance of substantial impact on landslide activity in natural slopes (Robinson *et al.*, 2017) and on the performance of man-made earthen structures (Vahedifard *et al.*, 2017; Jasim *et al.*, 2017), calling into question the current procedure for infrastructure design and risk assessment."

A proactive citizen response:

You can become aware of local conditions that could impact the road network, and your vital exit or relocation routes, in your area. You can report some issues to your county or to Caltrans; you may need to persevere to get action. Bigger issues, such as roads that hug canyon walls or run right alongside rivers, have no quick fixes. Bridge replacements are a similarly complex undertaking from the politics on up. Always consider your best relocation exit routes, early departures, and feasible destinations if you think your road connections may not be reliable in extreme weather. More than 80 state highway closures across Southern California on the morning of August 21, 2023, as Hurricane Hilary passed north, have given us a preview of which roads, and which terrain, could be vulnerable to travel and transportation disruption under sustained and intense megastorm conditions.

Side note: a comment on fuels

No matter what shape the roads are in, transportation is for now (in 2023) almost entirely dependent on availability of hydrocarbon fuels. In future, grid problems could increasingly impact EV travel. Fuels and energy will be commented on in the next chapter.

Conclusion: Movement of materiel and possibly of emergency personnel is likely to be problematic and impeded, and movement of civilians might be further restricted depending upon circumstances.

* * *

Further reading

California Transportation [Infrastructure] Asset Management Plan 2022 (draft): Caltrans. https://dot.ca.gov/-/media/dot-media/programs/asset-management/documents/draft-2022-tamp-01142022-for-public-review.pdf

U.S. DOT data on individual bridges: https://infobridge.fhwa.dot.gov/Data/SelectedBridges [or] https://www.fhwa.dot.gov/bridge/nbi.cfm

State Emergency Plan (2017): https://www.caloes.ca.gov/PlanningPreparednessSite/Documents/2017%20SEP%20Executive%20Summary%20ADA%20Edits.pdf

AghaKouchak, Amir, Elisa Ragno, Charlotte Love, & Hamed Mofakhari. (University of California, Irvine). 2018. Projected Changes in California's Precipitation Intensity-Duration-Frequency Curves. California's Fourth Climate Change Assessment, California Energy Commission. Publication number: CCCA4-CEC-2018-005. Projected changes in California's precipitation intensity-duration-frequency curves

Ersoz, T, and T. Topal (2018). Assessment of rock slope stability with the effects of weathering and excavation by comparing deterministic methods and slope stability probability classification (SSPC). Environ Earth Sci. https://doi.org/10.1007/s12665-018-7728-4 [paywalled] https://link.springer.com/article/10.1007/s12665-018-7728-4

NOAA, 2002. Technical Report NOS CO-OPS 035. HISTORICAL GOLDEN GATE TIDAL SERIES. https://tidesandcurrents.noaa.gov/publications/techrpt35.pdf

Sahagún, Louis. 'We've lost the aqueduct': How severe flooding threatens a Los Angeles water lifeline. Los Angeles Times, 25 March 2023. https://www.latimes.com/environment/story/2023-03-25/eastern-sierra-flooding-threatens-los-angeles-water-lifeline

Bedsworth, Louise, Dan Cayan, Guido Franco, Leah Fisher, & Sonya Ziaja. (California Governor's Office of Planning and Research, Scripps Institution of Oceanography, California Energy Commission, California Public Utilities Commission). 2018. Statewide Summary Report. California's Fourth Climate Change Assessment. Publication number: SUM-CCCA4-2018-013. https://www.energy.ca.gov/sites/default/files/2019-11/Statewide_Reports-SUM-CCCA4-2018-013_Statewide_Summary_Report_ADA.pdf

Radke, J.D, G.S. Biging, K. Roverts, M. Schmidt-Poolman, H. Foster, E. Roe, Y. Ju, S. Lindbergh, T. Beach, L. Maier, Y. He, M. Ashenfarb, P. Norton, M. Wray, A. Alruheil, S. Yi, R. Rau, J. Collins, D. Radke, M. Coufal, S. Marx, D. Moanga, V. Ulyashin, A. Dalal. (University of California, Berkeley). 2018. Assessing Extreme Weather-Related Vulnerability and Identifying Resilience Options for California's Interdependent Transportation Fuel Sector. California's Fourth Climate Change Assessment, California Energy Commission. Publication Number: CCCA4-CEC-2018-012. https://www.energy.ca.gov/sites/default/files/2019-11/Energy_CCCA4-CEC-2018-012_ADA.pdf

7

Impacts on California Energy and Fuels

California "is the third largest market for gasoline in the world."
—*Radke* et al., *2018*

This is a longish but very condensed treatment of a topic that is of paramount importance, not only because of the profound impacts to energy supply that can be expected, but also because nothing is more likely to bring home to you, the reader, a sense of the vast, intricate scope of how life in California could be disrupted. Below, I'll try to provide an overview of California's energy infrastructure and the weather and climate vulnerabilities it faces. The point of this review is to show you why you may not be able to rely upon having grid electricity, or fuels like gasoline, diesel, propane, or natural gas during an extreme weather emergency. If you find that hard to believe, then you'll be more interested in the detailed explanations and references provided below (in brief).

Hydrocarbon (mostly 'fossil') fuels are used to meet many needs including transportation, home heating and cooking, and electrical power generation. California as of 2021 generates more than half of its of in-state electricity from renewables, including geothermal, hydroelectric, solar wind plus some from (non-fossil) biomass. As of 2017 through 2021, half of the state's new installed solar electricity generation was on-site (residential and some commercial properties) and half was from 'industrial' solar farms. Nuclear was scheduled to be phased out by 2025; however, that has been extended following the announcement of the state's upcoming electric vehicle mandate.

That brings us to energy interdependencies: as of 2021, 40% of California's electricity is now generated at power plants fueled by natural gas. Conversely, hydrocarbon fuels cannot move through pipelines without grid-supplied electricity to operate the pumps and controls. State-sponsored assessments are aware of these vulnerabilities and of the potential for cascading failures. Both interdependent energy systems—electricity and hydrocarbon fuels—are discussed below.

Electricity: Generation / Power plants

Balancing electrical supply (generation) and demand is a much more complicated undertaking than it might seem. Imbalances between (low) production, (high) demand, and grid capacity can necessitate potentially cascading powerplant shutdowns (due to AC frequency drop) and, worst case, de-energizing of the entire grid until a gradual bootstrapping process allows safe operation to fully resume; if you are interested, you can look up "black start" online, and review the nature of the stresses on the Texas grid (a near miss) in February 2021. A significant loss of power generation could lead to a bigger problem than you might imagine, unless demand falls at least as fast, for example, due to local grid failures.

Conventional / Hydrocarbon-fueled (see also fuels section below)

The USGS ARkStorm study considered the issue of storm impacts upon power generation, concluding that some power plants may be vulnerable to flooding, especially in Santa Clara and Los Angeles counties. However, referring to maps published by USGS, a number of additional electrical generating plants around the Central Valley, *mapped but not otherwise commented on,* also appear to lie within the vicinities of, or at least very near to, areas expected to flood as a result of a megastorm like the ARkStorm. For example, the NCPA power plant in Lodi sits at 8–13' above sea level (per Google Earth Pro), about 53 miles from the Carquinez Strait as the crow flies, on very flat ground along I-5, where 10'–20' of flooding is predicted by USGS in an event like the ARkStorm. USGS pointed out that some substations may also be vulnerable even to relatively shallow flooding. *The degree of vulnerability of the power generation and transmission infrastructure was not addressed in any detail by the USGS study team.* So, power generation may be affected by extreme storm conditions including flooding. Major generation equipment, if damaged, could take a long time, optimistically many months, to replace and install.

Of course, fuel is required.

Hydroelectric power plants

Whether California's hydroelectric power plants would continue to operate under megastorm conditions was not addressed by the USGS study panel. Management of dams and reservoir levels may be one determining factor; resilience of grid connections is another. When hydroelectric turbines, as in the Hyatt Powerplant at the Oroville Dam, can't even pass water without a solid grid connection to absorb the substantial electrical power output generated, that's a constraint on reservoir management. Grid connection vulnerability was, in fact, one* of the issues that complicated management of the spillway emergency at the Oroville Dam in 2017, one that could potentially have restricted the emergency release of lake water even further (*another was that the dam's powerplant almost flooded after erosion around the damaged main spillway filled the river channel with rock and soil, damming the river and causing water to rise toward the powerhouse).

The potential flooding of powerplants located <u>above</u> floodplains deserves attention. Some hydro plants are located directly adjacent to the river channels that (may) supply the flowing water that turns the generator turbines. If you look at other rivers with hydroelectric plants, even those supplied by penstocks or canals from higher, more distant sources (to provide a more powerful 'head' of water), the powerhouses are often along the rivers' edge. Consulting the FloodFactor 1% annual chance flood mapping at www.riskfactor.com, the forecast methods developed by the First Street Foundation indicate that in a condition of uncontrolled flood flow (with upstream reservoirs at capacity), a modern 1% ACE or so-called '100-year' flood could put many powerhouses in the flood, or underwater. A megastorm could produce flooding at least that great.

Geothermal power plants

Assuming no physical effects (wind, surface water flow) acting directly upon the generation plants themselves, the biggest threat to remote plants would presumably be a loss of grid connection that would prevent distribution of any power generated, and require shutdown of the turbines.

Wind farms

Although wind turbines go offline when winds reach high speeds, by adjusting (feathering) their blades to shed the force of the wind, typically at 55 mph according to the U.S. Department of Energy, the towers themselves are also vulnerable to stronger winds. In one 2013 example from a review of typhoon impacts on Chinese wind farms (Chen *et al.*, 2015), one third of towers at one wind farm collapsed in storm winds with one-minute sustained velocities of 155 mph. According to General Electric (2018), normal turbines can withstand wind gusts of 94 mph; they reported work on a new type of turbine that could withstand gusts of 128 mph (designs evolve and statements like these come online and go offline). Since wind farms are often located in the windiest areas, including mountain passes, an extreme AR storm might put legacy towers at risk. Based on ARkStorm-model windspeed prediction mapping, an area like the Tehachapi Pass, as an example, in a region where megastorm wind speeds are predicted to exceed 100 mph, might be particularly vulnerable to equipment damage.

Solar farms

Large solar farms built on well-drained land may be vulnerable only to grid interruptions. However, some solar farms have been built at the margins of old 'dry' lakebeds. We expect to see refilling dry / desert lakes in a megastorm. The area near Rosamond, CA may be vulnerable to flood, per USGS mapping. Some solar farms are located around the edges of the Tulare Basin, which refilled in the 2023 floods. How flooding might affect equipment is not yet clear; surface water could be salty, and conductive.

Nuclear-fueled power plants

As of 2021–23, California only hosts one operating nuclear-fueled power plant, at Diablo Canyon. As with geothermal plants, a nuclear plant may continue operation unless storm effects (*e.g.*, surface water flows) or a loss of grid connection forces a shutdown.

Electricity: Distribution

The USGS ARkStorm scenario report released in 2011 makes some definite (if incomplete) predictions about impacts of an 1861–62-sized megastorm on California's modern electrical infrastructure, *but leaves other related points unexplored or only hinted at.* Because of limitations acknowledged in the 2011 report *(for example, PG&E, a large electric utility in Northern California, chose not to participate in the USGS 2010–11 study panel)*, this chapter will try to describe what's in those gaps.

Starting with the definite predictions from the USGS study, high winds produced by a megastorm like the ARkStorm could directly damage electrical transmission lines in some parts of the state, particularly to the southeast of the Sierra. Peak winds reaching 125 mph may be experienced in a few areas such as south of the Owens Valley, and such winds may cause direct damage to transmission lines. In other areas such as the western Sierra Foothills, wind speeds might not exceed 60 to 70 mph, and might not be a primary direct cause of power line failure (although the recently introduced Public Safety Power Shutoffs, or PSPS, assume that winds of that force are a direct threat to power transmission lines, which the utility companies de-energize pre-emptively). I'll note that recent smaller AR storms have produced extremely high winds (to 100 mph) along the coast.

The USGS panel <u>considered only predictions in which any/all wind-caused grid damage is caused directly by the wind acting on lines and poles (but not indirectly from trees, branches, or debris, nor from erosion, nor lightning)</u>.

Direct effects of strong winds are what caused so much destruction to Louisiana's power grid during Hurricane Ida in 2021. This 'direct-damage' limitation on the USGS estimates paints an incomplete, too-rosy picture about electrical grid resilience in the Foothill counties of the Sierra, and in similar terrain. As a result of this narrow view, Placer, Amador, Calaveras, Tuolumne, and other counties without substantial flood risk, with 'ARkStorm' winds not expected to exceed about 70 mph, all shared <u>the following prediction: only two people per thousand would, briefly, experience any megastorm-related power interruption.</u>

Well, I'll just say: that's ridiculous. *Around my area, if Rudolph sneezes (metaphorically) on Christmas Eve, a couple hundred people lose power for a day or two.* In the Foothills, we already regularly experience grid failures of up to one or even two weeks from smaller, ordinary storms, even when the utility crews have unimpeded access to their grid infrastructure. As I write this, a lightning strike during a mild fall storm has knocked out power to our neighborhood for the day. Relatively mild 2022-23 winter weather took out several powerlines and even a pole within a mile of my land.

Even if you don't live in the Sierra Foothills… based on the California Public Utilities Commission maps of Tier 2 and Tier 3 at-risk high- and extreme-fire hazard zones, *43% of the state land area, by my calculations based on CPUC map layers, is included and may have similar potential issues with 'indirect storm damage' to grid equipment if present within the forested areas.*

One factor that determines a hazard-tier classification is "abundant dry vegetation." The mapped zones indicate where overhead utility lines and equipment might interact dangerously with vegetation… <u>not</u> explicitly where vegetation might impact the electrical grid, but that's almost a hair-splitting distinction. The threat map provides an indication, to an approximation, of where vegetation, particularly forests, might represent a threat to the grid under storm conditions. You can look at the online CPUC map for where you live and get a sense of the local potential for vegetation x power-line interactions (if that's not already obvious to you from eyeball observation), and a further sense of how many communities could be affected by extreme winds and/or snow.

There is also a new PG&E rapid-shutdown 'fast trip' protocol whereby parts of the grid shut down immediately "if an object strikes a line." That's a good safety approach (it probably would have prevented the 2015 wildfire that a power line started on my land); however, the current protocol then requires every inch of line in the affected area to be visually inspected before the line(s) is re-energized. In rough weather, or dense vegetation, drones and choppers won't do the job. Boots on the ground, or in trucks, will take time to complete the required inspection, even more so if there are any storm-related access problems such as road closures. The company states that the 'fast trip' protocol will only be used during potential wildfire conditions (which are lengthening, year after year). I'll just note that we have had recent <u>winter</u> (the 'wet season') wildfires in the Sierra Foothills, and in October 2021, an intense, record-breaking AR 5 storm arrived the same week that the Governor declared a statewide drought emergency. How quickly will 'trip' protocols be changed if an AR storm arrives?

Regardless of equipment settings, if there is a fast, or slow, 'trip,' or actual damage, here is what PG&E had to say in 2021 about the power restoration process in this 'High Fire Threat District' terrain (remember, in winter storm conditions, the process will be more difficult):

> "The locations of these updated settings [for equipment] are typically in areas that are difficult to access and at higher risk for a catastrophic wildfire. Once there is an outage, patrols will be conducted either on the ground or in the air and may involve foot patrols in very steep and difficult terrain with limited access. Patrols also can only take place during daylight hours [meaning fewer hours in winter]. Crews will restore customers in stages, or steps, as individual portions of the circuit are deemed safe and ready for re-energization."

I was on a crew in 1974 that cleared ice-storm-caused forest damage from roads and trails in Santa Cruz County. Across one of our public roads through forest, a one-mile stretch had 200 trees down overnight, mostly Tanbark Oak. Snow in places like the Sierra Foothills, for example in February 2019 and December 2021, caused smaller problems which still resulted in extended grid outages.

My take: *Repairing extensive grid damage when the area is largely inaccessible is going to take a while. I'd expect that severe-storm damage to the grid in the Foothills and similar wooded areas would probably result in a large number of points of failure, requiring extensive repairs under difficult conditions in areas that may be hard for crews to access, under short-daylight conditions. In the worst-case scenario, with loss of road connections, the upper Foothills region might generally be hard for repair crews and equipment to reach at all. Utility repair fleet fueling, including aircraft, might become one further limitation.* Suggestions received by the USGS study panel included one to "Pre-position repair crews based on severe weather forecasts." I'd personally be happy to see repair crews embedded upcountry and wherever / whenever there is a risk of community isolation or loss of access (such as from Cat4 and Cat5 ARs). I can't predict what the priorities for power restoration might be *(but I can imagine that priorities might be based on the size of affected community populations, or on where emergency shelters are operating, or on accessibility, or on other factors)*. I suggest we allow for the possibility that back-country folks (I am one) might not be top-of-the-list.

On-site generation: solar, wind, micro-hydro, fueled generators

On-site (residential and commercial installations) solar PVE, whether 'rooftop' or ground-mounted, with off-grid capability, in principle overcomes any problems associated with remote generation facilities and/or grid reliability. However, there are some winter considerations: the daylight hours are fewer ('shorter'), sun angles are lower and produce less power for many fixed panel installations, and in cloudy storm conditions you might receive only 5-10% of the sunlight intensity your maximum ratings are based on. Snow on panels also stops or drastically cuts power generation. With a typical on-site system, without a working grid-tie, in winter storm conditions, expect to have to ration power, especially if you plan to operate an electric vehicle, unless you have over-built your on-site solar PVE production or storage capacity. Also, make sure you understand whether your installed grid-tied system can even operate without a live grid connection; many of the cheaper basic solar PVE systems (without battery storage) can't activate the panels and inverter when the grid is down (a real head scratcher, but a true fact). When 'going solar,' consider <u>all</u> that you will require of your system.

If you live on suitable terrain and have an interested in on-site wind turbine(s) or micro-hydro, and are DIY-handy with those systems, you may have even better winter / storm options than on-site solar. Unfortunately, they remain rather exotic and are not yet, typically, plug-and-play systems, but perhaps that will improve. The simplest systems might work best for battery charging, for example an electric vehicle (EV) if you are patient. If you are picturing a charging station near your creek, a steady power output for a small micro-hydro turbine might be 500 W/h, meaning you could capture 12 kWh in a continuous 24-hour period. A Mini-Cooper in 2022 takes 29 kWh to become fully charged while a Hummer pickup may require 200 kWh for full charge. [I'm waiting for a rugged, lightweight, high-clearance, decent-cargo-capacity, adequate-range EV.]

Fueled generators (using non-renewables) are a popular option, although (1) fuels have a higher cost per kWh than grid prices, and (2) with most installations you typically have to depend upon availability of your necessary (for extended operations) fuel from remote, possibly vulnerable systems, over road networks that may be disrupted. Fuels storage capacity requirements could be substantial; I discuss that, and on-site options, in more detail in the chapter on individual preparedness.

Hydrocarbon fuels

In the 2020s, we rely upon gasoline, diesel, fuel oil, natural gas and propane / LPG for many of our energy needs including power plants, routine personal transportation, trucking and heavy equipment operation, aviation, boating and shipping, and for backup electrical generators, home heating and other domestic uses. The 2011 USGS ARkStorm study did not provide much assessment of the impact of a megastorm upon California's hydrocarbon economy. In fact, for security reasons, after 9/11/2001 some information on energy infrastructure, designated Critical Energy / Electric Infrastructure Information (CEII), is now restricted by the Federal Energy Regulatory Commission (you can even see this stamped on some public dam failure inundation maps). The full picture is readily available only to relevant authorities and authorized emergency planners and managers. Bits and pieces are public. I'm only able to present some possible issues here but not to fully or authoritatively resolve them for readers.

Hydrocarbon fuels tend to share certain key features including production, transportation, refining, and distribution. I'll present some very condensed information on the fuels, from a California perspective, first, then some thoughts on their commonalities, and especially their vulnerabilities.

Absent coal, our hydrocarbon fuels are liquids or gasses, and can be divided roughly, as sectors, into Transportation Fuels, Natural Gas, and Other (propane, LPG).

Natural gas

About 11 million customers (accounts) in California have metered natural gas service. California imports about 85% of its natural gas through six large pipelines; it produces the other 15% primarily from hydrocarbon production fields in the Los Angeles area and the San Joaquin Valley. About 45% of the natural gas used in California powers electric plants. About 21% is used for residential needs including space and water heating, cooking, etc. Both heating and electricity needs increase in the winter / storm season.

Both PG&E an SoCalGas own and operate natural gas pipeline networks (maps are online) connecting supplies, mostly arriving from south of Las Vegas, NV, with customers located in densely populated areas and in simple terrain. The network does not reach most areas with low population density in hilly or mountainous terrain. Locations outside of this pipeline network have only propane as a 'gas' [not gasoline] option. SDG&E is a smaller third natural gas utility operating around San Diego.

A fuel that stays within a pipeline from its source to its end-user would seem to be a reliable energy source even during a weather emergency. However, pipeline vulnerabilities are known to exist and will be discussed below.

Propane

Propane is the common 'gas' fuel used at sites away from the natural gas pipeline network. LP gas can mean 'Liquified Propane' or 'Liquified Petroleum' gas (also called LPG). The 'propane' you buy may be LPG. In California about 60% of propane comes (as of 2018) from natural gas plants (*i.e.*, gas well facilities that also produce methane gas) and about 40% from incidental production by petroleum (oil) refineries.

> "…propane is transported from its point of production to bulk distribution terminals through a distribution system of pipelines, railways, trucks, barges, and coastal tankers. From the terminals, propane marketers fill trucks that carry the propane to end users, including retail fuel sites." (—U.S. Department of Energy)

> "There are no pipelines shipping consumer-grade propane out of western Canada, so propane is mainly shipped by rail or truck to the Unites States…" (—Canada Energy Regulator).

Gasoline

In 2015, Californians used 15.1 billion gallons of gasoline (= 41 million gallons per day on average). Ninety-seven percent of that is used to fuel cars, small trucks, SUVs, etc. Gasoline is produced from crude oil at refineries; California has two major refinery areas, in Los Angeles and near the northeastern end of the San Francisco / San Pablo Bay, as well as refining around Bakersfield, Santa Maria, and Oxnard. In California, by law, virtually all consumer gasoline is blended at the refinery or downstream with ethanol to make a 90/10 blend. A typical distribution network for gasoline is via pipelines to storage terminals or Central Distribution Terminals, then (sometimes by truck) to blending / distribution terminals, then by truck to fueling stations ('gas stations,' once called 'service stations'). Some gasoline (also diesel) is trucked directly to end-users.

Diesel

In 2015, California used 4.2 billion gallons of diesel fuel, mostly for large vehicles (like transport and delivery trucks), trains, ships, and heavy equipment. These are the machines needed to move supplies into and around California, to carry out road and infrastructure protection and repairs, etc. Most diesel fuel is produced from petroleum at refineries. Small amounts of Biodiesel and Renewable Diesel, made from soybeans, animal waste oils, and/or recycled oils, are also sold and used here.

As with gasoline, diesel leaves the refinery via pipeline to distribution (or storage) terminals. 75 to 85% of these fuels (and products such as jet fuel), are carried in those pipelines. Most distribution is via fleet trucks to fueling stations or end users.

Jet fuel

Without it, the planes won't fly. Some is distributed via pipelines.

Ethanol

Most U.S. ethanol is produced in the Midwest where corn (maize) feedstock is most available. California is home to seven ethanol plants, most of which use corn shipped in from the Midwest. 90% of U.S. ethanol is transported by train or truck, about 10% by barge, and minimal amounts by pipeline. California has two railway receiving stations for ethanol, which is then trucked to gasoline distribution terminals for blending. The 10% ethanol-blended gasoline in California, based on 2015 numbers, represents about 1.5 billion gallons annually of pure ethanol.

Fuels-infrastructure commonalities

Almost every liquid or gaseous hydrocarbon fuel in California comes partly or entirely from refinery or well production (ethanol is an exception but is blended with refined gasoline). While pipeline networks distribute natural gas more-or-less directly to customers in more densely developed parts of the state, most other fuels, including propane and 'Transportation Fuels' move, ultimately to end users, by a combination of pipelines, trucks, and to some extent rail and barge transport (collectively this entire system is the 'TFS')

Vulnerabilities

Apparent vulnerabilities in California's fuels infrastructure systems include the following:

- **Interruption of production or of arrival of feedstock supplies due to (1) weather impacts on and/or (2) grid electricity supply:**
  - ° production fields
  - ° pipelines including pumps, valves, and control systems
  - ° marine offloading terminals; tanker traffic
  - ° rail and barge traffic

- **Interruption of refining, processing, blending due to**
    - ° loss of grid power
    - ° inability to remove and dispose of refining waste products
    - ° weather impacts to central distribution terminals and blending terminals
    - ° physical damage or operating issues with pipeline systems

- **Interruption of distribution due to**
    - ° loss of road and/or rail networks
    - ° physical damage or operating issue with distribution terminals
    - ° lack of correct fuels for fleet trucks
    - ° lack of parts and maintenance for fleet trucks
    - ° physical damage or operating issues with pipeline systems
    - ° loss of grid power

If you want to go beyond the bullet list above, I'll provide further abbreviated highlights below, and then 'further reading' listing the source articles I drew from. I've included more explanatory details here because it's important to understand how and why our energy infrastructure could be severely impacted by extreme weather; we tend to overlook or dismiss that. And if you are skeptical, it's fair to give you more background. While this is very important information, you may not feel inspired to read it through in detail. The gist is that most energy systems are both vulnerable and interdependent, and a cascading failure across the energy sector is assessed to be a real possibility.

Radke *et al.*, in a 2018 sub-report for California's Fourth Climate Change Assessment, provide a detailed description of the CA Transportation Fuels Sector (TFS) infrastructure and its exposure to certain risks <u>associated with future climate</u> (coastal flooding, wildfire, and to a much lesser extent, inland flooding using what may be relatively benign assumptions about precipitation). To that assessment I've then added some key points from other of the 2018 CA4_CCA 'climate-focused' reports. The state is clearly interested in identifying emerging infrastructure (especially in energy) vulnerabilities due to climate change; however, <u>I have found far less information about assessments of existing, current vulnerabilities</u>. Fortunately, much of what has been identified as future vulnerability—when not using methods that underestimate risks—can also be regarded as a proxy describing current vulnerabilities under extreme storm conditions (most of the methods applied in the various 2018-era CA4_CCA reports stop short of megastorm-scale scenarios).

Sources, feedstock transport

Petroleum oil ('crude') enters and moves through California primarily by tanker ships into facilities such as those around Long Beach, San Pablo Bay and the Carquinez Strait, and by rail cars, many from east of the state, that offload at about a dozen rail transfer stations, perhaps 7 (or more) of which may be in flood-prone areas [cf. Wall Street Journal], and by a limited number of pipelines running predominantly through low ground, that move both California-produced and out-of-state crude oil to refineries.

Pipeline infrastructure is discussed below, and the significant rail and highway / road vulnerabilities to closures by flooding, erosion, and landslides are covered in the chapter on transportation impacts. Here, I'd like to highlight tanker terminals, crude oil storage facilities, and refineries, with some details about Northern California's refinery complex in the Richmond-Benicia area and the Southern California complex at Long Beach. In the abstract of a 2014 article by A. M. Nafday titled "Feasibility of Continuing Operations at California's Marine Oil Terminals during ARkStorm," he wrote:

> "California's marine oil terminals (MOTs) transport the bulk of the state's requirement of petroleum and petroleum products and constitute a vital infrastructure link to mount successful emergency response after disasters. The ARkStorm scenario may simultaneously affect multiple MOTs and potentially trigger a major disruption in crude supply to refineries and petroleum products to the public, cause likely closure of ports, and significantly impact the economy of the western United States. As disaster relief necessitates timely supply of petroleum products, the feasibility of continuing operations at the state MOTs during the ARkStorm scenario is assessed, taking into consideration the existing design, and operational and procedural safeguards that were primarily built in to address public safety, health, and environmental effects from other hazards. The expected runoffs from ARkStorm are estimated to overwhelm MOTs' drainage design and site-specific flooding analysis and review of mooring analysis for extreme currents is recommended. It is also prudent to formulate strategies to address regional and simultaneous impact of this common cause scenario."

It's worth mentioning that Herdman *et al.* (2018) point out that a storm in 1998 brought 30-foot waves off the coast of California, in addition to heavy rains and coastal riverine flooding.

Radke *et al.* in 2018 calculated refinery flooding vulnerabilities in California using a limited model <u>based on (and focusing on) sea level rise only</u> (including tides but omitting storm effects other than '100-year' storm surge).

> "Refineries in Northern California are predicted to be flooded as early as the 2020-2040 period. Our scenarios indicate a 176-223 ha, (14-18%) inundation of the Chevron refinery at Richmond occurs by 2040 (min, max scenarios) and by 2100, a 240-697 ha, (20-57%) inundation occurs. At the Andeavor Martinez refinery (min, max scenarios) 0.6-2 ha (0.4 - 1%) of inundation occurs during the 2020-2040 period and by 2080-2100, the range increases to 4-117 ha (2 - 68%). Together, the area inundated at all other SF Bay / Delta refineries is 10 - 22 ha (1 - 2%) by 2040; and 51 - 204 ha (5-17%) by 2100.
>
> In the LA / Long Beach region, the only identified refinery exposed to flooding is the Valero Wilmington facility located at the end of the Dominguez Channel in the Los Angeles Harbor. This facility's exposure is significant in terms of area: by 2040, 33-47 ha (40-50%) are inundated and by 2100, 65-84 ha (77-100%)."

I'll point out here that while Valero in Long Beach is probably the most ocean-ward petroleum facility in the complex, and by satellite appears to be at an elevation of 1–10' ASL, the entire area of refineries and terminals is also within the so-called 100-year floodplain of the Los Angeles River, which drains an 827 square mile area, and is specifically mapped by USGS as being flooded in an ARkStorm-scale event (otherwise comparable to a conventionally described so-called '500-year' flood event). Please remember that the conventional so-called '100-year' events are not our biggest concern.

Onshore, considering storm surge plus runoff effects in the lower reaches of large rivers, the following is from a study of the Napa River, which drains into the west end of the Carquinez strait, directly opposite the Phillips 66 marine oil terminal and refinery, part of the Northern California refining and terminal complex, about 4–5 miles from Benicia. The researchers found that in a fairly ordinary big storm, water level at the mouth of the river would rise by 3 to 8 feet depending on other variables, during their chosen basic 'less-than-100-year' storm scenario (or by 10 feet in a second scenario).

> "…maximal water levels will occur in a tidal river when high tides, storm surge, and large fluvial discharge events are coincident… The interactions between tides, river discharge, and storm surge are not simple, **indicating the need for more**

integrated flood forecasting models in the future." —Herdman *et al.*, 2018 [Interestingly, in this modeling study of the Napa river, a "realistic" scenario for runoff discharge rate was set at 10,382 cfs, even though there have been four peak discharge rates of 25,000–37,000 cfs recorded there by USGS since 1960, so the scenarios evaluated by Herdman *et al.* are not even 100-year storm events… let alone megastorm-scale events.]

Refined product distribution

Between the refineries and the rest of the distribution network of pipelines, truck and rail tanker filling points, etc., are terminals. The biggest are 'Central Distribution Terminals' (CDTs) and there are two in California, one in Concord, one in Long Beach. Radke *et al.* (2018) say this about the central terminals:

> "Central distribution terminals are critical assets to the operational success of the TFS as many refineries transport fuels to such terminals via pipeline for further distribution. The two highest product throughput volumes in the TFS (post-refinery) occur at the Concord terminal in northern California and the Watson terminal in southern California. Kinder Morgan, Inc. operates both and they are considered central distribution terminals. They represent fuel convergent nodes, one step before distribution. …**if these individual terminals fail, the inability to move fuel in the system could seriously disrupt the TFS**." [Note: If <u>both</u> fail at the same time, the situation would be far, far worse.]
>
> …
>
> "In Northern California, terminals tend to be more clustered around the greater Bay Area refineries—many of which are in shoreline locations. Most of these assets are exposed to coastal flooding, but only in the maximum flood scenario in the 2080–2100 period… Kinder Morgan, Inc. Station in Concord is not exposed to any projected coastal flooding." [Note: <u>Both</u> the Concord and Long Beach terminal areas might be exposed to runoff flooding from extreme precipitation events; see below.]

Because Radke *et al.* only considered flooding from sea level rise, I'll add back some crucial perspective on surface runoff flooding. Let's look at the Concord CDT terminal. Most of the hardware sits at an elevation of 16–30' ASL. The property is bordered on the west by Walnut Creek, which drains 146 square miles and which flooded at least from San Ramone north in 1862. It sits ~2 miles from an inlet to Suisun Bay, which feeds the Carquinez Strait, the outlet and to some extent a possible bottleneck for all drainage of inland surface water through the Central Valley and Delta. That area could flood more severely if a sufficient 'surge' rise in ocean and bay water, perhaps wind-driven, is restricting runoff floodwater drainage westward. All of this could be modeled and assessed by experts for extreme conditions.

Considering the CDT terminal in Long Beach, it is, like most of LA's petroleum infrastructure, located in a floodplain and possibly vulnerable to flooding from extreme surface runoff. Radke *et al.*, again only considering sea level rise, said this about the terminal complex there:

> In Southern California, terminals are more widely scattered throughout the LA / Long Beach area, many of which are away from coastal locations. In this region, 11 terminals are subject to maximum 2100 flooding and 6 exposed to minimum flooding." —Radke *et al.*, 2018 [This '2100' A.D. flooding can serve as a 'mini-proxy' for an any-year megastorm event.]

Now, when you add in the fact that the whole area is in a mapped flood zone with a FEMA-recognized 'hazard' from the so-called '500-year flood,' which is also the scale of the flood that could be expected in any year from a megastorm, you can see the vulnerability there, with dual exposure to both river and ocean. Extreme weather threats to both of the big California CDT terminals seem plausible, and in a true megastorm-scale event, *both could, as inferred from the USGS ARkStorm scenario and other studies, be disrupted at the same time.*

Refined product transport

Refined liquid petroleum products including gasoline and diesel move to some extent through two limited, isolated pipeline networks originating at refineries in the San Francisco Bay Area and Los Angeles. (Two other, separate pipeline networks carry crude petroleum to refineries, and natural gas for distribution.) Typically, by design, pipelines move their materials in only one direction, using pumps. Some products move by barge between the two centers.

Pipelines can be vulnerable to land subsidence or erosion, to flooding leading to corrosion, debris impacts, or watercraft impacts. The USGS predicted considerable damage to water / wastewater pipes under megastorm conditions but did not specifically discuss vulnerabilities to other pipeline systems such as petroleum / hydrocarbon feedstocks and products; it's reasonable to think that some vulnerabilities apply to all pipeline networks. However, hydrocarbon pipelines could go offline even before physical damage to pipes, due to either a loss of grid power for operating pumps and controls, or due to flooding of that electrical equipment.

> "Pipelines for refined transportation fuel products are the most critical asset and the greatest threat to breaking the flow of fuel within the TFS (Transportation Fuels Sector) network. Many of these pipeline assets are the singular link between refineries and intermediate transshipment nodes or end node terminals **with no redundancy** in place. **If these pipelines go out of service for an extended period of time, the TFS could suffer a debilitating or even devastating failure. An impact on a singular node or link, depending on where it is in the network, could result cascading and devastating impacts.**"

> "Pipelines are the main arteries of the TFS. If disrupted, the flow of finished product in the entire system is dramatically altered as **few pipeline redundancies are built into the system. If the disruption lasts for days**, access to fuel becomes critical in the region affected (J. Settles, personal communication, February 8, 2018). Although emergency preparedness exercises practice short-term repairs to the distribution network (such as truck, rail and marine transportation), **it would be perilous to assume these repaired operations would be effectively maintained over any longer periods.**" —Radke *et al.*, 2018

Refined liquid (or liquified) products also move through the state by truck or rail. Loss of road or rail networks (see the USGS projected highway closure maps, or online FloodFactor flood detail maps), or a lack of the correct operating fuel *(e.g.,* diesel), or if vehicle parts and maintenance are lacking, or if secondary terminals including blending facilities themselves are flooded, then fuels being refined cannot be distributed to customers. Furthermore, it would probably require an emergency order to temporarily suspend the requirement to blend ethanol (which also has a vulnerable supply chain and also increases TFS system complexity) with gasoline.

Fuels like propane will have very comparable production and distribution vulnerabilities.

> How bad could an interruption of the flow of TFS fuels to Californians be? **"California has an approximately three-day supply of transportation fuel on hand.**" —Radke *et al.*, 2018

Natural gas and other pipelines

Natural gas, on the other hand, is not a major TFS fuel, but is vital for power plant operation and home heating; it will presumably be primarily affected by production and pipeline vulnerabilities (in addition to grid power loss). Consider this assessment for Northern California:

"Of particular concern is the fact that California's natural gas infrastructure was designed and built in the previous century when climate-change effects were not as well understood nor considered (Radke, Biging *et al.* 2016). [Note: Nor were extreme weather events fully appreciated at that time, or perhaps even now.]

"The Sacramento Delta is a focal point for natural gas in the State. It hosts a network of natural gas supply pipelines to many points in the State and, in particular, to the urban population hub of the San Francisco Bay Area (Radke, Biging *et al.* 2016). … **"A large portion of the Delta's natural gas infrastructure is located within the Delta's 100-year floodplain and as such may be damaged and disrupted during flooding events." Inundation effects on pipeline infrastructure include: increased hydrostatic load; erosion, scouring and debris flows; corrosion; and restriction of access** (Radke, Biging *et al.* 2016). Given that SLR [sea level rise] rate is projected to accelerate throughout the 21st century (Board 2012), **the higher frequency, duration, and/or depth of inundation from future flooding could exceed pipeline design standards as seen in other recent high-water events** (Needham, Brown *et al.* 2012)." —Brooks *et al.*, 2018.

According to DWR's 2022 UCIP data, there are almost 8,000 utility pipeline crossings of levees and channels in California's Central Valley and Delta. Some number of these are natural gas or hydrocarbons pipelines. All are inspected on a rotating five-year basis, and routinely, ~7% are found to have "urgent maintenance needs" while 59-73% have been found in recent years to need non-urgent maintenance. Urgent here means "Visual observation indicates pipe integrity **or levee integrity issues, or imminent flood risk during a high-water event.**" Of the levees themselves, other DWR sources document that between the SPFC levees and those in other projects like CVS-FFPS, dozens to hundreds of issues have been found in recent years, often indicating points assessed to be likely to fail in the next one or two high water events.

The 'floodplain islands' of the Delta are already as much as 30' below sea level in places, and, with their levees, are subsiding at a rate even faster than sea level is rising. "Previous research with airborne laser scanning measured the subsidence of the levees, and new measurements for the Fourth Assessment found mean subsidence rates of ~1–2 centimeters per year (~0.4 to 0.8 inches per year) (Brooks *et al.*, 2018)." —CA4_CCA report overview. The Brooks *et al.* study considered the impact of a standard 1970s-era 'observational concept' of a so-called '100-year flood' and decided that the levees protecting this natural gas pipeline infrastructure would meet federal and state 'freeboard' (or elevation safety margin) requirements for a few more decades; *I'll suggest this needs confirmation under updated realistic scenarios.* Maendly (2018) looked at the same issue and found that an estimated '200-year flood' during mid-21st century conditions would overtop today's levees in a number of places. USGS said that even bigger floods could happen at any time (and forecast numerous levee breaks in that event); so do 'simulation' methods of estimation (which don't rely upon small samples of 20th century weather observations). Referring to the Brooks *et al.* study on possible flooding of gas pipeline routes in the Delta, the 2018 CA Climate Safe Infrastructure Working Group report stated:

> "At that point, the safety of natural gas pipelines could no longer be guaranteed."

Earthquake vulnerabilities of Delta-region levies and pipelines are already on the energy threat radar; storm and flood threats are taking their place alongside them. Much of Northern California's fuel infrastructure runs through, and is exposed in, this small region.

In Southern California, another 2018 sub-report, by Bruzgul *et al.*, from the state's CA4_CCA report, summarized some vulnerabilities of the San Diego-area SDG&E natural gas pipeline network <u>due only to some selected climate change impacts</u> (which are similar to, and could be replicated or compounded by, extreme weather impacts):

> "The research team analyzed the exposure of gas assets within the SDG&E Company Service Area to climate change-driven coastal hazards (wave flooding, tidal inundation, and coastal erosion) and inland hazards (inland flooding, wildfire, extreme heat, and landslides). This analysis found that many gas assets will potentially experience increased exposure to these hazards. By mid-century:
>
> - **over 6,500 point assets (which are located at a particular point, such as substations; rather than spread over a distance, such as transmission lines) and 120 mi. (193 km) of line length are projected to be exposed to 100-year coastal wave flooding, over 5,600 point assets and 75 mi. (120 km) of line assets could be exposed to annual tidal flooding, and nearly 4,000 point assets and 60 mi. (96 km) could be exposed to 100-year event low-lying erosion;** these

exposed assets represent <1% of the total assets in the study area,

- **over 13,000 point assets and nearly 270 mi. (435 km) of line asset length lie within 100-year floodplains** (representing <2% of point assets and line asset length), and

- **over 43,000 point assets and over 340 mi. (547 km) of line asset length lie within landslide and slide-prone formations** (representing <5% of point assets and line asset length)."

[Remember, present-day vulnerabilities to extreme winter storms, particularly the effects of inland surface runoff or riverine flooding, were not evaluated in this report, but are clearly suggested by the above observations.]

So, the 'timetable' failure projections above are based on assumptions which do not include extreme storms. The latter two points, and coastal inundation, are of greatest import to megastorm impact estimation. This sub-report, like some others, makes a rather rosy summary assessment of the reliability of this particular SDG&E pipeline network, by excluding the possibility of an abrupt, extreme weather event which could impact most of the above vulnerabilities simultaneously, *with the addition of runoff flooding that is not considered* in the Bruzgul *et al.* report. Note that if one used existing mapping of a so-called '500-year-floodplain,' in this area (and others), that would correspond more closely in scope to the potential inland impact area for megastorm flooding, per USGS in 2011.

On-site fuel solution: wood

Wood is the one fuel that, for most rural Californians, is abundant, locally available, in reliable supply, and which requires minimal processing before use. If it fits your lifestyle, wood heat / energy, from wood stoves or similar already-installed appliances, could be the one fuel source that you could depend upon during a prolonged period of disruption or isolation. A wood-fueled stove (or boiler) is a very practical backup heat source in more rural areas. In my view, this could be a particularly important consideration for emergency shelter facilities in rural areas.

Interdependencies

On one level, in a complex society like ours, almost every infrastructure system depends upon several other systems. Redundancy is expensive, and optimism, however arrived at, lowers up-front costs. Consider some crucial observations by Radke *et al.*:

> "...**few pipeline redundancies are built into the system**."
>
> ...
>
> "We find that **transportation fuel product pipelines and central product distribution terminals are the most critical assets within the TFS network, and that the network is dependent on supporting sectors such as electricity and natural gas.**
>
> **During extreme weather events pipeline operations are most vulnerable to pump failure due to loss of power** from interconnected electrical partners. Where backup generators exist, they are mainly in support of pipeline communications and keeping the loading racks operational at distribution terminals. Loading racks in distribution terminals are key units responsible for trans-loading fuel products from pipelines into tanker trucks for further distribution (Langenkamp, 2014). **Aboveground pumps and valves are also susceptible to damage, which in turn could stop the flow of fuel.**" —Radke *et al.*, 2018

Some views of consequences

It may seem obvious that without product inputs from refineries or gas fields, fuels won't be flowing through pipelines, but it's worth remembering that pipelines flow because new inputs must push, via pumps, on the fuels already in the pipes. No inputs, no push, no flow.

Product supply or pipeline failures could also cause disruptions in Reno, Las Vegas, and Phoenix. 90% of Nevada's refined petroleum products, and 50% of Arizona's, arrive via pipeline from California. This could affect relief operations from likely staging areas.

Using propane as an example of some of the 'lifeline' complexities around energy, availability may be limited under severe and prolonged storm conditions. Eight propane business facilities including fleet transfer stations from Merced northward to Manteca along U.S. 99, at elevations of 50' to 150' ASL, are projected by USGS (per their flood mapping) to experience up to 3' (in the south) or up to 10–20' of predicted flooding (near Manteca) during a megastorm. Four other facilities further north, from Walnut Grove to Sacramento, are at elevations ranging from 18' to 43' ASL in predicted 10'–20' flood depth zones (levees 'not withstanding'). If equipment is ruined, distribution of propane may be impeded even after waters recede. Road access to and from such facilities may also be limited. Somewhat similar issues could arise with terminals and fleet distribution of gasoline and diesel, and of ethanol supplies.

Distribution fleet capacities for propane, gasoline and diesel are not easy to pin down, but a simple calculation provides some rough insight. Basically, deliveries match retail sales (consumption). That means a one-day supply is carried in the fleet of delivery trucks on any given day (a 1.4-day supply if there are no regular weekend deliveries). If a typical propane customer gets winter-season deliveries every 30 days, that means that about 3–5% of fuel needed in the service area is on the road on any given day or business day. Residential propane deliveries usually are aimed at, and prioritize, customers with tanks that are down to a 20–30% reserve; this is practical, just-in-time supply, which reduces the number of delivery trips but keeps a number of customers near empty at all times. If fuels delivery fleets stop operating for any reason, some degree of shortages affecting unlucky customers will start to appear within a few days at most. A week of non-delivery, continuing, could shortly impact up to 15–25% of the local customer base, not even counting those who are self-rationing.

With respect to gasoline, homex.com states that "The majority of neighborhood gas stations sell around 2000–4000 gallons a day," and that such a station takes delivery every 2–3 days. A tank for any one type of gasoline is typically 12,000–24,000 gallons. Depending on whether customer topping-off or stockpiling is occurring, *a single gas station, selling three fuel grades, after a delivery might have as much as a 10–12 day inventory, but is likely to sell out before that if storm alerts or evacuations are getting underway.* Radke *et al.*, above, stated that California has a 3-day supply of transportation fuels on hand.

Transport (in 2023) typically requires fuels, either directly or for non-renewable electricity. Orderly, effective evacuation requires fuels. Shelter facilities require fuels or energy. And there will be less obvious TFS impacts and consequences: storage tanks are an example:

> "Liquefied petroleum gas tanks and underground storage tanks can break away from their supports and float in flood waters, causing hazards from their released contents." — USACE, CVIFMS draft watershed plan, 2015

A loss of grid power has both obvious and less obvious consequences. If your home is dark and you can't charge your cell phone or hit the Internet, or run your well pump, you notice. Less obviously, if you have a public water or sewer service, you may not at first think about purification and pumping of potable water, or pumping and treatment of sewage, as being grid-dependent. One Foothills water agency has had a policy of keeping a two-to-three-day supply of diesel or propane fuel at each plant, to allow on-site electrical generation and to sustain operations when the grid goes down. Ordinarily, fuel deliveries will be possible within that two or three-day window. But under extreme conditions, with damage to local and regional road networks, and perhaps more fundamental supply disruptions, fuels might not be able to reach local distribution fleets, and fleet trucks might not be able to reach more remote upcountry, or low-lying, facilities where road conditions are a problem. Those public water and sewer services could end within days. Vulnerabilities to these and to wastewater systems will also be discussed in the next chapter.

Basic human needs are far easier to provide for, including to displaced persons, if electricity, or fuels for producing electricity, are available.

Most communications depend upon electrical power at all points in the chain, and coordinated emergency management and disaster response, and in-field rescue and repair efforts, depend on electronic communications.

Limited fuels availability might also hamper roadwork and other repairs, if maintenance agencies do not maintain adequate fuels reserves, and materials and equipment are not pre-positioned in areas most at risk of overland isolation. Even snow removal will require fuel.

In conclusion

The infrastructure lifelines that supply energy for basic human needs and for all supporting operations are both interdependent and potentially vulnerable. In an extreme weather scenario, disruptions could arise at several points and their consequences could rapidly propagate much more widely. *I hope that issues of fuels and energy production, reserves, and distribution / availability issues will be fully explored in future storm planning studies by emergency managers and state officials.* The CA4_CCA studies are not comprehensive; they have an overly narrow focus and consider too limited a range of scenarios to provide the full picture we need. Meanwhile, it seems clear that in a megastorm situation it could become much more difficult to produce and to move refined petroleum fuels by truck or rail, and possibly by pipeline, around and across California, to end users. It also seems likely that major impacts to electricity generation and distribution will occur, *and this should be reviewed and clarified.*

No matter where we live, disruptions to these broad-scale energy 'lifelines' are issues that could affect us, often profoundly, during extreme weather. Energy should be a consideration in any storm / megastorm preparations including sheltering in place and providing shelter services.

* * *

A note on carbon

This book doesn't focus on climate change, but it's a factor that will 'boost' future storms and megastorms, and it also looms large in infrastructure assessment, as we have seen above, and infrastructure design and investment planning, so here are three paragraphs on carbon. From the pages above, you will see that places like California literally burn through a massive amount of carbon-based fuel every day. A small amount of that, from ethanol, biodiesel, co-generation, wood chips or pellets, and firewood, represents biological carbon that has cycled through the atmosphere and biosphere for thousands of years. Those cycles and relationships have led to a relatively stable amount of carbon in the air for millennia.

What's new is the injection, into the atmosphere, of <u>geological</u> carbon in fossil (previously buried and 'locked up') fuels being extracted and burned since the industrial revolution. Prior to the 18th century, volcanoes were typically the main source of geological carbon dioxide injections, and even that was in a roughly balanced cycle of millions of years. All the non-renewable hydrocarbon fuels now being burned are a new source for CO2 (and CO) entering the atmosphere, where it will linger for a long time. While it lingers, it helps trap heat (= energy) in the atmosphere, and then the oceans, and the land: the greenhouse effect. This 'blanket' effect has been known and reported on since at least 1912. The 'greenhouse gasses' (GHGs) also include unburned methane (natural gas), a much more potent GHG that leaks from gas wells, compressors, etc.

Scientists trying to model future climate and weather behavior use a set of scenarios for how quickly GHGs will reach certain concentration levels in the future atmosphere, which are related to forecasts of global temperature. The worst standard scenario, called RCP8.5, is actually the "Business As Usual" scenario in which we just carry on as usual, without making any reduction in GHG emissions or trends. How significant is all of this? It's the "BAU" RCP8.5 scenario that leads computer models of future weather to predict (among other problems) that by 2100, we may be having megastorms in California about once every 40 years, on average, or more often according to the latest studies; also, worse droughts and more of them. Hence the concern about hydrocarbon emissions, and the interest in deploying old and new strategies and technologies that will reduce GHG emissions. The more than 50% share of renewable electricity in total current production in California is significant; ideally, that will continue to increase even as 'watt-thirsty' electric vehicles (EVs) enter service in greater numbers. These are public policy / public welfare issues.

* * *

Further reading

2021 Texas grid problems; "Black Start": https://www.
youtube.com/watch?v=08mwXICY4JM

Nafday, Avinash M. Feasibility of Continuing Operations at California's
Marine Oil Terminals during ARkStorm. Natural Hazards Review, A6014001-
1 to -4. 2014. Abstract at: https://trid.trb.org/view/1426745

Bedsworth, Louise, Dan Cayan, Guido Franco, Leah Fisher, & Sonya Ziaja. (California
Governor's Office of Planning and Research, Scripps Institution of Oceanography,
California Energy Commission, California Public Utilities Commission). 2018. Statewide
Summary Report. California's Fourth Climate Change Assessment. Publication number:
SUM-CCCA4-2018-013. https://www.energy.ca.gov/sites/default/files/2019-11/
Statewide_Reports-SUM-CCCA4-2018-013_Statewide_Summary_Report_ADA.pdf

Radke, J.D, G.S. Biging, K. Roverts, M. Schmidt-Poolman, H. Foster, E. Roe, Y. Ju, S.
Lindbergh, T. Beach, L. Maier, Y. He, M. Ashenfarb, P. Norton, M. Wray, A. Alruheil,
S. Yi, R. Rau, J. Collins, D. Radke, M. Coufal, S. Marx, D. Moanga, V. Ulyashin, A.
Dalal. (University of California, Berkeley). 2018. Assessing Extreme Weather-Related
Vulnerability and Identifying Resilience Options for California's Interdependent
Transportation Fuel Sector. California's Fourth Climate Change Assessment, California
Energy Commission. Publication Number: CCCA4-CEC-2018-012. https://www.
energy.ca.gov/sites/default/files/2019-11/Energy_CCCA4-CEC-2018-012_ADA.pdf

Herdman, L. M., Erikson, L. H., and Barnard, P. L. 2018. Storm surge propagation and
flooding in small tidal rivers during events of mixed coastal and fluvial influence. Journal of
Marine Science and Engineering pp. 1–26. https://pubs.er.usgs.gov/publication/70201673

Brooks, Benjamin A., Jennifer Telling, Todd Ericksen, Craig L. Glennie, Noah Knowles,
Dan Cayan, Darren Hauser, Adam LeWinter. (U.S. Geological Survey). 2018. High
Resolution Measurement of Levee Subsidence Related to Energy Infrastructure in the
SacramentoSan Joaquin Delta. California's Fourth Climate Change Assessment, California
Energy Commission. Publication Number: CCCA4-CEC-2018-003. https://www.
energy.ca.gov/sites/default/files/2019-11/Energy_CCCA4-CEC-2018-003_ADA.pdf

Bruzgul, Judsen, Robert Kay, Andy Petrow, Tommy Hendrickson, Beth Rodehorst, David
Revell, Maya Bruguera, Dan Moreno, Ken Collison. (ICF and Revell Coastal). 2018.
Rising Seas and Electricity Infrastructure: Potential Impacts and Adaptation Actions for
San Diego Gas & Electric. California's Fourth Climate Change Assessment, California
Energy Commission. Publication Number: CCCA4-CEC- 2018-004. https://www.
energy.ca.gov/sites/default/files/2019-11/Energy_CCCA4-CEC-2018-004_ADA.pdf

[CA] Department of Water Resources. 2022. Inspection and Local Maintaining Agency
Report of the Central Valley State-Federal Flood Protection System. https://cdec.water.
ca.gov/reportapp/javareports?name=2022_Combined_Report-Body_Without_Appendix.pdf

8

Impacts on California Water Infrastructure

"Greater Sacramento, California, is often considered to be the most at-risk region in America for catastrophic flooding, relying on an aging system of levees, weirs and bypasses and Folsom Dam to reduce its flood risk. But that system, just like a chain, is only as strong as its weakest link." —U.S. Army Corps of Engineers

Water infrastructure refers to water storage and flood control and diversion systems (dams including hydroelectric plants, canals, bypasses, levees), clean water supply and distribution systems, and wastewater treatment and disposition. Water redistribution infrastructure such as the massive State Water Project (SWP) and the Central Valley Project (CVP), which send water from Northern California southward, won't be specifically discussed here, except to note that the canals may be vulnerable to storm damage, according to USGS (drought issues are beyond our scope here but are briefly referenced elsewhere in this book). Federal, state, and smaller local agencies and private owner-operators all maintain some water infrastructure. This chapter will just cover some highlights of how a megastorm like the 2011 USGS ARkStorm simulation (or like the real 1862 storm) would affect water systems in California.

Levees

Flood control infrastructure includes the dams and levees that ordinarily constrain and regulate much of the surface water flow and movement in California. Levees separate low-lying land areas from waterways, protecting property on the dry side. California's levees were built at different times (beginning around 1850 and more formally, with federal support, getting underway in the early 20th century), using different designs, materials and techniques, for different purposes; these levees, many aged, presently exhibit a range of conditions, including continuing subsidence among others. There are 3,789 miles of levees in the Sacramento Valley (north of the Stanislaus River) and Delta, more in the San Joaquin Valley, and a total of 13,800 miles of levees around California.

> "Let no one believe that because you are behind a levee, you are safe." Galloway (2005), quoted in Pinter *et al.* (2018)

In 2011, the USGS expert panel

> "…felt that [in the ARkStorm simulation] urban levees might be threatened or overtopped at 60 to 75 critical sites, and that 15–20 breaches might realistically occur. The panel believed that 30 breaches of Delta levees were realistic, with 2–3 breaches occurring per island. The panel felt that **a total of 50 levee breaches was realistic**." [If you look at a map of urban levees in the Central Valley, you can pick up to 15 or 20 urban locales that might flood, plus 10 to 15 Delta islands, and then try to imagine it.]

If you look at comprehensive maps of the USACE-estimated 1% AEP floodplain in the Central Valley, the levee-protected areas are within the 'maximum extent of flooding.' Without over-interpreting how 'maximum' applies, it is clear that in expert planning scenarios, these areas remain vulnerable to severe flooding events. This was the USGS conclusion. Levees in several California counties failed or were overtopped in 2023.

One article on Sacramento-area levees presented an observation by geologist Nicholas Pinter:

> "With recent devastating wildfires and longer, hotter and drier summers, even **Californians are prone to forget floods caused the most disasters in this state.** 'An estimated 7 million residents and $575 billion in infrastructure [quoted in 2018] are at risk of flooding,' according to Dr. Nicholas Pinter in his book, Geology of Sacramento and Surrounding Area. 'Of the 85 major disaster declarations in California, over half (47) have involved flooding.' "

Waves like those that "beat farm homes in pieces" across the Central Valley in 1862 might also pose a threat to levees. If one levee fails, the resulting 'lake,' and wave effects, increasing in strength over longer reaches, could cause damage to further parts of the levee system. While I haven't seen this discussed specifically anywhere as a consequence of flood and expanding levee failures, the following quote from the U.S. Army Corps of Engineers (2015 Draft CVIFMS Plan) is relevant:

> "Anticipated sea-level increases due to climate change will also increase water-level stages in the Delta and lower reaches of the Sacramento River. Sea level rise **would increase existing structures' exposure to waves and wind setup, and increase the hydrostatic pressure on levees**, especially on low-lying land currently below sea level. **These effects increase the possibility of catastrophic levee failures** that could inundate communities, damage infrastructure, and interrupt water supplies (Hanak and Lund, 2008). …
>
> (Wind setup is the vertical rise in still water at the face of a structure or embankment due to wind stresses. The term is usually used in discussions of reservoirs or small bodies of water; comparable to "storm surge" used to describe similar activity for oceans or larger bodies of water.)"

Much more could be said, and is said in other reports, about the age, intended purposes, effects and conditions of levees. I provided some details earlier, in Chapter 7.

Dams

Dams are another 'simple concept, complex subject.' And dams and dam safety are a hot button issue for officials and agencies; information on them may not flow freely (see Cox, 2023). *Even the USGS ARkStorm report tiptoed around impacts to dams:*

> "The ARkStorm [report], therefore, does not posit any dam overtopping failure to DSOD [state] regulated dams… Because of **the extremely sensitive nature of a dam-damage scenario**, the selection of a particular dam to imagine as hypothetically damaged in such a way is left to emergency planners."

Dams can provide flood control… until the reservoirs behind them become filled. Dams in the Sacramento and Lower San Joaquin River Basins have a combined maximum volume of incidental and dedicated flood control capacity (*i.e.*, a regulatory target to be reached by each December: space reserved to 'buffer' heavy wet season runoff inflows) of about 2 cubic miles, more than two trillion gallons. Total reservoir capacity above the Central Valley is about 7 cubic miles; combined capacity of the 200 largest reservoirs in California is about 12 cubic miles.

Compare that with the amount of rain and 'snow water equivalent' that is expected to fall during a megastorm: recent estimates range from 45 to 60 cubic miles, statewide; however at local and regional scales, some precipitation intensity and proportional total amounts will be more extreme. In a megastorm, depending on several variables, including initial reservoir capacities and down-channel constraints on preemptive releases, 'run-up' weather (determining soil moisture condition and pre-existing base flows in streams), timing and rhythm / intensity of rainfall and snowfall, runoff efficiency (*i.e.*, what fraction of rainfall becomes immediate runoff), runoff lag and travel times, temperature and rain-on-snowpack effects, and others, a large volume of water could be flowing uncontrollably over dam spillways. Reportedly, preliminary USACE assessments of recent simulation data from the ARkStorm 2.0 project found that some dams could be overtopped by a plausible modeled megastorm (Cox, 2023).

Even preemptive controlled releases must sometimes, unavoidably (at least as designed), exceed levels safe for downstream channels including levees, sometimes causing damage, as for example at and below the Terminus Dam on the Kaweah River above the Tulare Basin in the spring of 2023.

Are these volume numbers unrealistic? From the USGS description of a 4000 square mile lake forming in the Central Valley, and taking 10' as a very rough average of USGS-projected flood depths there, that alone would represent around 20 cubic miles of water accumulating and slowly working its way toward the Carquinez Strait and the San Francisco Bay. (6000 square miles at up to perhaps ~12' to 15' average depth, *a la* 1862, would be… more.) And still more water would be flowing in and flowing out.

The high inflow 'pulse' of runoff down to the Valley floor could last for four weeks in the ARkStorm (and longer in a bigger or more prolonged megastorm) depending on when and where reservoir flood control capacity is exceeded. When this volume of water reaches the Valley proper… The thing about levees is, they restrict water that would normally spread across the floodplain into much narrower channels. That may be obvious, but I suspect few people pause to imagine what a flood of those megastorm proportions looks like in those artificially narrow channels when levees attempt to prevent it from spreading across its natural territory. This might help: 'Lake Sacramento' could become 20 to 60 miles wide, whereas the Sacramento River above the Yolo Bypass is about 650' wide, levee to levee; in Sacramento the river channel is about 750' wide. Elsewhere in this book you can read more about behavior and vulnerabilities of levees.

If you want to think about similar runoff volumes in Southern California, recall that the ARkStorm projections call for 7.5 feet of rain in the mountains between Los Angeles and the Mojave Desert, 11 feet in the Southern Sierra, and around 18–19" in urban Los Angeles, in this simulated 23-day event. One watershed, that of the Los Angeles River, covers 834 square miles from mountaintops to the sea.

When water behind a dam begins to flow down an auxiliary or emergency spillway, possibly in addition to other 'controlled' channels—and specifically, when the 'surge capacity' <u>above</u> the level of the dam's highest spillway is also being used or exceeded—the river is in uncontrolled or unregulated flow, only occasionally seen since the 20th century dam building era. Meanwhile, large quantities of water, and potential energy, are stored behind dams (a 10,000-ton chunk of the concrete St. Francis Dam near Los Angeles traveled ¾ of a mile when the dam failed in 1928). Any dam or spillway damage or failures would be serious, and the topic must be discussed responsibly. I'm not an engineer or a hydrologist and I won't offer opinions. On some topics, inexpert speculation is unhelpful and irresponsible. That said, the U.S. Army Corps of Engineers in 2016 rated 833 of California's dams as having "high hazard potential," meaning that failure would result in loss of life (nationally, the number was 15,498 high-hazard dams), according to AIR Worldwide (see Sources). Understand that <u>this is not a description of their condition</u>, nor a prediction that those dams <u>would</u> fail. That said, Associated Press reported in 2022 that "more than 2200 high-hazard dams [are] in poor or unsatisfactory condition across the US."

There is a federal National Inventory of Dams website online (see below). Although it is cumbersome to use, in theory one can extract information about 'high-hazard' dams and dams having a particular condition assessment such as 'poor.' However, most dams in the Sierra are assigned to the "condition assessment not available" category. The information exists: the AP report describes their "… review of federal data and reports obtained under state open records laws…;" however, it is deliberately sequestered. One official reason for restricting this information has been offered (below); other possibilities are left to our imaginations.

> "Dam conditions are supposed to be rated as unsatisfactory, poor, fair or satisfactory. But the ratings are subjective—varying by state and the interpretations of individual inspectors—and are not always publicly disclosed.
>
> Since the Sept. 11, 2001, terror attacks, the U.S. government has cited national security grounds in refusing to include dams' conditions in its inventory, which was updated most recently in 2018. But the AP was able to determine both condition and hazard ratings for more than 25,000 dams across the country through public records requests." —AP

Without dwelling on or speculating about dam safety, here are three examples of what might be causes for concern, or at least for awareness. First, Oroville in 2017:

> "The real near-catastrophe in 2017 was the failure of the main spillway and near-failure of the emergency spillway on Oroville Dam, on the Feather River upstream of Sacramento. Although eventually controlled and now largely repaired, the events at Oroville resulted in the evacuation of nearly 200,000 people and **came within hours of what could have resulted in a large loss-of-life failure.**" —Pinter *et al.* (2018). [2017 was not the first time that the Oroville Dam had come within hours of a dangerous uncontrolled release of water.]

Next, here are some observations from the 2011 USGS ARkStorm report. There are about 1500 of what could be called 'significant' dams in California; about 1250 are regulated by the state DSOD [California Division of the Safety of Dams; USACE sets the operating regulations for most big dams]. From the USGS 2011 study:

> "A DSOD panelist felt that, close to the reservoirs, this [the ARkStorm] could cause minor spillway damage or erosion in downstream channels. However, expressing a greater level of concern, a dam owner panelist felt that **"minor spillway damage" may be an underestimate**, saying **"When spillways sit untested for years, then are subjected to continuous flow for an extensive period, damage is possible or even likely."**

The latter perspective seems prescient in retrospect, because six years later, the Oroville dam, owned by DSOD, effectively lost safe use of both of its spillways to damage. For a good review of the very complex situation at Oroville in 2017, the book 'Spillway Emergency' provides a wealth of information on the events at Oroville, both the situation at the lake and dam (hydrology, infrastructure, and flood control), and the emergency response.

Lastly, one dam, at Whittier Narrows in Southern California, recently has been assessed as potentially not being able to withstand the effects of a severe storm. Correcting problems with that dam has been identified as a top federal priority; about half of the roughly $600 million price tag was approved by Congress in 2020, and the remainder was included in the Administration's proposed budget for 2021. Repairs are scheduled for 2025-2030. About 1.2 million people live downstream from that dam. USGS in 2011 also indicated that some other infrastructure in California may not be immune to damage from uncontrolled spillway releases from flood control dams (levees presumably top this list).

As this book was in final edit, an excellent article by Christopher Cox appeared in the New York Times (cited below). With a focus on dam safety, runoff flows and capacity exceedance, the report also touches on many other themes found in this book. If this book has your attention, you will appreciate the Cox article.

Flood control, generally

It may also be useful for those who live in low areas, where they must depend on flood control systems, to review their assumptions about flood control. If you think that the huge expenditures made thus far have promised to eliminate all flood problems, you are mistaken. <u>Flood control infrastructure was designed and built (in part) to reduce the frequency and likelihood of flooding, and reduce impacts, not to prevent all flooding</u>. It does help, up to a point, when in good repair, and operated correctly, to prevent flooding from major storms. But it has been understood from the beginning that it cannot handle the biggest of all future storms. The 'gambler's problem' lies in estimating when or how often those problem storms might arrive (actually, in estimating the odds at any time), and in imagining how big the storms might be. [Service life and deterioration is an additional estimate.] For different projects, and different studies, in different decades, those estimates have ranged from 10,000 years, to 500 years, to 70 years, to 30 years, to… Clearly, the problem of good estimation is complicated, difficult, and serious. The problem for legislatures and agencies is to apply those estimates (whether good or bad) within cost / benefit analyses, under various constraints including the challenge posed by the reality of diminishing returns at larger scales of capability.

A more troubling aspect of these issues is noted in Chapter 3 (see Pajaro, CA): do your public agencies, in cost / benefit analyses, even calculate that you and your community are valuable enough to be worth protecting or prioritizing?

Water treatment and delivery systems

There are many public water systems in California. USGS in 2011 noted that some facilities are vulnerable to flooding that can damage or contaminate various equipment including wellhead seals, electric pumps, and electronics. Others may be vulnerable to contamination of the aquafer by sewage flows when wastewater systems fail. One water district panelist said that

> "...its wellheads are supplied by backup power—emergency generators powered by natural gas with some onsite storage—**although because the electrical equipment is located at ground level**, the generator and its electrical equipment would be damaged, rendered nonfunctional, and have to be replaced."

Locally, in the hinterlands, I'm informed by a local water agency that they keep a 2–3-day supply of backup fuels for off-grid operation, while depending on delivery trucks to use the road network to resupply operating fuels. In short, in some areas, if lacking fuel and/or roads, safe water being actively pumped by a public or private water authority may be in short supply during and after an AR-megastorm. USGS stated: "The Central Valley counties with the most severe flooding are Glenn, Butte, Colusa, Sutter, Yuba, Yolo, Sacramento, San Joaquin, Merced, and Kings; for these we assume that **50 percent of water supply is lost during the duration of flooding and for 14 days thereafter**." "Duration" could mean months of draining in some areas. Repair cost estimates ranged from 100 million dollars for one relatively small water district to up to 10 billion dollars for a single large district. There are between 8000 and 9000 water districts and agencies in California. Many of the 600,000 private water wells, which serve about 1.6 million Californians, might have similar vulnerabilities, depending on where the wellhead is situated, and they generally rely upon electricity, including grid electricity, for operating pumps.

Wastewater treatment

We probably spend less time thinking about wastewater systems including wastewater treatment plants (WWTPs) and lift stations (pumps). In fact, the 2011 USGS study panel could not locate any comprehensive database of WWTPs in California, and therefore pulled together an incomplete inventory from various sources. In that (incomplete) survey, the Sierra Foothills region had few if any WWTPs threatened by flooding. In some other parts of California, it will be a problem. Sewage systems run on gravity, with lift pumps as needed. Per USGS, "WWTPs tend to be in low-lying areas and, therefore, more subject to flooding than the population served." Similarly, lift stations pump waste from low areas to higher ones. Flooding will damage unprotected equipment including pumps, more so if the systems have not been de-energized (shut down) first. Sewer pipes are also vulnerable to damage from landslides; the USGS panel estimated that repairs to sewage pipes would cost $300 million statewide. Regarding sewage, one USGS panel estimated that, in Marin County, given an extended grid outage, 2 to 5 percent of street miles might have raw sewage on roads due to pump shutdowns (bookmark this sort of possibility if you might have to rely upon home purification of surface water for domestic use). Although a USGS panel felt that replacement of WWTP electrical equipment might take 3–6 months, the study concluded that "we have perhaps optimistically assumed that service is restored within 4 weeks after floodwaters recede from WWTPs. **This assumption needs checking**." [Yep!] Let's remember, regarding clean water and wastewater system repair timelines, that in some areas it would take weeks, and even months, just for floodwaters to recede.

On higher ground, as in hill country including the Sierra Foothills, clean water (public and private) and wastewater services are likely to be more dependent upon working grid electricity or else backup hydrocarbon fuels availability (and good road access) to keep otherwise serviceable equipment operating. For individuals and remote communities, and for emergency shelter operations, a possible need for alternatives to public services and electrically pumped wells should be anticipated in any planning process.

* * *

Further reading

https://www.abc10.com/article/news/history/when-sacramento-became-levee-city/103-48d5063b-ad48-4b32-9709-c7ca4fe8ea79

Central Valley Flood Protection Plan [CVFPP] Update 2022. Public Draft. CA DWR. https://water.ca.gov/-/media/DWR-Website/Web-Pages/Programs/Flood-Management/Flood-Planning-and-Studies/Central-Valley-Flood-Protection-Plan/Files/CVFPP-Updates/2022/2022updateCVFPP22_layout_v9_plus_Append_BC.pdf

https://www.geiconsultants.com/wp-content/uploads/2017/10/The-Origin-and-Evolution-of-the-California-State-Plan-of-Flood-Control-Levee-System.pdf

http://www.safca.org/Images/Maps/AR_SR_FLOODDEPTHZONES.pdf

Sager, Willian, and Wayne Wilson. Spillway Emergency: The Story of the Failure of the Oroville Dam Spillway and the Evacuation of Oroville. Independently published, 2019. Available from amazon.com.

Adams, Nathaniel and Matthew Hergott. 2017. Imagining the Worst: What if the Oroville Dam's Auxiliary Spillway Failed Catastrophically? Paper published online by AIR Worldwide. https://www.air-worldwide.com/publications/air-currents/2017/imagining-the-worst-what-if-the-oroville-dams-auxiliary-spillway-failed-catastrophically/

Sahagun, Louis. Rare L.A. mega-storm could overwhelm dam and flood dozens of cities, experts say. Los Angeles Times, February 18, 2019. https://www.latimes.com/local/california/la-me-ln-mega-storm-dam-failure-20190218-story.html

U.S. Dams: https://www.fema.gov/emergency-managers/risk-management/dam-safety/national-inventory-dams

https://nid.sec.usace.army.mil/#/

Rott, Nathan, and Clare Harbage. California's epic snowpack is melting. Here's what to expect. NPR, May 5, 2023. https://www.npr.org/2023/05/05/1173069933/snowpack-california-2023-flooding-what-to-expect

Cox, Christopher. The Trillion-Gallon Question [Extreme weather is threatening California's dams. What happens if they fail?] New York Times, June 22, 2023. https://www.nytimes.com/2023/06/22/magazine/california-dams.html?smid=nytcore-ios-share&referringSource=articleShare

9

Impacts on California Communications

"…all mails are cut off… The telegraph also does not work clear through, but news has been coming for the last two days. In the Sacramento Valley for some distance the tops of the poles are under water!" —William H. Brewer, Journal entry for January 31, 1862, writing from San Francisco

"A dispatch received from Mokelumne Hill: "Hell has broken loose here, look out down below in Stockton." And then the telegraph went dead." —Sacramento Daily News, January 16th, 1862

In storm-impacted areas, postal mail service and newspaper production and delivery may become sporadic or cease altogether for the duration. Electronic telecommunications, both one-way and two-way, potentially may be among the only 'modern' ways to distribute or exchange information in or into remote and/or impacted areas (word-of-mouth, bulletin boards, etc. may serve some neighborhood needs). However, all electronic communications systems are potentially vulnerable in at least some areas, beginning with power supply and/or charging. Many modern people might experience communications difficulties and any limits on access to information as one of the most distressing aspects of life under megastorm conditions, assuming that they are warm, dry, fed and hydrated. The 2011 USGS ARkStorm scenario study considered impacts to telecommunications infrastructure and operations in detail. Notably, both overuse and power failure can cause service interruptions without any physical damage having occurred. That said, the systems are also vulnerable to physical damage. Finally, communications are vitally important to the successful coordination of response, relief, and repair operations.

Two-way telecommunications

Both landline systems (for convenience I include both Plain Old Telephone Service [POTS] and 'cable' service systems here, which may carry voice, broadband Internet, and/or programming channels) and cellular transmission systems typically have electrical power backup systems, with battery capability for hours of off grid operation (for cellular 'Base Transceiver Stations', or BTS, which your phone connects to, three hours of battery backup is typical per USGS in 2011). Both systems can dispatch mobile units to affected stations to supply generator power and switching capability. However, the question is: how many mobile units are available to be put into the field? There are a lot of cell tower transceivers (between 400 and 40,000 per each 100-mile square). In a prolonged regional loss of grid power, any existing fleet of mobile cellular transceivers would presumably be able to provide only patchy and weak cell service to the customer base. Scattered equipment able to operate within prevalent area-wide failures might be overwhelmed by call volume from the service base. Finally, cell phones may lose charge more rapidly if network or local signal strength is weakened, as when more distant transmitters must be reached.

Phone landlines, cable and fiberoptic systems have both similar and different vulnerabilities. Buried cables can be damaged by soil failure and by flooding that leads to water infiltration. Switching and power equipment are typically located in central offices; because of its weight much of the vital power equipment there is typically located on the ground floor, where it is most vulnerable to flooding.

The USGS provided estimates of the length of megastorm-caused telecommunications service interruptions for each county in California. *However, their estimates are derived in part from other estimates of electrical grid power interruptions, and as I've written before, I believe that those estimates are likely to be too optimistic and should be reassessed.* At this point, I'll just say that it's reasonable to expect that some loss or deterioration of typical consumer two-way communications services can be expected in various areas affected by the storm, for unpredictable but possibly extended periods of time.

Satellite phones would <u>seem</u> to be more reliable, but the service can be affected by weather, and by anything affecting ground stations. Review more information on this topic before assuming that 'sat phones' are an ideal solution. Newer satellite systems are currently being planned or have been put into operation. Finally, specialized portable GPS devices and the newest smartphones may have direct satellite uplink capability, allowing emergency texts to be sent from almost anywhere. Remote call centers may be able to forward such messages, but in the event of widespread regional disruption (as in a megastorm) the ultimate fate of such messaging is uncertain.

There are various kinds of two-way radios used by amateurs and civilians, by agencies including law enforcement and other responders, by companies with personnel operating fleets of vehicles, and by the armed forces. All have their uses and limitations. If civilian / amateur radio is a topic that interests you, with respect to emergency scenarios, I encourage you to learn more. In theory, a ham radio in an isolated community could become a key point of contact with the outside world, including with regions not affected by a megastorm. In practice, response and relief agencies often incorporate ham radio as one significant communication channel.

> "Radio Amateur Civil Emergency Service (RACES) RACES (pronounced RAY-seez) is an emergency-communications service that operates under the auspices of the Federal Emergency Management Agency (FEMA). Many government agencies across the country train their Auxiliary Communications Service (ACS) volunteers using the RACES protocol." —FEMA

You may find it interesting to connect now with local ham radio operators and learn about that option. You can check with your local fire department, CERT team, or county OES. Ham trainers can describe the licensing / training process, and the availability of classes in your area. Becoming a ham radio operator requires some commitment. Becoming an ACS volunteer in your area may appeal to you.

All radios, excepting crystal sets and the occasional dental filling, need some source of external power.

One-way telecommunications

Having just mentioned ham radio, you may want to have a multi-band radio, or, if you are more computer oriented, you may want to look into SDR (Software Defined Radio). An inexpensive USB antenna kit and some software (some is free) can turn a personal computer into an all-band radio receiver. By all-band I mean everything except restricted frequencies. Because it is one-way (listening only) radio, you do not need an operating license.

Television, radio, and Internet (with one-way streaming) may continue to operate 'within limits.' Broadcast transmitters on elevated towers may be among the most vulnerable to wind-caused damage, lightning strikes, etc. They will require power to operate. Internet services (including static pages, streaming and two-way communications) are most often provided via phone or cable service, or occasionally satellite, meaning that (as discussed above) they will have to be able to reach you using your established service (your ISP), which is not guaranteed.

Communications impacts on emergency activities
… with more general notes on emergency response coordination

Emergency alerts from county, state, or other agencies may not reach persons or areas if they can only be communicated over locally non-functioning systems. But a deeper problem may affect emergency management and response activities depending on location and vulnerability of facilities, equipment, and infrastructure. For example, consider the flooding of an optimistically but poorly situated (in my view) radio station carrying the Emergency Broadcast System alerts in the 1986 floods in Northern California: that EBS signal went off the air and station personnel were evacuated by boat.

California and its counties have moved to Web-based emergency management and virtual Emergency Operations Centers. That all makes perfect, modern sense, unless Internet connections, or hardware damage, or a lack of power impacts communications. Here are some positive highlights.

The City of Sacramento Emergency Operations Plan (2018) provides an example of some thought that has gone into this issue at state and local levels:

> "The city EOC can communicate with the OA EOC to access the State OASIS satellite system. OASIS can support the operational area entities by allowing for direct satellite communication with the State's Regional EOC (REOC), and the State Operations Center (SOC). OASIS voice transmission works like a standard telephone and data transmission is similar to a computer modem.
>
> City Operations and Responders. The City of Sacramento operational staff in the field implement interoperable communications through the use of 800 MHz radios to facilitate communications with all responding departments and city entities. Alternate forms of communications such as the use of cell phones, text messaging, email, amateur radio etc., may be utilized if determined necessary. The use of the interoperable radio system allows for communications between DOCs, EOCs, and the Incident Command Post (ICP) that is located near the site of a field emergency incident. Communication channels will follow the communication structure that is defined by the City of Sacramento emergency management organizational chart. DOCs and dispatch centers for private entities (*i.e.*, private EMS providers) are responsible for maintaining communications with the city EOC when it is activated. More details are provided in the Communications Function section of this plan."

Electronic telecommunications are at the heart of today's operational coordination. It makes sense, and is essential, to stress test communications systems and protocols between agencies, as well as command and coordination frameworks, in advance of an emergency. It is also essential to consider vulnerabilities in the essential communications equipment, facilities, and services, as well as in the physical EOC facilities and field / operating facilities as well. Even for facilities above the floodplains, will hurricane force winds, for example along the coast, leave transmitter towers and aboveground grid, landline, and fiberoptic systems operational? Do facilities with backup generators have a 'Plan C' in case fuels like diesel, propane and gasoline become unavailable? All contingencies should be prepared for.

Communications Impacts on Recovery

Some disasters have shown that general infrastructure repairs may be hampered or delayed if the cellular network is not restored first (per USGS). Crews and dispatchers who rely upon cell phones for assignments and instructions may be unable to undertake repairs until that service is restored.

Final point

Any device you use personally for electronic communications is going to require a source of electrical power. I review some solutions elsewhere.

* * *

Further reading

Abbot, Jake. Impacts, Lessons from Oroville Spillway Crisis. Marysville Appeal-Democrat, January 02, 2018. https://www.govtech.com/em/disaster/impacts-lessons-from-oroville-spillway-crisis.html

https://caloes.ca.gov/cal-oes-divisions/regional-operations/cal-eoc

https://www.cityofsacramento.org/-/media/Corporate/Files/Emergency-Services/2018-City-of-Sacramento-Emergency-Operations-Plan.pdf?la=en

https://hamradioprep.com/ham-radio-in-emergencies/

Introduction to Software Defined Radio, from a software vendor: https://www.sdr-radio.com/

10

Impacts on California Populations, Shelter, and Supplies

> *"A week ago today news came down by steamer of a worse condition at Sacramento than was anticipated. The news came at nine o'clock at night. Men went to work, and before daylight tons of provisions were ready—eleven thousand pounds of ham alone were cooked. Before night two steamers, with over thirty tons of cooked and prepared provisions, twenty-two tons of clothing, several thousand dollars in money, and boats with crews, etc., were under way for the devastated city."—William H. Brewer, Journal entry, January 19, 1862*
>
> *. . .*
>
> *"It is with the poorer classes that this is the worst. Many of the one-story houses are entirely uninhabitable; others, where the floors are above the water are, at best, most wretched places in which to live." —Brewer, Journal entry, describing conditions in Sacramento on March 7, 1862*

A future AR-megastorm will disrupt people's lives in many ways; having to leave one's home (some people will and some won't) will be one of the more serious ones, sometimes merely inconvenient but often genuinely traumatic. Populations living in low-lying coastal and inland areas, with or without levees, or near rivers that might leave their usual banks, or below dams if any are threatened, will often have to relocate. People in other, unflooded areas might relocate to areas with more reliable electrical, water, and wastewater services, more access to goods and materials including food and fuels, more access to emergency services including medical personnel and facilities, and out of areas that face long term overland isolation due to landslides, road and bridge losses, or other factors. Scattered homes may be damaged by wind, falling trees and limbs, earth movement or debris flows, or may be without heat, such that they no longer provide adequate shelter. Ultimately, many people without other options may have to seek emergency shelter.

Dislocation and evacuation

USGS in 2011 looked at population displacement in a single "inland area" of the state comprising 21 counties from Kern to Modoc, and including Solano and Contra Costa Counties to the west. That corresponds primarily to the Central Valley and Delta. In those areas, per USGS, 20% of the population, meaning 1.5 million of 7.5 million people in 2011, live in areas that would be flooded in an ARkStorm-scale event. San Joaquin and Sacramento Counties would <u>each</u> have more than 400,000 residents affected by flooding. Nearby, 97% of Sutter County's population lives in areas that are expected to flood. USGS stated: "The Central Valley counties with the most severe flooding are Glenn, Butte, Colusa, Sutter, Yuba, Yolo, Sacramento, San Joaquin, Merced, and Kings." Of those 1.5 million likely evacuees, about 220,000 'refugees' from 23 counties would need access to emergency shelters on higher ground upslope from the Valley, or elsewhere, according to federally accepted calculation methods used by USGS.

Later that decade, Cal OES developed a severe storm impact assessment for just 10 Delta and Sacramento Valley counties (north of the Stanislaus River). Their estimates projected that 1.46 million people (34% of the population) <u>from that area alone</u> would be exposed to flooding and potentially displaced, with 330,000 (22.5% of 34%) requiring full emergency shelter and care. Impoverished people comprise disproportionately higher percentages in those totals.

These numbers establish the general scope of flooding impacts anticipated for some defined areas of California, and may represent a rough estimate of people who would be forced out of their homes by flooding alone, disregarding other causes (the official language "exposed to flooding" and "affected by flooding" avoids saying "displaced by flooding," an estimate which is needed for response and relief planning). Even one foot of water can cause cars to start to float, and homes may be uninhabitable. A more precise estimate is difficult to make. USGS accepted in 2011 that the flood-affected 1.5 million people in the Central Valley or 'inland' region would be forced to leave their homes and relocate to higher ground, or else travel much further away if possible (1.5 million is also the number of Central Valley residents or workers within the so-called 1% / '1-in-100-year' floodplain, according to the 2017 California CVFPP document, whereas USGS projected ARkStorm flooding extending across the larger so-called '500-year' flood zone in the region surrounding Sacramento and Stockton).

What the other 1.28 million 'not as desperate' displaced Valley persons (using the USGS 'affected' estimate, or more, if the Cal OES indications were extended to additional counties) would do is not answered, but they will presumably be on the move somewhere. As of 2023, California has 1,063 Bed & Breakfast establishments… not nearly enough for a big flood. Evacuees proactively able to reach family or friends on high ground, and who have taken planning and preparedness seriously, will be the fortunate ones. Others will reach hypothetical relocation sites for tents and RVs. More than half of that exposed population lives east of the San Joaquin and Sacramento Rivers, and so may be most likely (or able) to relocate toward the east, possibly in the Sierra Foothills counties.

Assumptions that Donner Pass on I-80 at, 7056' elevation, into Reno will remain open are uncertain or doubtful; USGS predicted extended closures for <u>all</u> Sierra passes and highways (and flooding issues for northbound and southbound routes). USGS estimated that the ARkStorm would cause I-80 west of the pass to be closed for at least 30 days, and limit its usability for several months (flooding on I-80 east of Reno might also be an issue for evacuation and logistics). Even assuming that the pass could be kept open, here is a perspective recorded in the 2013 ARkStorm scenario preparedness exercise attended by officials including emergency managers in the Tahoe / Reno area:

> "Given an ARkStorm-type scenario, a general consensus believed that **the state of California would not be able to provide significant emergency management support to Nevada, because resources would be stressed in dealing with large storm impacts and disruptions in California.** Stakeholders raised significant concerns about the availability of, and competition for, a variety of resources given likely significant requirements and federal declarations elsewhere in California. **Indeed, in such an event, California populations would be expected to evacuate into the Reno / Tahoe region, adding to the emergency conditions and requirements there. Thus, the regional capability to absorb significant self-evacuees traveling to Reno / Tahoe from impacted areas of California is a major concern.**"

Translation: officials in the Reno area were doubtful about Nevada's ability to provide emergency services to displaced Californians (assuming they can reach Nevada). Also recall that the Carson Valley got about 9–10' of rain in six weeks in 1861–62, and that the 1997 AR-storm caused major flooding and damage in Reno and throughout the Carson Valley.

A quick look at a map indicates that a handful of Foothills counties, from around Nevada Co. or El Dorado Co. in the north to Tuolumne Co. or Mariposa Co. in the south, might bear the brunt of sheltering displaced persons from the hardest hit areas of the Central Valley, assuming they can't or don't travel further.

Areas along I-80 and U.S. 50, up to about SR 49, are relatively developed and may be relatively better able to provide mass shelter services, compared to Amador, Calaveras, Tuolumne, and Mariposa. [Note: Population in the area has increased since 2010–2011. The population of unhoused people, without transportation or alternate shelter options, has also sharply increased.]

I have not located any specific public plan for who would be evacuated to where, but a comparison of some population numbers is illuminating. From the USGS report and census data, here are comparisons of low-lying counties situated east of the main rivers, and their adjacent Sierra Foothills counties.

'Valley county'	Evacuees (USGS)	'Foothill county'	Population (2020)	
Sutter	94,024	Nevada	102,241	
Yuba	56,262	Placer	403,490	
Sacramento	527,885	El Dorado	191,185}	
		Amador	40,474}	231,659
San Joaquin	480,106	Calaveras	45,292}	
		Tuolumne	55,620}	90,812
[Total	1,158,277		838,302]	

These numbers present a very simplistic picture, particularly northeast of Sacramento, where the terrain and the developed landscape are complex. But in the Foothills from El Dorado Co. or Amador Co. south through Tuolumne Co., the impact of over a million displaced persons and potential refugees (a large proportion needing full emergency shelter services) on the lifeline systems in place for a settled population roughly one-third that size would be massive. How would they be accommodated, beginning with physical space? Note that this <u>simple</u> set of numbers ignores any Foothills residents also needing relocation and shelter.

As a relevant example, one local county fairground also designated for emergency operations and potential shelter space has about three acres of paved parking and an estimated ~17 more unpaved, ready to use acres (in dry weather) on a partly undeveloped 55-acre site. It's difficult to park 100 full-sized RVs on one acre. With <u>best</u> design, 162 cars can park on an acre. County-level ESF-6 (Shelter & Mass Care) planning can begin with assessing and cataloging the physical space options available at suitable sites within the county. Note: in 2022, CDFA made awards to 12 in-state fairgrounds (not ours), ostensibly to improve their emergency shelter capabilities.

The total number of persons potentially uprooted from this 21-county region, projected at 1,538,032 by USGS (2011), includes populations living in several counties west of the big rivers, who would presumably not travel east. However, it is also an estimate based solely on flooding impacts. Other circumstances could also lead people in these counties <u>and other counties including those in the Sierra</u> to try to relocate to find shelter and services. Bear in mind, California has 58 counties, and all may be affected by storms and floods, landslides, road closures, and loss of power, fuel, and other necessities.

It's important to remember that, as in 1862, there could also be major flooding in western California, in valleys which are now often heavily populated, and in Southern California, on flat plains, river floodplains, and in coastal areas vulnerable to storm surge. Any concerns about dams could exacerbate this relocation situation. In a statewide event, numbers of displaced persons would be much higher than just the numbers from the Central Valley or 'inland'. I won't offer a useful estimate here, but my rough calculations put that number much higher (guessing very roughly, 2 or 3 times?) than 1.5 million people. For example, <u>considering flooding alone</u>, in a much broader assessment than what USGS released in 2011, CA DWR in 2013 stated that 1,414,000 Californians lived within so-called '100-year' floodplains and 7,274,000 within so-called '500-year' floodplains. The flood modeling team in the USGS ARkStorm scenario study determined that flooding from such a megastorm event would cover the traditional so-called '500-year' floodplain zones in much of California. As noted by Nicholas Pinter of the University of California at Davis (and co-authors), a DWR-estimated $575 billion (in 2013 dollars) in infrastructure, presumably including residential, agricultural and commercial structures, is at risk of flooding. USGS (2011) predicted that

> "…the models estimate that **almost one-fourth of the houses in California would experience some flood damage** from this storm." —Lucy Jones, USGS MHDP Chief Scientist

Damage to structures will disproportionally affect residential structures. Depending upon structure inhabitability and services availability, dislocations and relocations of some duration affecting a mass of people possibly approaching a quarter of the state's population (excluding many multistory apartment or condominium dwellers), so perhaps several million persons, could be plausible. Not all flood damage would automatically lead to relocation, but remember, flooding isn't the only hazard or hardship that will drive people from their homes.

[As a side note, USGS in 2011 estimated ARkStorm evacuation and relocation costs statewide at $2.5 billion. That might equate to hundreds of dollars per person affected. *Is that realistic?*]

The point is that, in a situation like the ARkStorm or the 1861–62 megastorm, emergency managers, agencies and NGOs, as well as many families and friends, churches, and community and benevolent groups, all across much of the state and beyond, will have displaced persons, often in unprecedented numbers, to shelter and care for. It is not likely to be possible to simply shift resources including personnel and materiel (emergency supplies and equipment in this context) from one county to another. Disaster relief will be a broadly regional issue, and not restricted to California alone, if 1862 conditions reoccur. Prudent planning will allow for an expandable response making full use of <u>all</u> resources.

Let's consider the question: Where will people go? Until official evacuation routes and destinations are determined and publicized, we won't have clear answers to this question, but, generally speaking, to higher ground, of course, but not very high, because generally above around the 1000' to 1500' elevation level, for example in much of the Sierra, other problems will be occurring due to winter weather, mountainous terrain, forest vegetation, few developed facilities, access issues and infrastructure impacts including losses of road networks.

Emergency management and relief agency officials will, I believe, give a high priority to establishing relocation centers where there is a road network that can be maintained, both locally and with through connections to any sources of goods, supplies, and personnel. Looking at the USGS maps of highway vulnerabilities, and travelling actual roads and terrain, we can visualize some areas that are more practical (than others) as relocation destinations. As an example, local and familiar to me, SR 49 and various feeder connections from the Valley, from around Coulterville or particularly Jamestown in the south, through Placerville and perhaps further north, is one area that is likely to logistically support providing for the needs of a displaced East Valley population. There is a similar predictable need along the length of the coast ranges during such extreme weather; much of I-280 and I-680 provide a model of what is sufficient, as contrasted with low-lying stretches of U.S. 101.

In your area, if you are above any floodplain or zone, you can assess where suitable terrain, reliable road access and service infrastructure exists to facilitate providing for the needs of however many people ultimately relocate (or are relocated) there. In state emergency planning, if the state becomes involved, Caltrans advises and coordinates with CHP on evacuation and transport routing. What maintainable routes are likely to be available in your area?

In some counties your office of emergency services, or your sheriff's office, may have done some planning along these lines, especially where floodplains exist; you could inquire (and let them know you care!). If planning has been done, has it been communicated to the public? Is there any signage in place to clarify routes and familiarize residents with them?

USGS in 2011 pointed out something that may seem obvious, but because flooding is not uppermost in everyone's minds nor potentially in their planning, here is a useful observation that anyone can make use of at a basic level:

"Elevation data can be used to identify suitable shelter sites. Integration of various spatial information will be useful for regional evacuation planning. One example of spatially integrated information at the local level is the evacuation mapping designed by Baldwin (2010) for San Joaquin County." [See below; the site has local neighborhood maps with rally points, and brochures for each neighborhood; a good model approach.]

The Red Cross usually has a lead role in organizing shelters and caring for displaced persons. A megastorm may have such extreme impacts that no single agency or NGO (Non-Governmental Organization) could be responsible for all shelter needs. The 1986 AR storm here (and some other events elsewhere) exhausted the resources of the Red Cross locally and nationally. *This is a prime example of one of many issues that should be stress-tested or 'war gamed' in advance by emergency managers.* The 2017 Oroville Dam evacuation of 188,000 people provided Californians with an uncommon chance to develop—on very short notice—and later review relatively large-scale evacuation and shelter approaches under winter storm conditions. One positive sign in that crisis was the number of churches and non-governmental organizations that set up additional ad hoc shelters on their own; this is a function that Foothills community groups with facilities or other resources can start to think about and prepare for well in advance, to reduce the ad hoc element. To be clear, inaccessible or remote communities will have different, more local challenges and agendas.

Feeding, clothing, sheltering, treating, and caring for 'refugees'—by estimates, hundreds of thousands of them—requires both access to goods and materials and the ability to deliver them. Power and fuels for heating and cooking might be particular challenges for some storm shelters. Roads must be open and fuels must be available to transporters. But in addition, *it must be possible to <u>secure and access</u> stores of food, fuels and supplies. This is another topic that the USGS study team did not address;* I make a few comments below.

Finally, if you still wonder why I decided to write this book, consider the number one conclusion of the large USGS AR-megastorm study team in 2011:

"An ARkStorm raises serious questions about the ability of existing federal, state and local disaster planning to handle a disaster of this magnitude."

And, from an overview presentation on the unreleased Cal OES NCCFRP document, assessing possible impacts of a catastrophic flood in the Sacramento Valley:

"Unknown casualties. Mass fatalities may result during an unexpected levee break or if people refuse to evacuate."

There are reasons to think that given the overwhelming scale of the event, and its humanitarian challenges even where populations will more safely congregate, help may be unlikely to reach remote areas in a timely manner. If you live or shelter 'off the beaten path,' navigating the challenges may be up to you and your community.

As I wrap up this chapter, in June 2022, Bangladesh is flooding. Much of the land area of that country is a floodplain that lies at the same elevations as those in the California Delta and adjacent Valley; Bangladesh lacks the flood control infrastructure—dams, levees, etc.—that usually protect floodplains in California from most storms. I'll link the Reuters article below, but here are some excerpts, to assist your imagination around some of the possible realities of flood-driven dislocation, that could apply generally both to Bangladesh and to an <u>unprepared</u>, megastorm-flooded California:

> "Authorities in Bangladesh intensified efforts on Wednesday to deliver food and drinking water to millions of people struggling after heavy rain unleashed catastrophic flooding across a quarter of the country... "We deployed different agencies, including the army, navy and air force to rescue people. In some areas, we have ensured that people are airlifted"... Authorities said at least 36 people had been killed and **about 4.5 million people stranded so far.** The floods are also threatening to disrupt agriculture, infrastructure, and clean water supply. Mohammad Mosharraf Hossain, Sylhet division's chief administrator, said 365 medical teams were trying to reach flood-affected areas **to provide tablets to purify water for drinking.** "We are making frantic efforts to ensure there is food and drinking water for all the affected people," said Atiqul Haque, director general of Bangladesh's Department of Disaster Management. Large swathes of farm villages were submerged. Rescue teams used boats to supply drinking water, medicine and food to people perched on higher ground and government buildings. "Many people are in dire need of food and drinking water," said Enam Ahmed, 45, a resident in worst-hit Sunmaganj district. "There is water everywhere but **no drinking water. Flood shelters were crammed with people but they are not getting enough food**," he said... "Shelters are overwhelmed as many schools and other shelters where people would normally take refuge were inundated with

water as well," said Hossain I. Adib, acting country director for WaterAid, Bangladesh… **About 5.5 million people have been displaced, of which about 3.7 million are staying in government-run makeshift shelters on raised embankments or other higher ground.**"

There is always room to tuck ample water purification tablets, and a bottle, into a go-bag. We'll delve deeper in chapters on preparedness.

Comment on a related point: supply-chain issues

The ongoing need to replenish or restock supplies including food, materials, parts, and all other goods is a universal challenge, but one felt most acutely by displaced persons and in relief operations generally. Let's take a moment to consider supply chain issues during a megastorm.

Manufacturing, warehousing, and transport facilities, designed for functional efficiency, essentially require flat ground. The flattest ground in many areas is also low, floodplain ground, making such core elements of our supply chains particularly vulnerable to flooding. For example, at least some large warehouses are in low-lying areas of the Central Valley, where it is cheapest to build them, including in the lately-popular 'tilt-up' construction style, and where in normal times there is very direct access to major transportation routes (which themselves may also run across low ground). When planning for personal or community emergency needs, you may want to consider the number of warehouses and supply / distribution facilities located in the low Central Valley, particularly from about Woodland and West Sacramento south through Manteca and beyond.

Some other Central California facilities on higher ground are west of the San Joaquin River and might be inaccessible from the east, or else might be committed to provisioning the populations west of the Valley. *I have not found clear assessments of what supply-chain components will actually be available during megastorm conditions,* and so I'm not going to speculate here, but until some capable team assesses this issue, you are welcome to do some research and develop your own picture of where storehouses of food, medicines, medical supplies and equipment, all other kinds of supplies and materials, spare and replacement parts, heavy equipment and everything else are located. If warehouses and distribution centers of food, supplies, repair parts and equipment are either isolated by local conditions, or subjected to flooding, then any of those needed supplies and materials will probably not be available from that source. At least one warehouse of emergency relief supplies and equipment (and possibly more than one) is located in a flood-prone area. Flood risks appear to be strangely absent from the calculus of critical supplies lifelines.

This uncertainty is a big reason to consider stepping up proactive grass-roots preparation, by families, communities, and even local relief agencies. As a first step, in my view, relief agencies and organizations should be sure that their emergency stores are kept where:

- they will be secure in extreme weather,
- accessible to 'invulnerable' extended transportation routes, and/or
- will be 'staged' in advance (*i.e.*, permanently, with rotation) and locally available to communities that might be cut off from transportation and supplies and/or to displaced populations in shelters.

In many kinds of emergencies, supplies can be moved rapidly from any warehouse to wherever they are needed; however, extreme storm scenarios are very different. It may only be workable to have supplies already prepositioned in smaller, dispersed storage facilities throughout local regions and communities where people will be in need. There is very little downside to warehousing emergency and relief supplies in a network of smaller, wisely situated and well-protected facilities across a region. In smaller-scale disasters there is only a relatively small extra cost for moving supplies from Point A to Point B, and in many instances, they will already be closer to the area of need.

* * *

Further reading

An overview presentation on the (non-public) Cal OES Northern California Catastrophic Flood Response Plan: https://caresiliency.org/wp-content/uploads/2020/01/NCCFRP-Presentation-for-CA-Resiliency-Alliance.pdf

San Joaquin Co. evacuation maps and brochures: https://www.sjmap.org/evacmaps/

https://www.reuters.com/world/asia-pacific/bangladesh-india-race-help-millions-stranded-deadly-flooding-2022-06-22/?taid=62b36330892b0a0001d91695&utm_campaign=trueanthem&utm_medium=trueanthem&utm_source=twitter

11

Costs and Losses

Consequences for property, wealth, business, agriculture, revenue

"You can imagine the effect it must have on the finances and prosperity of the state. The end is not yet. Many men must fail, times must be hard, state finances disordered. ... I see no help, and on whom the blow will fall remains to be seen." —William H. Brewer, Journal entry for January 19, 1862, writing from San Francisco

The United States Geological Survey's 2011 report on a study of the effects of a simulated AR-megastorm, dubbed the ARkStorm, avoided making any specific predictions about human hardship (other than evacuation impacts for the interior region, and the particular needs of certain demographics) or loss of life, while clearly describing a deadly dangerous situation. (Cal OES, referring to a similar scenario for the Sacramento Valley in an overview of its non-public NCCFRP document, treats it as a potential mass-casualty event.)

Instead, the USGS report used dollar costs as an indicator to describe the scale of some of the immediate and longer-term impacts of an extreme weather event on California property, infrastructure and operations. The topics in the report included impacts on seven 'lifelines:' highways, power, water supply, wastewater treatment, dams, levees, and telecommunications. It also considered losses to property, to business activity, and to agriculture. Dollar cost and loss estimates provide a perspective on the magnitude of megastorm impacts on California, leaving human costs to the imagination. In reality, a 'big' megastorm would likely affect several states, not only California; however, impacts including dollar losses were only estimated for California alone.

A trillion dollars, or...

The USGS damage cost / loss estimate—with one focus on property—is probably the most convoluted and intricate section of the 2011 ARkStorm study report, so it might not be shocking that the report summary and the report details sections present different cost / loss numbers. I worked with the various detail elements in the cost calculations, and attempted to update them for inflation and appreciation, while considering 12 post-2010 years of growth, development, economic expansion and infrastructure rollout and replacement.

However, I don't think the general reader will be very interested in the details. If I'm wrong, I refer you to the ARkStorm study itself, and to some later follow-up papers cited below (bring a calculator). The two acceptable options here are 'rough numbers' and expert analysis; for many reasons, rough numbers must suffice for this book, while expert re-analysis elsewhere would be very welcome. Different expert approaches will have different scopes of inclusion, and different concepts and calculations.

You may be satisfied for now to know that the media have settled on the one-trillion-dollar figure, which is more-or-less in line with an updated, selective view of the ARkStorm report conclusions from 12 years ago. A reported number like this may typically represent only an immediate property (and infrastructure) damage estimate, consistent with the attention span of a typical news cycle. But you may want to bookmark my thoughts that the immediate and short-term (2–5 year) costs tallied from the USGS report, updated, allowing for economic expansion, fully considering business interruption costs (those 'BI' costs alone, per USGS, would now be close to a trillion inflation-adjusted 2023 dollars), allowing for some apparent USGS underestimates, taking into consideration numerous apparent study gaps in the damage and repair / replacement costs to lifeline infrastructure (dams, spillways, bridges, culverts, grid, pipelines, etc.), could be closer to two trillion dollars.

That's just for California. Multiple states could also experience catastrophic impacts. Looked at in these ways, it would be the most expensive disaster in US history, and potentially also the deadliest. Clearly, the specific damage, losses and costs depend upon the size and characteristics of any eventual megastorm(s), a term which would include smaller and more frequently recurring megastorm events (the USGS ARkStorm model may be on the smaller side) as well as larger, rarer megastorms (compare 1862 and the 'ARkFuture' simulation of Huang and Swain, 2022). If you say 'low trillions' you'll be in the ballpark.

An economist could tell you whether it's fair to include the ripple effects and indirect effects, including increases in insurance premiums, including for flood insurance, or greater future loss exposure due to potential unavailability of insurance in the California market and others, in borrowing rates for local and state governments (and the value of the currency), in deficits and borrowing costs arising from lost tax revenues, in economic dislocation caused by insolvencies, in the national prices of foods and other products originating in California, in the actual demand surge for materials and equipment needed to rebuild structures and lifeline infrastructure (USGS capped this estimated pricing surge effect optimistically at 20%), in environmental impacts and remediation costs, and in health and healthcare cost impacts due to injuries, weather exposure, limited medical care access, diseases favored by floods, contact with once-buried or released materials and chemicals, damp and decay, and emergency relocation and shelter conditions:

> "The ARkStorm Scenario predicts that a prolonged winter storm event across California would cause extreme precipitation, flooding, winds, physical damages, and economic impacts. This study uses a literature review and geographic information system-based analysis of national and state databases to infer how and where **ARkStorm could cause environmental damages, release contamination from diverse natural and anthropogenic sources, affect ecosystem and human health, and cause economic impacts from environmental-remediation, liability, and health-care costs. Examples of plausible ARkStorm environmental and health concerns include complex mixtures of contaminants such as petroleum, mercury, asbestos, persistent organic pollutants, molds, and pathogens; adverse physical and contamination impacts on riverine and coastal marine ecosystems; and increased incidences of mold-related health concerns, some vector-borne diseases, and valley fever. Coastal cities, the San Francisco Bay area, the Sacramento-San Joaquin River Delta, parts of the Central Valley, and some mountainous areas would likely be most affected.**" —Abstract, Plumlee *et al.*, 2016

An ethicist could discuss whether loss of life, injury, illness, or other hardship should be placed within a context making it a formal part of the 'damage description,' usually dollar-denominated, of a major catastrophe Is there a loss of life calculation that reaches a trillion-dollar mark? The September 11, 2001 attacks were a unique event that led to federal compensation enacted by Congress (a body subject to political forces); while responses to other mass-casualty events cannot be predicted, the 9/11 fund approach developed by the Special Master might provide an illuminating model:

"The economic portion of the award is calculated by determining the victim's post-tax income and then, adding in the victim's employer-provided benefits, such as bonuses and 401K matches. This figure is then increased based on the victim's work-life expectancy and an applicable wage-growth rate. A percentage representing the victim's share of household expenditures and consumption is subtracted, and the final amount is reduced to present value.

The non-economic portion of the award (pain-and-suffering) has been presumptively set at $250,000. For a death claim, $250,000 is awarded for the decedent, $100,000 for the spouse, and $100,000 for each dependent. For physical injury claims, the $250,000 presumptive award can be increased or decreased by the Special Master based on the individual's circumstances.

...

There is no maximum payout established by the Act or the regulations. However, the regulations establish a minimum award for a single deceased person, before collateral income sources are deducted, of $300,000, and for a married deceased person or a deceased person with a dependent of $500,000. As of June 16, 2003, the average award for a death claim was $1.44 million, and personal injury awards ranged from $500 to $6.8 million." —DOJ OIG Audit Report 04-01, October 2003. [$5.12 billion was initially allocated to this compensation award fund. Additional funds have since been allocated, while programs to cover emerging related health care costs have also been funded.]

California's Fourth Climate Change Assessment (CA4_CCA) in 2018 took the USGS megastorm damage loss estimates seriously and married a $750 billion '2010-dollar' figure from the 2011 report to a progressive (accelerating) estimate of 21st century megastorm occurrence probabilities published by Swain *et al.* in 2018, to come up with a future <u>mid-century</u> actuarial figure estimating the average expected, 'amortized' megastorm damage cost <u>per year</u>. [OK, for wonks, I'll note that there are evident errors in the described computation in the CA4_CCA summary report on page 97, starting with which graphical figure data in Swain *et al.* 2018 is applicable (it should be 2c, not 1c), what the graphed data represent (half the models forecast between 1 and 2 megastorms between 2018 and 2060 under RCP8.5 assumptions; the trendline at 2060 shows a 100% median cumulative expectation, not 50%), and the irrelevance of the obsolete pre-industrial projection to a total cost (not increased cost) calculation. CA4_

CCA gave an (erroneous) average amortized cost per year of $8.4 billion, whereas a 2.5% annual event probability by 2060 gives a per year amortized cost of $18.8 billion in that period, accruing each year. Now if you double the starting estimate of total event cost to $1.5 trillion, that's real money.] Event probabilities are reviewed in the next chapter, and Chapter 20.

Even using an appropriate calculation (in future, we can hope), it makes little sense to imagine costs of a singular event as being spread out over all years (or five years in this CA4_CCA case), unless a capital reserve fund accruing annual allocations is being implemented. This would be fiscally possible, in budget surplus years, but surely a political target (I remember CA budget surpluses being called 'obscene' in my youth); a more likely palatable approach could be to increase annual funding for infrastructure hardening and improvement, and for evacuation, shelter and mass care preparations. As a clarifying comment, the risk is <u>already</u> real at greater than a 1% annual chance, per models; it is the increasing annual risk that is attributed to trends in the climate.

Liability

Even how pain, suffering, injuries and death are valued is relevant, for example if liability for those intangible losses is assigned to private entities or public agencies. Of particular concern to the state, and other public entities and agencies, should be the liability implications of the Paterno Decision. In 2003, the California Supreme Court determined that the state was liable for damage resulting from the 1986 Linda Levee collapse in Yuba County. Consequently, the State of California had paid out $464 million in damages by 2007. If 25% of the structures in California were damaged or destroyed by megastorm flooding, and if federal, state, or other agencies were held responsible for any failure (or inadequacy) of flood control infrastructure, a long, litigious decade or two of musical bankruptcies, or fiscal hobbling, could follow.

> "The Paterno decision's precedent makes it possible that the state could ultimately be held responsible for the structural integrity of all SPFC facilities." —CA Legislative Analyst's Office, 2017

> "California gave assurances to the federal government that it would oversee and maintain the "State Plan of Flood Control" (SPFC) system along the Sacramento and San Joaquin Rivers. This system includes 1,600 miles of levees, four dams, and seven flood bypasses." —CA Legislative Analyst's Office, 2019

The Paterno Decision was followed by further cases, ramifications and administrative responses; a short summary linked below is worth a two-minute read. Imagine a worst-case scenario, from a public-funds perspective: paying billions for flood control, thus establishing responsibility, and then also paying billions in damage liability awards. Alternatives come to mind.

* * *

Some particular economic topics will be of greater interest to the general reader. First, consider insurance coverage. USGS in 2011, looking at coverage on properties likely to flood in the ARkStorm, estimated that only about 6–12% of the value of at-risk properties was covered by flood insurance. With property losses predicted to reach into the hundreds of billions of dollars, that's a huge amount of loss exposure for individuals, families and (when coverage caps on required policies are too low) mortgage lenders. Insurers will also have the piper to pay, though the bill for NFIP payouts in excess of reserves presumably goes ultimately to the U.S. Treasury.

> "…there is a low penetration of flood insurance policies in California, and the small number of policies means many owners of damaged properties may not have access to immediate funds to pay for repairs." —USGS, 2011

> "Only perhaps 12% of California property is insured, so millions of building owners may have limited or no ability to pay for repairs. That degree of damage would threaten California with **a long-term reduction in economic activity, and raise insurance rates statewide - perhaps nationwide or more - afterwards**." —USGS

> "Standard homeowners insurance does not include flood coverage, even though, according to a recent survey, 47 percent of Americans assume that it does. Just 1.33 percent of California households [among the 230,000 flood-insured structures here in early 2023] have standalone policies through the National Flood Insurance Program, a federal-run system that makes up 95 percent of flood coverage in the United States. The share of private flood policies in California is even smaller. Yet as of earlier this month, 90 percent of the state's population was under flood watch… In recent years, the number of Californians holding flood insurance policies has been declining in line with a national pattern." —Blanca Begert, PreventionWeb, 18 January 2023

I'll take this opportunity to remind readers that, as far as standard homeowner's insurance policies are concerned, flood damage is not covered, and flood damage might be <u>anything caused by the movement of water over the ground to the insured structure</u>. In fact, water from a roof-gutter or downspout that hits the ground and then flows into your home will cause damage that <u>might</u> not be covered by a standard policy. Ask your agent. You may also want to review coverage caps on flood insurance policies, which may be much lower than the value of your property; while you're at it, ask about how your flood policy, if you have one, defines 'flood;' you might be surprised (*e.g.*, two or more properties). In particular, ask "What covers my home for damage from surface water affecting only my home?" Earth movements are also typically excluded causes, except possibly for mudflows.

If you live <u>outside</u> of a recognized flood zone, you still need to understand how water could flow on the land around your house. Based on what you can see happen there during rainstorms, you may learn where you need to add drainage ditches, hook downspouts into a runoff drain system, alter the slope of land, put durable berms along a driveway, add a culvert, etc. Surface water management improvement costs will typically be less than uninsured water damage losses. In some situations, for example on some streets, you might have to throw together a wall of sandbags (you will need to have sand and bags ready; some Public Works yards and emergency services stations may offer limited supplies if you can reach them while they last). You can also ask your insurance agent about adding flood insurance coverage, even if you are not in a zone where mortgage lenders require you to have flood insurance. Earlier in this book I noted that flood risks extend beyond the old FEMA SFHA zones determined and mapped by traditional standard methods. Be sure you understand your coverage; RiskFactor.com can provide perspective that may help you assess your risks.

After flood damage, whether to rebuild / repair, sell cheap and take the loss, or let the bank foreclose depends on several variables, as does who exactly loses what. But it's a lot of money. USGS looked only at an assumption of full replacement of damaged and destroyed properties, but I suspect that write-offs would follow a different arithmetic of loss. Complicating the loss picture would be any decreased desirability and valuation of properties in neighborhoods with demonstrated or obvious exposure to recurring hazards. If different land use policies follow one or more floods, that will affect property values too.

Summing up

Estimating losses from a future disaster is speculative and numbers depend upon the magnitude of the event and its details, on the methods, assumptions and scope of the analysis, and other economics and accounting practices. For a megastorm, the numbers will be big. Storms and floods are already long considered to be the leading cause of property damage losses in the West, and the trend is for greater losses in coming decades: for a very recent trend analysis of sharply increasing sub-megastorm AR damage costs, from 1990 through 2090, see Corringham *et al.*, 2022.

Remember, money spent post-disaster on rebuilding, higher insurance premiums, novel health care costs, and unplanned environmental remediation, to name just a few cost-sinks, is unavailable for other economic activity and/ or public works, and that is generally a drag on the greater economy. In a truly comprehensive assessment of the full economic impacts of a megastorm, beyond direct damages, all of these persisting ripples in the economy should be accounted for.

For comparison, per one source, Hurricane Katrina in 2005 caused about $81 billion (2005 dollars) in damage (insurers including the Federal Government absorbed about $60 billion of those losses); California could experience a similar intensity of damage, but over a larger area and population, with a much higher total cost. Complicating the picture, tax revenues would be sharply reduced at the state and local levels, and noticeably at the federal level, for some time, while public debt would be increased. Insurance losses would be large, insurance rates would be reset going forward, and flood insurance programs including risk estimates and coverage rates might be overhauled. NFIP frameworks for floodplain-communities development also might be overhauled.

Take-home message: In dollars and impacts, a single megastorm (ARkStorm-scale) has been said, informally, to be as big as seven or eight 'Katrinas' and much bigger even than that when compared to 'big' earthquakes like the USGS 'ShakeOut' magnitude 8.0 scenario. It would represent the largest domestic relief and reconstruction challenge the United States has ever taken on. *It seems like a good idea to have a plan for that.*

* * *

Further reading

Flood insurance facts: https://www.valuepenguin.com/flood-insurance/ how-much-flood-insurance-do-you-need-requirements

Paterno decision: https://www.watereducation.org/aquapedia/state-liability-flood-protection-and-paterno-decision#:~:text=Liability%20for%20 levee%20failure%20in%20California%20took%20a,also%20had%20long-term%20legal%20ramifications.%20The%20Paterno%20Decision

https://lao.ca.gov/publications/report/3571#Flood_Management_Responsibilities

https://lao.ca.gov/handouts/resources/2019/Flood-Management-050919.
pdf#:~:text=%C2%84%20California%20gave%20assurances%20
to%20the%20federal%20government,established%20state%20
liability%20for%20maintaining%20the%20SPFC%20system.

https://riskfactor.com/

Extreme weather in the U.S. cost 688 lives and $145 billion last year, NOAA
says. NPR, 11 January 2022. https://www.npr.org/2022/01/11/1072077479/
extreme-weather-in-u-s-cost-688-lives-and-145-billion-noaa

When extreme rainfall goes up, economic growth goes down, new research
finds. NPR, 12 January 2022. https://www.npr.org/2022/01/12/1072433290/
climate-change-extreme-rainfall-economic-growth-weather

Plumlee, Geoffrey S., Ph.D.; Charles N. Alpers, Ph.D.; Suzette A. Morman; and Carma
San Juan. 2016. Anticipating Environmental and Environmental-Health Implications
of Extreme Storms: ARkStorm Scenario. Natural Hazards Review, Vol. 17, Issue 4.
https://ascelibrary.org/doi/10.1061/%28ASCE%29NH.1527-6996.0000188

Corringham, T.W., McCarthy, J., Shulgina, T. *et al.* Climate change contributions
to future atmospheric river flood damages in the western United States. Sci
Rep 12, 13747 (2022). https://doi.org/10.1038/s41598-022-15474-2
[or]
https://www.nature.com/articles/s41598-022-15474-2

Wing, Ian Sue, Adam Z. Rose, & Anne M. Wein. 2016. "Economic
Consequence Analysis of the ARkStorm Scenario." Natural Hazards Review,
Volume 17, Issue 4:A4015002. https://open.bu.edu/handle/2144/27348
Permanent Link: https://hdl.handle.net/2144/27348

Bedsworth, Louise, Dan Cayan, Guido Franco, Leah Fisher, Sonya Ziaja.
(California Governor's Office of Planning and Research, Scripps Institution
of Oceanography, California Energy Commission, California Public Utilities
Commission). 2018. Statewide Summary Report. California's Fourth Climate
Change Assessment. Publication number: SUM-CCCA4-2018-013.

https://www.energy.ca.gov/sites/default/files/2019-11/Statewide_Reports-
SUM-CCCA4-2018-013_Statewide_Summary_Report_ADA.pdf

A useful site for area and property flood risks, a more comprehensive approach
that the FEMA/NFIP mapping through 2021, and using different, more inclusive
methodology that integrates changing climate effects: https://floodfactor.com/about

https://www.npr.org/2020/10/18/918725965/undisclosed-most-
homebuyers-and-renters-arent-warned-about-flood-or-wildfire-ris

https://www.cbc.ca/news/canada/marketplace-home-insurance-1.6262386

https://oig.justice.gov/reports/plus/a0401/final.pdf

Accounting for flood risk would lower American house prices by $187bn. The Economist, April 12, 2023. https://www.economist.com/graphic-detail/2023/04/11/accounting-for-flood-risk-would-lower-american-house-prices-by-187bn?utm_content=article-link-8&etear=nl_today_8&utm_campaign=a.the-economist-today&utm_medium=email.internal-newsletter.np&utm_source=salesforce-marketing-cloud&utm_term=4/12/2023&utm_id=1559893

Begert, Blanca. California's storms are almost over. Its reckoning with flood insurance is about to begin. PreventionWeb, 18 January 2023. (Sourced from Grist Magazine) https://www.preventionweb.net/news/californias-storms-are-almost-over-its-reckoning-flood-insurance-about-begin

12

Risks and Probabilities: 'All Bets Are On'

What are the actual odds of experiencing an AR-megastorm in California?

"Our results suggest that such an event is more likely than not to occur at least once between 2018 and 2060, and that multiple occurrences are plausible by 2100 on a business-as-usual emissions trajectory." —Daniel Swain et al., 2018

Are megastorms flukes, or rare but normal, and how frequent are they?

In the first chapters I looked at California's Great Flood of 1862, and at the origins of the megastorm that caused it. The United States Geological Survey's 2011 ARkStorm report provided a more detailed description of what a near-future megastorm in California would be like, which I explored in earlier chapters. There is a reason why USGS developed a preliminary analysis of what megastorm impacts would have on <u>present-day</u> California: we could be hit by one of these extreme winter storm systems in any winter, in any year—if the right conditions develop—including the next one.

But you still really want to know when another AR-megastorm like 1861–62 would hit here, right? So, important questions are: how common are megastorms and their floods, and do they follow any kind of cycle or pattern? Unfortunately, there is no definite rhythm or pattern (but see below*) that we can detect or understand based on past history going back 1800 years (though the odds might increase after a drought). There are so far only some indications that we might be able to develop short-term forecasts: a recent report supports the idea that moderate to strong El Niño conditions may be conducive to megastorm sequences (thus with some possible predictive potential, with respect to 'the odds,' on a scale of months: Huang & Swain, 2022). Also, droughts are increasingly ended by unusually stormy years (as in 1861–62, Los Angeles in 1938, recently in Australia, and other examples); this 'whiplash' weather phenomenon and trend were documented by Swain and colleagues in 2018; this might have some predictive value, in which case it will be important to anticipate the psychological inertia and then mental whiplash that this pattern can induce. In a good example, one can see a stronger 'whiplash' pattern (some authors use the term 'dry-wet knockout') after 1970 in the total flows on the Cosumnes River, which lacks significant flood control, east of Sacramento; these and many other raw data are online.

On the other hand, we have a good count and timeline (based on sea floor and lakebed sediments) of seven uncommonly large storms in California, plus somewhat less-extreme storms, during those 1800 years. And there is a range of intervals between the extreme storm years, and we understand those interval <u>ranges</u> pretty well. In very rough numbers, the intervals between 'big' or statewide megastorms appear to have been around 150 to 400 years, averaging about 275 years. Again, these numbers are for huge storms, apparently as big as 1861–62 <u>or bigger</u>. There are also other 'almost as big' megastorms, possibly more like the ARkStorm simulation, possibly more regional in scope but still extremely intense, that are more frequent (in the 100–200-year range):

> " 'We think this event happens once every 100 or 200 years or so, which puts it in the same category as our big San Andreas earthquakes,' said Lucy Jones, chief scientist of the USGS Multi-Hazards Demonstration Project and architect of ARkStorm."

In Northern California, as detailed below, there is evidence for six (or seven) great 'regional' or larger storms in the past 700 (or 800) years.

So, what are the current year-to-year risks, for these events which are not precisely predictable but are nonetheless considered inevitable? From the past histories (at multiple locations) we can estimate what the odds have been for a return event in any one year, at least what those odds have been until recently, into the twentieth century. Naturally, we are more interested in the future. Experts are seeing changes and new trends in recent weather patterns, and the changing odds based on the best current information and calculations are getting worse for us. Possibly, a lot worse.

The evidence left by megastorms

The oral histories of the indigenous Mi-Wuk people of the Sierra region, shared with the early European settlers (who may have had trouble believing them until the winter of 1862), told of a history of earlier floods, and some older, astonishing high water marks are reported to have been pointed out to the new immigrants. But establishing dates now for storm events prior to the 1800s, based on oral history later recorded in written records, is not feasible. Instead, for establishing the hard evidence, including dates and severity for other megastorms prior to the 1861–62 Great Flood, the most useful approach has been the study of sediment deposits.

Surface runoff waters cause land erosion and transport soils, clay, silt, sand, and more over distances. Greater distances, and larger particles, both correspond to an indication of greater velocity and force (and volume) of the moving water that transported and deposited them, even while moving offshore. The thicker the particular (usually annual) layer or 'varve' of sediment present, the greater was the overall erosional effect, in proportion to the volume and flow rates of storm waters on the upstream land. To do this analysis, scientists sample and measure the yearly sediment layers that build up at the bottom of bodies of water that are relatively still and undisturbed (lakes, ocean depths). Each layer is like a tree-ring, allowing dates to be determined by counting backwards from top to bottom, then confirmed by carbon dating. The layered sediment deposits that are studied can either be inland lake deposits, given the size and topography of the Central Valley, or ocean floor deposits, particularly in the offshore region near Santa Barbara. San Francisco Bay deposits, at least until human disturbance of the Central Valley drainage, are also informative. The storm histories revealed by these studies from, for example, the Sacramento River Valley and the Pacific Ocean near different rivers, including offshore near Santa Barbara, show both similarities (especially for the largest storms) and differences (which indicates that some big storms have narrower or shifted tracks and geographical impacts).

In the past few years, there have been several such studies on the 'geological history' of California weather. The conclusions from different studies at different places are generally similar, and can be summarized rather simply:

1. Offshore sediment studies have identified, between 200 A.D. and today, California 'megaflood' events that appear to have been <u>as big as 1861–62</u>, <u>or bigger</u>. Some were apparently a <u>lot</u> bigger, for example in 1605. The megastorms do not appear to follow a simple cycle pattern [but see below*]; intervals between two 'big' megastorms have been as short as 163 years or as long as 400+ years. An average would be about 275 years. We are now 161 years past our last 'big' megastorm.

2. Other sediment studies have indicated that additional, somewhat narrower or smaller megastorms locally approaching an intensity range similar to 1861–62 appear to have occurred at intervals of about 100–120 (–200) years. One such study was done on inland sediments from Little Packer Lake north of Sacramento. This type of inland study is particularly important

for Northern California. The scientists found a total of 6 floods "comparable to 1861–62" [perhaps only at regional scale] in the past 700 years. Big floods dated to 1805 and also in 1862 tell us that the Mi-Wuk people in the Gold Rush era had seen two great storms about 57 years apart. [Math: a 120-year average interval could be interpreted as an annual megastorm risk of about 0.83%; a 100-year average would mean an annual risk of about 1%, or 1-in-100 in any year. And this is a chance for me to remind the reader that these are <u>not</u> so-called 'hundred-year-storms,' these would be ongoing roughly estimated storm risks of 1% each year, averaged out from possibly chaotic or semi-random events, and under as yet incompletely understood conditions in Pacific and global weather systems… <u>and</u> that the risks and odds are now apparently changing along with weather patterns. Also, these events do not fit properly into the FEMA/NFIP '100-year-storm' estimates; they represent <u>additional</u> risks.]

Some authors have written that we are "due"* or "overdue" for a megastorm and flood. I don't like that kind of thinking because AR-megastorms don't seem to punch a timeclock (or, if they are somehow long-range predictable, we don't understand how to do it). Instead I would say that after 160+ years we are "well within the known window of possibility" when it would not be surprising to have another megastorm. In fact, from simulation studies, it seems that we have beaten the odds during the last 160 years, with the sort of luck that cannot ever be relied upon. If the latest estimates are accurate, some Californians now (or soon) living, including our children and grandchildren, would be likely to experience a megastorm event (or more) at some point during their lives.

[*However, here I reluctantly must take a detour; if I don't, some readers will wonder why. Research papers by A. Schimmelmann and colleagues, beginning in 2001-2002, used data from a 2000-year record of sediments offshore of Santa Barbara, plus other hemispheric and global-scale event correlations, to propose that extremely large floods or megafloods have occurred in California on a roughly 200-year cycle, with some 'skips' to 400 years. Ingram and Malamud-Roam (2013) have also cited those original arguments; USGS in 2011 accepted the facts, though without comment on the theory. If this is a real cyclical pattern, it would mark these extreme Pacific AR megastorm sequences as a distinct type of weather phenomenon, not just 'big storms' to be fitted to year-by-year probability curves. No interval shorter than 163 years is known for the megafloods in the marine record from Santa Barbara, suggesting a possibly non-random pattern (though not necessarily a cycle; possibly just a lull).

But focusing just on the reported Santa Barbara sediment record, and to explain my reluctance to embrace this regular-cyclical theory (if you consult the authors noted above): one problem with this 200-year idea is that there are some inconvenient 'skips' in the sequence for the past 2000 years. In fact, over the past 1800 years, only three of the 'accepted' flood events came <u>roughly</u> 200 years after the preceding one, while there have also been three 'skips.' Another wrinkle in that sediment record is that the 0.3"-thick layer from the strong 1958 storm is not considered as evidence of a megaflood, while 0.1" layers beginning in AD 212 are accepted. In fact the 1605 layer is 20 times thicker than the 212 or 1029 layers, so what, exactly, is a megaflood? And there's this oddity: the 1861-62 Great Flood megastorm that affected most of California and much more of the West Coast is not represented as any sort of noteworthy flood in the Santa Barbara sediment record, so, along with the 1800's, is effectively a 'skip' in this cycle theory.

Humans are wired to see and infer patterns (which can lead to confirmation bias); it may be too soon to say whether the 200-year pattern might be genuine. If the arguments for this skipping 200-year recurrence idea, but taking an 1862 starting point, are persuasive to you, you would want to plan accordingly approaching the mid-21st century. However, the theorists themselves have pointed to a possible ~400-year recurrence dating from 1605 (now in 'overtime'). I'm not going to suggest that you should give weight to any of these predictions, but if they motivate you, enduringly, fine. See the last pages of this book for a dive into what the latest simulation work is indicating: accelerating recurrences without reference to cycles.]

That was then: Changes

Computer models indicate that occasional megastorms will continue to occur here, they will become more frequent, and they will tend to be bigger. The Earth has become warmer, and there is now capacity in the atmosphere for up to about 7% more water moving overhead (globally) than there was during the Gold Rush. Capacity means that air rising from the ocean surface, as in the tropics, can capture and transport more water vapor, potentially coming ashore along the West Coast. But, also unfortunately, warmer air with increased but <u>unused</u> absorption capacity can also rob land and vegetation of moisture at an increased rate, making droughts worse and extending the dry season in the West. This is one basis for trends toward more extremes of weather, both wet and dry, into the 21st century. Many people may find the increases toward both extremes confusing.

A 2020 study from UCLA by authors Huang, Swain & Hall calculated that under current trends, even for smaller storms, moisture transported in future atmospheric river storm events, by 2070, will be 23% greater than now; the resulting precipitation amounts in different terrains in California and Nevada are indicated to increase by a range of 9% to 46+%. Precipitation intensity is expected to increase by 27% in the Sierra and 32% in adjacent regions (on average), and to tend toward exceeding 1" per hour. If sustained for hours, the resulting stream or river flows will be extreme.

Similar results have been obtained in other modeling studies of what future weather will look like in the West. Precipitation amounts and intensities typically are seen to increase in future decades, as will longer dry spells and droughts. There is less agreement about expectations for winds; some studies indicate that surface winds are also now increasing in speed and force.

Trends in changing weather patterns since the mid-20th century are being observed and incorporated into, or confirmed by, the most comprehensive new computer models available to weather and climate scientists. Some well-supported projections come from a 2018 study published by Daniel L. Swain of UCLA and colleagues. The past 1800 years appear to furnish what has become an obsolete and potentially misleading predictor of how the atmosphere will behave going forward. Here are two estimates offered by the UCLA authors in 2018:

- Between years 2020 and 2060, weather trends indicate that there may be a better than 50:50 chance that California will experience another AR-megastorm, perhaps in the range of the 1861–62 event.
- By the year 2100, the best available estimate is that California may be likely to experience, on average, 2 or 3 megastorms (or "severe storm sequences") per century, *averaging* one year out of 40; that's about 5 times the estimated "1-in-200" annual probability we lived with into the 20th century (when none occurred).

Megastorm probability forecasts are a bit slippery because such extreme weather events could have a range of different 'shapes and sizes,' and thus different probabilities. Things like geographical scope, duration, intensity, run-up conditions, temperature conditions, and total volume of precipitation could all differ, and each of these may have separate probabilities only now being glimpsed in the earliest computer simulations of future weather events. However, even the smallest events being referred to as megastorms by experts are expected to have the potential to cause great damage at least at regional scales.

A recent (2022) paper by Huang & Swain suggests that within the next ~80 years, if current trends continue, smaller to larger megastorms could occur up to five to six times (the most likely range, on average, with smaller ones more frequent). (Some of the late-decades details depend on the future greenhouse gas trajectory.) This is an example of why the popular concept of "hundred-year floods" is obsolete ("OK, pal, <u>which</u> hundred years? Last 100? Next 100?").

For comparison, the risk of serious local damage from a major (Richter 7.0+) earthquake in any county of western California appears to be not more than about 0.5–1% per year, per USGS; by several kinds of estimates, megastorms are already more likely than major earthquakes in any year. What do risk levels like these mean to us? How do our minds process uncommon and unfamiliar, but always possible, event risks? What should we do? I take a brief look at the psychology of risk perception and estimation in a later chapter.

This book you've been reading has tried to describe what will happen in a future megastorm event, to help people imagine it, to let that sink in, and to possibly motivate readers to begin to think and prepare. With planning and preparation, a state of readiness, and a forward-leaning response posture, a disruption of a few weeks is survivable for most of us (the more, the better!) without extreme hardship. Six weeks without reliable access to goods and services might be a realistic forecast for many communities, but you can assess your own situation as being more or less vulnerable to isolation or disruption, then adjust your planning target accordingly. I think "Six Weeks" is a useful middle of the road planning scenario and target (hopefully incorporating a safety margin) that most people can understand and manage. For example, six weeks = 126 meals per person at 'three squares a day' (official relief operations may provide for two meals per day). In the next part of this book I'll present some ideas on preparation for individuals and families, for networks of friends and neighbors, and then for communities. I'll then take a first look at California's official preparedness and response posture.

End note: change

It's very unfortunate that the topic of 'climate change' became politicized, making it much harder to discuss. One indication that weather patterns are changing: the Federal National Flood Insurance Program (NFIP), using its early flood risk calculations, broke even financially from 1968 through 2005, but in the following 12 years, went $25 billion into debt (due to both changing weather norms and to fiscal policies set by Congress). You can also search the Internet for news stories on (so-called) 'thousand-year floods' and see how many have been happening lately (dozens), even this afternoon (Fort Lauderdale, FL, April 12, 2023). What many people may find confusing is that current trends are for <u>all types of weather to become more extreme</u>. Both storms and drought—not one or the other—will become bigger problems in the West, sometimes back to back. 2021 through 2023 brought California floods during drought.

* * *

Further reading

ARkStorm: California's other 'Big One'. Science Daily, January 18, 2011. https://www.sciencedaily.com/releases/2011/01/110117142512.htm

Study on Little Packer Lake flood history: https://cepsym.org/Sympro1996/Byrne.pdf

Hunsaker, Leon, and Claude W. Curran. "Lake Sacramento" —Can It Happen Again? Copy Quick and Academy Printing, Grants Pass, Oregon, November 2005. https://cepsym.org/history/LakeSacramento_book.pdf

https://www.llnl.gov/news/increase-atmospheric-moisture-tied-human-activities

Swain, Daniel L., Baird Langenbrunner, J. David Neelin & Alex D. Hall. Increasing precipitation volatility in twenty-first-century California. Nature Climate Change volume 8, pages 427–433, [23 April] 2018. https://www.nature.com/articles/s41558-018-0140-y [paywalled] https://ucanr.edu/sites/MarinFoodPolicyCouncil/files/311178.pdf

Huang, X., *et al.* 2020. Future precipitation increase from very high resolution ensemble downscaling of extreme atmospheric river storms in California, by Xingying Huang, Daniel L. Swain, & Alex D. Hall. Science Advances, 15 Jul 2020, Vol 6, Issue 29. https://www.science.org/doi/10.1126/sciadv.aba1323

A graphic from UCLA about changing weather: https://www.ioes.ucla.edu/project/future-extreme-precipitation-california

Huang, Xingying, and Swain, Daniel L. 12 August 2022. Climate change is increasing the risk of a California megaflood. Science Advances 8:32. https://www.science.org/doi/10.1126/sciadv.abq0995

Papers from 1996 on California weather extremes: https://cepsym.org/proceedings-1996.php

Dettinger, Michael D., Fred Martin Ralph, Tapash Das, Paul J. Neiman, and Daniel R. Cayan, 2011. Atmospheric Rivers, Floods and the Water Resources of California. Water 3(2): 445–478. https://www.mdpi.com/2073-4441/3/2/445/htm

Dettinger, M. D. Climate change, atmospheric rivers and floods in California—a multimodel analysis of storm frequency and magnitude changes. J Amer Water Resour Assoc 47:514–523 (2011).

Schimmelmann, A., C.B. Lange, and B.L. Meggers (2003). Palaeoclimatic and archaeological evidence for a ~200-yr recurrence of floods and droughts linking California, Mesoamerica and South America over the past 2000 years. The Holocene 13 (5), 763-778. https://doi.org/10.1191/0959683603hl661rp

Ingram, B. Lynn, and Frances Malamud-Roam. 2013. The West Without Water. University of California Press, Berkeley.

https://silverjackets.nfrmp.us/Resources/Risk-Communication-Resources

https://www.fema.gov/flood-maps/tools-resources/risk-map/products

For a comparison to seismic risk assessment, risk mitigation, and preparedness: Yanev, Peter I. 1991.Peace of Mind in Earthquake Country. Chronicle Books, San Francisco, CA. 218 pp.

13

Planning and Preparedness for Individuals, Families and Households

Empowering the grass roots (this means us)

"The time to begin taking action is now, before a devastating natural hazard event occurs," said USGS Director Marcia McNutt.

I've included a lot of material in this positive, can-do chapter, in the hopes that you may feel not only motivated, but empowered and supported, towards preparing for an extraordinary but expected event with considerable challenges that can be anticipated and dealt with.

Whenever the next extreme atmospheric river storm sequence—an AR-megastorm—hits California and the West Coast, the impacts could be, and are predicted to be, severe and extensive… like nothing living Californians have seen here. Some of us have experienced flooding or other aspects of extreme winter storms, but for the most part not such intense or prolonged effects, and not over such a vast area, causing so much disruption. The same applies to all emergency management agencies; the scale of megastorm impacts will be greater than what has been experienced in previous disasters; demands on responders, shelter providers and all levels of government and NGOs will be unprecedented(!) under such conditions. Put another way, the choppers may not be parachuting pallets of Spam into your isolated neighborhood.

The odds of experiencing one (or more) of these extreme winter weather events are increasing, according to weather models (discussed earlier), and some experts tell us it's likely that Californians alive today will have to deal with this kind of event at some point. Experts also tell us that there will be greater numbers of 'very wet years' like 2022-23, (in addition to the more extreme events like megastorms), so smaller localized storm disruptions, including runoff and flooding issues, will affect some communities more often than at present. Sorry to say, drier seasons and drought years will also become more common; change is toward precipitation extremes in both directions. Awareness, knowledge, planning and preparation can make a huge difference in coping with a situation that has a long lead time (= long recurrence interval), which is what we would normally expect for a megastorm. Each year, the months of the long dry season in California provide time to get (re-)organized for winter. And drought periods are the right time to think about storms and floods, due to the 'whiplash' shifts in weather patterns.

This chapter aims to help people <u>start</u> thinking about preparations for a short disruption of normal life, by presenting a number of issues, ideas, and suggestions. It is not comprehensive; it does not cover every issue and situation, but it discusses several that may affect many people. It's a beginning and a series of positive steps to take in the face of what might seem like great challenges, as is my brief review of coping strategies and solutions. I encourage you to consult other sources and adapt all information to your present and future situations.

We'll get to essentials (energy and fuels, food and supplies, clean water, medications, clothing and gear, equipment) in a moment, but let's start with the key decisions you'll need to make (in advance, because if a megastorm event is already getting underway, your options have started shrinking).

> 1. Will you stay in your home, stay with others in your area, relocate to a less impacted area in California, or try to escape the storm system altogether? What if you are evacuated?

> 2. During a developing extreme storm event, when will you set your storm response plan in motion?

I recommend that—now—you assess your home and neighborhood vulnerabilities to storms and floods, so that you can focus on appropriate plans. If you live on low ground including floodplains, you will probably relocate (sooner and wisely is better). If you are on stable high ground, if you can meet your own needs and cope with developments, you may be inclined to stockpile provisions (well in advance!) and shelter in place. If you or your community <u>might</u> become cut off from services or necessities, you would do well to weigh the pros and cons of relocating vs increasing your personal and local resilience. Every summer is a chance to figure these things out.

My personal assessment, for my own situation on high ground in a potentially isolated community, is to make all reasonable preparations to shelter in place. Your home is yours, it's familiar, and you may have prepared it to weather almost any storm. You may have a network of family, friends and neighbors. You may know your other community resources, responders and service organizations.

On the other hand, leaving your home without enough lead time, without a clear plan and a workable destination, can expose you to a host of uncertainties and unforeseen circumstances. If you are able to shelter in place successfully, in my view that could well be your best option. Community preparedness (see the next chapter) is also a key aspect of sheltering in place.

To help answer these questions, or start a conversation about them, let's assume for planning purposes that any storm-related period of isolation or extreme disruption could last six weeks (a return to full normalcy could take much longer for many communities). Please understand, that seems like a plausible 'ARkStorm-scale event window' for many well-drained areas; depending on where you live, you might opt to use a different prediction about a period of disruption, but remember, shorter-scale preparation is riskier. In the Central Valley, areas may be under water for weeks or even months, but at somewhat higher elevations your most urgent alternate shelter, lifeline services and supply arrangements presumably would be coming back under control in a matter of weeks. Let's also assume that the storm will cause significant problems well beyond the borders of California, as in 1861–62.

Shelter in place?

On question 1: If you live on high ground in a safe (look at slopes, water channels and drainage, and especially at nearby or overhanging trees) and sturdy home, can provide for your basic needs 'for the duration,' are generally pretty fit and self-reliant and have reasonable skills and a can-do attitude, then sheltering in place may be a good option (better than a tent city; cheaper than a tropical vacation). There are a fair number of actual pioneer families still on the land out west, and they remember a lot about how things were done in the past, and often keep those skills and strategies in current use. Thinking of a disruptive storm event as 'a taste of the pioneer days' might help you approach the challenge, especially if you have young people in your home or circle (teach them the word 'old-fangled'). Maybe your kids and others in your area are learning skills in 4H Club or Scouts. Being part of a strong local community will help. Some communities will be less isolated than others; you can assess that for yourself, based on location, terrain and road network. The next chapter in this book discusses community-scale preparation and planning.

It may be that the home of a family member, friend or neighbor, where you would be welcomed, could provide a better option. Depending on your relationships, and on timing of events, that move might be some driving distance away or within your own local community. It's well worth discussing in advance, before a situation becomes urgent and stressful. In some cases, 'many hands' while sheltering together will make necessary tasks easier than going it alone.

Some potentially limited resources, and I'm thinking first of fuels / energy, heat and light now, would be better conserved by sheltering together. Three homes with half-full propane tanks could provide warmth for three times as long if people did some sequential home-sharing. Maybe you have the perfect home for sheltering. Is there someone you would offer shelter from the storm to? You can reach out to discuss that at any time of year. If you get along well, gathering with others may help keep spirits up and avoid the sense of isolation. If you don't get along as well, you could play poker for money.

Relocate?

If yoat thu are determined to escape the storm completely, and willing to drive hundreds, or a thousand or more, miles to do so, especially if seats on planes, trains and busses are selling out, then you will always be thankful for having left early. One reason will be evacuation congestion on roads, possible fuel shortages, and 'no room at the inn,' something many Californians have not experienced. Remember, first come, first served. Amenities and services are sparse on many of those routes, heading eastward away from the coast. (Officials in the Reno, Nevada area have expressed concern that in ARkStorm circumstances, California would not be in a position to help Nevada provide for the needs of refugees that might be able to make it over the Sierra.) But more importantly, storm and road conditions could make travel difficult, potentially for hundreds of miles inland. Most people might first think of heading straight east, but the Sierra highway passes may generally be closed by extreme winter storm conditions and major damage to roadways. Even heading north, USGS (based on mapping that begins on page 29 of the 2011 report) expects I-5 to be closed in many places from Dunsmuir south, due to flooding, three days after the ARkStorm (the computer simulation) hits Northern California, and to remain impacted or closed for at least 90 days. I encourage you to give some thought to route and destination planning. Even if you get east of the Sierra, if the storm is like that in 1861–62, you could encounter flooding or flood damage in places over a very wide area (such as Utah, New Mexico...). And water may begin to flow where it is not typically seen, creating difficult or tragic surprises.

As an armchair exercise, try assessing routes through the western deserts using topo maps or satellite mapping, looking for 'dry' lakebeds or washes where storm runoff might accumulate. Could you still use SR 190 to cross the Panamint Valley? After I wrote that here:

> "Death Valley National Park, famous for its parched, otherworldly landscapes, closed completely Friday due to historic rainfall and flash flooding, **trapping about 500**

visitors and 500 staff members in the park after the closures. No major injuries were reported, though about 60 vehicles were damaged. The park experienced **"unprecedented amounts of rainfall"** of 1.46 inches measured at Furnace Creek..." — Los Angeles Times, August 5, 2022 [YouTube offers videos of flooding in the Panamint Valley. 'Unprecedented' is a favorite description of events which could have been foreseen or predicted with a bit of thought.]

Could you rely upon SR 58 past Edwards AFB? SR 247 through the Lucerne Valley? I-15 east of Barstow, or around Primm? I-80 east of Fernley or Golconda?? U.S. 95 in various places? I don't have the answers; these are just areas I flagged from satellite data; please check the upcoming 'Lessons' chapter and read about extensive road damage, for example in the Carson Valley, in the 1997 AR storm floods. Further disruptions could arise from avalanches, as happened on U.S. 395 near Mono Lake, where an avalanche caused a prolonged closure following the February 2023 snowstorms and a record snowpack caused by a long sequence of ARs.

Without direct inspection of the roadway and the terrain, you can still at least map and flag some hazard questions for further research as you work out planning for preferred routes. I have to mention, emergency agencies and highway engineers could assess (and advise on) roads, routes, and storm scenarios now; there would be no* reason not to make recommendations (about routes and destinations in certain forecast situations) available to the public in advance [*although it is my impression that some public officials may be reluctant to remind people, during bucolic years, that they might get caught up in a mass evacuation.] For now, you can start by checking the impacts maps of the major routes in California in the ARkStorm report (Porter *et al.*, 2011). You can also look at flooding maps from FEMA / NFIP, from www.riskfactor.com, and from USACE in reports like the 2015 CVIFMS draft plan, or interactively using online mapping displays from www.cal-adapt.org and other sources, and note where roads and highways run. It may be harder to find assessments of out-of-state routes. RiskFactor may be the single best nationwide tool at this time. If you tracked the more than 80 state highway closures across Southern California on the morning of August 21, 2023, as Hurricane Hilary passed north, you've been given a preview of which roads, and which terrain, could be vulnerable to travel and transportation disruption under sustained and intense megastorm conditions. Many additional local roads were also affected

Route closures would greatly magnify the traffic complexity and congestion during a mass exodus, especially if communications drop out and traffic control is incomplete. Another reasons for committing to an early start would be the route and traffic controls that Caltrans and CHP would at some point put into place (in CA; other states could follow), possibly followed by further restrictions as deemed necessary by Cal OES, Cal Guard, or other emergency authorities. Eventually, if you reach a non-impacted area, the question will be: what is available there for you and the other refugees who have joined you there? Less affected areas in the off-coastal states may be busy as staging areas for personnel, supplies and equipment, and thus preoccupied with channeling their energies and resources toward urgent relief efforts into the far West.

I'm pointing out again here that the 2011 ARkStorm study and computer simulation only dealt with effects in California. The 1861–62 megastorm sequence strongly affected three countries and several states and territories.

On Question 2: First, you probably want to know how much warning you're going to have. That's a problem; there will be a warning, but it may not look like a warning.

With a hurricane, you start hearing about a tropical depression, that might become a tropical storm, then a hurricane with a name, and you hear where its track is probably headed, how fast it is moving, when it will probably arrive, and how bad it might be. But a hurricane is basically one self-contained storm (a cyclone) amenable to such predictions.

An atmospheric river event or series is different. Like the name says, it's like a river (or a series of them) in the air, and it's going to flow continuously, or more likely as a series of segments or pulses, until it stops. We can now see and evaluate them, using satellites, up to about 7.5 days in advance, forming and stretching across the Pacific toward California, which is a journey of several days, but we can't see exactly how that river is being generated, supplied or sustained, or really theorize well (yet) about details of the process, so we can't predict when or how it will continue or stop flowing. Possibly future computer models will give us that long-horizon predictive / forecasting insight, but apparently not soon. And complicating the picture is the fact that smaller atmospheric river events are not uncommon, and most folks would be reluctant to cry 'wolf' when one begins, in spite of the media inevitably looking for sensational news.

With the new AR category rating scale it will be easier for communicators to cite the objective weather services rating for any approaching AR storm. However, by design that system only looks at a 72-hour 'onshoring' forecast, which might correspond to one 'pulse' in a longer AR sequence, such as in a megastorm. Regarding warnings or alerts, California's State Emergency Plan (SEP, discussed in a later chapter) describes the system of warnings being sent by the state to local authorities as the primary method for alerting the public about emergencies, but it does not specify a uniform policy for disseminating those warnings at the local level. Be sure to sign up with your county's 'alerts' system, and if you are unsure whether you are receiving weather-related alerts, have a conversation with your county OES staff. They (or your sheriff) can also brief you on evacuation protocols and let you know if your home is in an assigned zone.

The issue of timing may be most important to people who may have planned in advance to travel long distances to safety in an AR-megastorm event. <u>Sooner is infinitely better</u>. As conditions deteriorate, options trickle away. If being teased about being a 'nervous Nellie' might actually bother you, grow a thicker, safer, dryer skin.

If there were a question 3, it would be: how long will you wait to make arrangements and stock up on things that you will need? Here's a tip: most essentials will last on your shelves for years. Why wait if you can afford not to wait? (I realize that not everyone can easily afford the additional pantry and other resiliency purchases on their own; that's a societal issue that should not be ignored in public policy and charitable efforts.)

If you are going to relocate with (for example) a motorhome, your choices for a six-week stock of food and supplies may differ from how you would stock a home pantry; compactness, and perhaps weight and convenience considerations, might orient you toward more specialized purchases more easily sourced in advance. If you are going to shelter in place, and if you're reading this and you've done your planning and preparation homework, then you'll probably just gather any remaining items early on and batten down the hatches as things progress. You won't need any specific warning at all. If you are going to shelter with other people, renew those conversations early and keep talking as the situation progresses, being mindful of even local travel complications. If you have prepared and can stay on top of what needs to happen, it can all be done at the right time.

Sheltering in place: if you might become isolated

I'll put down some planning and preparation thoughts for the individual, for the family (I say, get the kids involved, gently, in an adventure, with meaningful responsibilities… the old computer game, "Oregon Trail," can still be played online), or for the group that has agreed in advance to shelter together at the best location. It will be obvious to you, reading this, that these planning suggestions apply most directly to persons and communities in more rural or remote areas, or in difficult terrain. What might not be obvious to you, if you live 'in civilization,' even above the floodplains, is that some things you take for granted may be unavailable to you during a period of disruption. What if your neighborhood is surrounded by water? What if goods and supplies aren't reaching your neighborhood? Think carefully about your situation. Some of what you read below may apply to you, some may not. If you live in a West Coast city and have done your earthquake preparations, you will already be several steps ahead with overlapping winter storm preparation.

I'm also going to assume that if there is storm water flowing through your home, across the floor, you're out of there. If you don't have a dry home with solid ground outside, you face a serious challenge. It won't be warm, unlike the hurricane-caused floods you've seen on TV; there will be cold water and possible low-elevation snow.

For planning I recommend that you work with the following assumptions; they do lean toward 'worse' plausible cases, but that's what safety and preparedness are about. 'Six weeks' is somewhat arbitrary but, in my assessment, may be typical for the acute disruption many shelter-in-place communities might experience, and a good starting target for planning purposes. (Assumptions for other communities may differ; for people displaced from floodplains and low elevations, shelter / relief options may be completely different:)

Assume up to six weeks of lifeline disruption <u>without</u>:

- Grid electricity
- Landline, cable, fiberoptic connections (voice, Internet)
- Cell service (or limited or intermittent)
- Available supplies (food, fuels, batteries, medications, clothing, gear, parts, equipment, tools, materials, etc.); no available refined fuels for
    ◦ Vehicles and equipment
    ◦ Generators
    ◦ Saws and powered tools
    ◦ Heat
    ◦ Cooking
    ◦ Light
- Propane or utility-provided natural gas service
- Running potable water (some public systems, some private wells with pumps)
- Functioning septic service (some public systems, non-gravity-flow septic systems)
- Services (possibly including medical, fire, law enforcement, repair, other)
- Reliably intact road network

Let's work through a <u>preliminary</u> list of solutions and options; you can always consult more comprehensive published or online preparedness guidelines. If you live in the outskirts, you may already be way ahead of me. If you're not, there are a lot of stores and catalogues you can browse.

Energy

Fuels can do many things, and any adult, and sometimes teens, can buy them. They pack energy, and are flammable or even potentially explosive, and its best to store them—even firewood—away from the house. Some commercial fuels (propane, diesel) are more stable than others. Gasoline instability is a particular issue, more so when blended with ethanol (which is now standard); here are some options. You can buy and add stabilizers to increase gasoline storage life. For small two-stroke engines, chainsaw shops carry ethanol-free gasoline pre-blended with oil. It's possible to track down and buy ethanol-free unleaded racing fuel in five-gallon cans. A few gas stations are listed online as sellers of ethanol-free gasoline.

Be sure you understand safe use and handling of fuels. Avoid using them indoors other than in an approved appliance, if possible. Install, check and trust carbon monoxide detectors; even a gas furnace or a wood fireplace, improperly maintained or operated, can be dangerous (even deadly). That said, I believe that a reasonable guideline is: (1) a few candles or a kerosene (oil) lamp should be safe in a typical room, if kept away from flammables, on a non-flammable, heat-proof surface; (2) if you must cook indoors on a portable propane or similar stove, first create necessary safe conditions including proper ventilation (partially open window); (3) portable propane or kerosene space heaters, as might be used in some warehouses or construction sites, are often considered unsafe inside a residence; (4) best bet is always to use carbon monoxide (CO) detectors. [Note that increasing concerns are emerging about other non-CO combustion products, for example with unvented gas stoves and ranges.]

Some manufacturers of small modern propane heaters sell them as being safe for use in enclosed spaces; I've seen evidence that this is accurate. Don't assume this is true for just any random propane-fueled heater. Check the product packaging for the manufacturer's safe-use guidelines, and use a trusted carbon monoxide alarm (also: stock batteries for the CO monitor!).

In prolonged rural isolation, wood is likely to be the most reliably available fuel for heat, cooking, and water treatment. If your house has a wood-burning stove, <u>safely</u> installed and ventilated (used with a carbon monoxide alarm), and if you have laid in a good supply of dry, seasoned firewood, you are much better prepared for a period of isolation or shortages than a house without wood heat. However, this note from 1862 makes clear that a wood stove is not always the right choice for every home!

> "The Myers and Schaffer families, of Yolo County, put two chests of choice possessions in a boat, already nearly full of goods. The boat was tied to a tree in the farmyard where it turned this way and that with the shifting wind and steep

waves. The raging storm made it impossible for them to escape to high ground across the new inland sea. They returned to the house and went upstairs where a fire was lit in the stove. At 9 o'clock in the evening the house toppled over. They were not hurt, and safely reached their boat. In a few minutes the house caught fire from the stove. Between the fire, wind, and water the house was completely destroyed, but they lived to tell the tale." —Taylor & Taylor, 2007

Off-grid-capable solar electricity will be helpful if there are grid failures, but stormy short-day winter skies will provide only a fraction of any system's rated kWh power output (10% or less is typical on stormy winter days), so available electricity may be weather-limited, especially in snow. Avoid over-optimism. If you have or install 'solar,' make sure you understand whether your system can operate off-grid; that's not a given! Without battery (or grid) power, most 'solar' PVE systems will not activate or produce power when the sun rises.

Electric vehicles (EVs) may become the backup batteries of some home systems, at least in part. A concept that is beginning to receive attention is called V2G (Vehicle-to-Grid); a web search will provide many useful links to this information. As one element, V2G fits with the utilities' plans for consumers to build out the grid's battery storage capacity (and pay for it). Currently available consumer EVs store from about 30 kWh to around 200 kWh of electrical energy in their batteries. At least one electric pickup truck now on the market can store up to 132 kWh of power, and is sold with the option of an intelligent connection system that can tap that power for emergency home use (at present I'm informed that this device requires an otherwise battery-free home system). We can expect to see more of these coming to market. From another direction, one (or more) manufacturer of vertically integrated on-site solar electric systems (for homes and larger installations) has announced that its own (proprietary, system specific) intelligent V2G connectors for all EVs will come to market in 2024. A typical V2G setup runs through the home to the utility's service entrance, so these also can be thought of as vehicle-to-home (V2H) systems. It may become routine to see fully charged consumer trucks or SUVs parked at residences as storms approach, to provide emergency backup power during shelter-in-place situations. My off-the-cuff assessment is that with strict rationing of power to only the essentials, and with another source of heat, a compact household might just barely be able to operate for up to two weeks on one 'truckload' of stored energy. Most modern Californians might struggle with that level of power rationing. However, properly implemented V2H should also allow basic solar PVE systems to reboot each morning without grid power.

Electric vehicles may seem appealing for transportation when hydrocarbon / petroleum fuels are unavailable, but when the grid is down, it may be a challenge to allocate enough residential solar or generator electricity, during winter storms, to recharge a passenger or working-duty vehicle. On the other hand, many people love horses.

Fueled generators can be reliable but often will use more fuel in six cold, dark weeks than what is typically stored at a residence. Here are some published figures to give you a rough yardstick (precise run times depend upon electrical load). Five gallons of gasoline will run a 5 kW generator for ~8 hours. 100 gallons of propane will run a 12 kW generator for ~36 hours. A 20 kW generator at ¾ electrical load uses ~1.3 gallons of diesel fuel per hour.

Micro-hydroelectric and wind turbines are more exotic, but on the positive side, wind and water will be abundant in storms, so if you are living 'on the land' and a serious techno-opportunist, you might consider such a system, for example for battery charging; increasingly, ownership of an electric vehicle in areas with an unreliable grid makes diverse on-site and renewable generation options more appealing. A small micro-hydro unit operating continuously typically produces about 12 kWh per day; a charged EV could drive that energy to a home with a V2H connection. Perhaps more 'plug-and-play' wind and water-powered charging systems will come to market.

You can buy small hand-cranked generators for charging phones, etc., but be prepared for a lot of cranking. Many small auxiliary batteries with USB ports are available for small electronic devices; larger versions can start your car too. There is a growing market for even larger 'power station' or 'solar battery' devices that are portable battery storage / inverter units with multiple connections for charging and for powering devices, plus some intelligent power management. Several can accept solar panel connections. Power tool makers have entered this market. At present these battery units are much more expensive, up to ~$1500 per kWh, than home-scale battery storage banks using technologies like AGM, but you can lug power centers around with you, and they can be versatile. [If you have basic skills, you can assemble a no-frills version, with ~2 kWh storage capacity, out of basic parts for around 25 to 35% of the cost; several videos are on YouTube.] Finally, camping stores have sometimes carried wood-burning camp stoves (outdoor use only) that can produce an electrical charging current through built-in USB ports.

Generator manufacturers are also now integrating storage-battery capability into their backup whole-home generator systems. This does improve fuel efficiency somewhat, as excess power is captured and stored while the generator is running, but generators will still be fuel-limited. We are going to see increasing deployment of residential storage battery systems in California, in part due to utility company and CPUC moves including the new NEM3 solar grid-tie agreement conditions. While household resilience is not a strongly promoted aspect of these moves, it will definitely improve somewhat as battery deployment proceeds; however, no-one is likely to be able to store six weeks' worth of power.

Simple twig / stick-burning 'rocket stoves' for last-ditch outdoor heating or cooking are cheap ($5), easy to make in advance, and effective; see next chapter and online information.

One safety tip about old-style radiant electric heaters (the kind with visible wires that glow red). They can start fires when used carelessly, too close to combustible objects or material. I've thrown my old ones away. Newer sealed heaters are much safer. If you are able to use portable electric heat, and need to, you will have one less worry that way.

For illumination, flashlights, headlamps, batteries, candles, fueled lamps, chemical light glow-sticks and occasionally flares (outside!) for six weeks may be appreciated. It's hard to have too many inexpensive sources of light. If you can find a quality hand-cranked flashlight, you might appreciate one of those. Luminous or reflective dots on important places and things can save you time and trouble in the dark.

<u>In summary</u>, make sure you have a flexible combination of energy sources, including appropriate fuels, in enough quantities such that you may always have one or two ways to accomplish anything you need to do.

Food and household supplies

Do you have shelf-stable food to provide meals for at least six weeks of disrupted supply? That is 42 x 3 = 126 meals per person (plus snacks). OK, how many persons are you going to take responsibility for? That's a big reason for discussing this with your family or 'circle' well in advance (and once a year). <u>Shelf-stable</u> is an important, relevant concept. Can you keep your freezer running? Maybe, maybe not. If not, cook and eat your most perishable food items first, and then your thawing frozen food next. Don't forget, in winter it may be colder outside than in an unpowered freezer. Cooking raw food in advance before spoilage extends storage time by a few days, assuming cooling is available (remember, it's winter). The good news is that there is nothing particularly exotic about shelf-stable foods. Canned foods are usually stable for at least year or two (some for more), though I've had problems with some imports, and acidic tomato products. Here's what the Utah State University has to say about the shelf life of canned goods:

> "As a general rule, unopened **home canned** foods have a shelf life of one year and should be used before two years. Commercially canned foods should retain their best quality until the expiration code date on the can. This date is usually 2-5 years from the manufacture date. High acid foods usually have a shorter shelf life than low acid foods. For emergency storage, commercially canned foods in metal or glass will remain safe to consume as long as the seal has not been broken. (That

is not to say the quality will be retained for that long). Foods "canned" in metal-Mylar®-type pouches will also have a best-if-used by date on them. The longest shelf life tested of this type of packaging has been 8-10 years (personal communication U.S. Military MRE's). Therefore, storage for longer than 10 years is not recommended.

<u>Use from Storage</u>. Always use FIFO (First-in, first-out), meaning use your oldest cans first. Before opening, discard any badly dented, bulging, rusty, or leaky cans or jars that have broken seals. Open cans or jars to view and smell contents. When opening, discard any can that spurts. Discard contents (do not taste) if there is a strange odor or appearance."

So, discard any cans or jars that bulge, leak, burp, spurt, fizz or stink. Food pouches of 'wet' foods (like tuna, chicken, Indian vegetables, some soups) should be good for at least as long as canned goods. Dried foods are stable for longer than that if they are tightly sealed in insect-resistant material (meaning, no thin plastic bags). Dried or wet prepared foods can develop off-colors or off-flavors, including bitterness, over time. Prepared foods usually have sell-by or use-by or best-by dates on them, which is not the same as 'unsafe after' but still offers a <u>minimum</u> safe-use suggestion (especially for refrigerated foods). Simpler basic foods kept dry (dried beans and legumes, rice and grains, flours and pastas) keep for a long time, so long as little insects don't get to them. Home vacuum+heat-sealed bags are a good option, especially if given a 72-hour freezer treatment after sealing. There are other rigid sealed plastic containers on the market; post-seal 72-hour freezing is always a good extra step. Got 'fresh' yeast, baking powder, baking soda?

Using this approach, with common retail items, you may need to make a bit of extra effort to plan to use (rotate and replace) your food reserve before it ages out. Processed foods, rather than 'dry goods,' will need the most attention. Two approaches to simplify and manage this process would be (1) to use / retire and replace processed (including canned) foods every 2–3 years, or (2) group your processed foods by date and replace only the oldest portion each year. Note that, if you are in the habit of shopping at discount grocery outlets, many items sold there are often already close to their 'best by' dates; for longer-term pantry stocking, it may be better value to stock up at conventional stores and capture the longer shelf-life of items there. What to do with still-safe items you are replacing? Donate to food banks <u>before</u> things expire (and capture a tax deduction). Throw food parties. Share. Do stocking stuffers.

Another option is to buy stable, staple foods in bulk (for example, 24 lbs., or up to about 240 servings of rice) in specially sealed containers from specialty providers, and this has some advantages. Benefits may include high-quality bug-

and rodent-proof storage containers and seals, and long shelf-storage life (under good storage conditions) of up to 30 years, even for canned goods. This can mean that you stock your cool, dry pantry only 'once in a generation,' you don't have to worry about tracking, managing and rotating your stock, and you don't have to repurchase it multiple times. Sometimes these bulk-purchase items are no more expensive than what supermarkets charge for the same quantity sold in small, thin plastic or paper bags.

There are also more convenient items, shelf-stable for many years (read labels carefully), that provide an array of pre-made meals in packets in sealed bulk pails or cartons. Some such meals may require rehydration or heating; military grade MREs (Meal Ready to Eat) usually include a chemical heating pack, and are much more expensive.

My personal suggestion for most folks is to not buy a pallet of something unfamiliar. If you do want to try specialty long-term storage products, look at online retailers and suppliers, and try a few items for starters, possibly including some of the ready-made meals. You can also always experiment with camping foods from outdoor stores (check the use-by dates for best flavor). Either way, why not have a taster party with friends and neighbors, and decide what you might like? (We used to see vanloads of people doing this with sale-priced wines in the parking lot at Trader Joe's every weekend). Most aisles in the supermarket are full of the familiar shelf-stable foods that you enjoy, including comfort foods and treats to keep your spirits up. Some things like powdered eggs, and powdered refried beans, you might have to look harder for (perhaps online), and some 'bulk' things at big-box stores might appeal to you.

One tip: Many (but not all) commercially produced tortillas have a stable shelf life of months, much longer than many loaf-bread products. Try flour tortillas for PBJs. English muffins are also durable for weeks.

Balance comfort with nutrition. The hardest food group to source 'not frozen or in cans' may be vegetables; I like Indian food, and that's the easiest source of shelf-stable veggie packs. Dehydrated 'soup mix' vegetables are available. Occasionally you may find packets of 'toasted' vegetable snacks. Vitamin supplements may complete the ensemble.

There are lots of sources of information on the topic of emergency food planning, some of it apocalyptic in tone, but you can keep it simple: all we're talking about is expanding your pantry somewhat, mostly with ordinary items, or with special purchase staples and ready-meals, and then rotating and replacing what's in it (if necessary) to keep it all in good condition.

Shopping tip: do NOT wait until the last minute. Or the last week. Look at photos online of empty store shelves during a crisis like a hurricane. Or recall the toilet paper aisle when Covid-19 hit. You're going to be much happier doing rational preparedness shopping over time, and expanding your pantry when the sun shines, rather than trying to join in a frenzy of panic buying when it's becoming harder to travel to (or resupply) stores. And consider this: <u>if you stock up long in advance, the supply chain adjusts and expands, the economy ticks up one small notch, a few jobs are created, no one loses, and panic buying at some future date is lessened</u>. It's the sort of win-win good deed that helps you too! Tell your friends. By the way, emergency preparedness is not hoarding.

Do you hunt? Forage? If you have a garden, do you put in winter vegetables? My broccoli just won't quit. Do you have nut trees? Do you can or dehydrate summer fruits and vegetables? If you have the skills and opportunity, or interest, to do those things safely (novice foragers sometimes make mistakes), you may have more options during those rare tough times. There won't be much to forage in January–February (though chanterelles do like wet weather...).

Note: Much of the above assumes that you will have the ability to heat water and cook food. If that is not the case, you have a bigger problem. There will be a more limited selection of ready-to-eat shelf-stable food. For some people, it may make sense to have some self-heating meals, like MREs (Meal Ready to Eat) originally developed for the military; often available at well-stocked outdoor stores. Having at least one hot meal per day could make a difference, even psychologically. You can learn more about MREs online.

Supplies that are grocery store or pharmacy-aisle items go into this category. You'll probably remember toilet paper! Will you remember matches or lighters? Don't forget 'soft drugs' like coffee and chocolate.

Potable water

What happens if your water utility shuts down, or you can't pump from your deep well? There will be lots of water around, but it will not be safe to drink once it's hit the ground or unwashed surfaces. Untreated creek water is not really, reliably safe. Maybe you pre-purchased a ton of bottled water (that's 240 gallons). And more and more people are adding clean-water storage tanks to their rural homesteads, relatively inexpensively, considering potential benefits; although most often installed to manage summer drought, like small private reservoirs, they will be at least as useful as a source of stored potable (drinkable) water in a winter emergency.

More information on water treatment is widely available; I'll just cover the basics. There are four common, effective ways to treat 'wild water' from lakes and streams, and, to be safer when doctors and hospitals are unavailable, even rainwater. By wild water I mean water free of chemical pollutants (and/or sewage, hopefully).

1. Heat. Boil water for at least 1 minute at sea level and for up to 10 minutes at high elevations. If conserving fuel, a pressure cooker may be more efficient. Sustained heat kills disease-causing microbes.

2. Chemicals. A wide variety are available at camping, hunting and outdoor stores, and online. Follow directions. They use various chemistries and have different pros and cons. They kill disease-causing microbes. [Note: If you don't mind the taste and odor of bleach, the Navy has a great .pdf (at www.cnic.navy.mil) on Emergency Water Purification, explaining (briefly here) that 8 drops (use a dedicated eyedropper, or figure that ¼ teaspoon holds about 24–25 drops) of standard household laundry bleach per 1 gallon of clear water should make it safe. For muddy water use 16 drops per gallon. Wait 30 minutes before use; if you can't smell chlorine, add another 8 or 16 drops of bleach and wait another 15 minutes. After that, letting it 'breathe' uncovered for a while will get rid of some odor and taste. Fun fact: one gallon of household bleach can treat 3800 gallons of water. Be careful with liquid bleach; gloves and safe eyewear are appropriate.]

3. Ultra-violet light. Camping stores have small, battery-powered UV 'pens' producing high-energy light that kills disease-causing microbes in water. These do not work well in dirty water, so settling or some kind of filtration as a first step may be needed. Note: 'Psychedelic black-lights' do not have the right energy spectrum to kill germs.

4. Ultra-filtration: Camping stores offer a wide range of ultra-filters that remove most disease-causing microbes (but not the smaller viruses) as well as particles from wild water. You can use them on muddy water if necessary, and get safe water, but that clogs filters sooner. They range from personal 'straws' to larger units that can provide for a hunting camp.

Always use one of these four methods if you are not sure of the safety of drinking water.

If your best water source is muddy, you can try using cheesecloth, paper towels, or coffee filters as a pre-treatment step, <u>before</u> using options 1, 2, 3, or 4 above.

If you don't have wild water, and you suspect chemical pollution in your <u>best</u>, or only, water source, you can add an <u>additional</u> pre-treatment step with a charcoal filter, such as are found in many home water filtration pitchers, before using options 1, 2, 3, or 4 above. It can't hurt, it might help, but it may not remove every pollutant, especially as the filter ages. Chemical odors are signs of some, but not all, pollution problems. Best options aren't always perfect.

Rainwater may be abundant and it's easy to catch it in clean containers, but remember, rain is washing everything else out of the air, like dust, bacteria and spores, so it's fairly clean but not squeaky clean. Without a doctor, pharmacy or hospital available, it's safer to treat it if you can. If you can't, so be it.

I'll suggest that you stock plenty of your favorite inexpensive chemical water treatment and/or a gallon of household bleach that you never open except for this emergency use. Then decide if there's some other treatment method that you might prefer. I guarantee, if push really comes to shove, there will be folks around who will be very grateful to receive those water treatment chemicals if you don't need them (re-read the report from Bangladesh in the 'Population' chapter). Many people would do well to keep some coffee filters and (in some cases) a spare household 'water pitcher' system with extra charcoal filter cartridges around too. Get a big box, label it 'Rainy Day Stuff,' pack it away (don't forget where), and sleep better. Ditto, extra purification tablets and a bottle in a go-bag.

Regarding human waste disposal: If flushing is impossible, do you have a 'roughing it' alternative? Camping stores do. If you have working septic / sewerage, but no running water, rapidly pouring (into the bowl) a bucket of two or three gallons of any old water will flush a toilet… an almost forgotten art in the modern world.

Medications

Do you have a six-week or more emergency reserve of your prescriptions in a cool place (if appropriate)? An M.D. friend tells me that many prescribing doctors will support this, and may have ideas about keeping costs low if insurers won't agree to cover. Some pharmacies may help with costs. You'll need to check with your team. Do you have a good first-aid kit and plenty of over-the-counter medications? You may be doing more tasks that leave you prone to cuts and sprains. If you have a serious medical condition or critical pharmaceutical need, you may want to reconsider any plans to shelter in place. If you relocate to an emergency shelter, relief staff can assist you with obtaining prescription medications.

Clothing and gear

Do you have all the winter weather layers you want and need? Are they stormproof? Do you have wet-weather gloves, rubber boots, waders, full poncho? You may be outdoors more often, in very wet conditions, dealing with situations. Do you have dry backup items? If your residence or shelter is damaged, do you at least have a good tent, sleeping bags, cushioning pads or cots (cots may be better on wet ground), if no better shelter is available? Do you have tarps and rope for whatever? Do you have enough extra to share? Pulling together with others to pull through may have lasting positive effects.

Do you have a pack or knapsack for essentials in case you have to relocate on short notice? A checklist? In some cases, something you can carry while on foot will be appreciated. Waterproof hiking boots you could travel several miles in?

Snowshoes? XC skis? A sled you can pull? As I revise this section in early 2023, California is having a very strong, very low-elevation snowstorm event;

I'll be snowed in tonight (only for two days, as it turned out). In a megastorm there could be a lot of snow on the ground at times even at low elevations, and snowplows may not be in service due to fuel limitations. Snowmobiles are useful as long as you have snow and fuel… and snow is not a given, as the climate warms. Nor is fuel.

Equipment

In the forested Foothills, I always think first about a chainsaw. Do you have a saw for downed trees and branches, that will run on whatever fuel or energy is available several weeks into the storms? I keep hand-powered bow saws, gas-powered saws and rechargeable electric saws ready, and the newer battery-electric ones are good or adequate for all but the big jobs. A spare saw chain or two could be precious. Do you also have a 24–30" muscle-powered bow-saw as a backup? Do you have a pole saw or pruning saw for handling overhead limbs or hard to reach tree damage (a hard-hat is recommended while doing overhead cutting)? A shovel? An axe? A winch or come-along? Tarps? Rope and cord? Bags for sandbags (available at good hardware stores; might save your driveway… will you need sand too)? Will you need to split firewood with hand tools (including hand-powered hydraulics)? Do you have fire extinguishers? Batteries for smoke and carbon monoxide detectors? This could be a long list. You could do a careful eyeball walk-around and make lists; capturing and saving video for any future insurance claims could be part of your process.

Do you have spare parts for any vital equipment? You can buy parts ahead for one repair / maintenance cycle.

Flotation, watercraft

If you are experienced with boating or rafting, you may (or may not) have a reasonable option for relocating if floodwaters isolate your location and put you at risk. If you <u>don't</u> have serious boating skills, it may be safer in many circumstances to await rescue. I am <u>not going to encourage anyone to attempt swift-water boating, or swimming in flood waters</u>. In both cases, particularly if attempting swimming, there are too many extremely dangerous hazards in swift or cold water to list here, including entrapments, but as an example:

> "Standing or working in water that is cooler than 75°F (24°C) will remove body heat more rapidly than it can be replaced, resulting in hypothermia (decreased body temperature). Survival curves show that an adult dressed in average clothing may remain conscious for an hour in 40°F

water and perhaps 2-3 hours in 50°F water. Physical activity such as swimming or other struggling in the water increases heat loss, reducing survival time to minutes. Without thermal protection, swimming is not possible and the victim, though conscious, is soon helpless. Without a life jacket, drowning is unavoidable. [Winter flood waters here will be <u>cold</u> and will possibly include snowmelt.]

...

Encounters with raccoons, opossums, and squirrels could result in bites that require medical attention or may lead to rabies... Snakes will also have their nests disturbed by flooding..." —USACE, CVIFMA Plan, 2015 [The animal hazards noted above are not specifically related to swimming or boating, but to flooding generally.]

These on-or-in-water choices would be <u>options of last resort</u>, attempting to save an endangered life, in my view, and would depend upon also having a strategy for reaching a safer location in the shortest possible time, and then regaining any lost body heat (for example with reflective blankets that you kept with you). That said, if you are anywhere on or near low ground, you may be very glad that you have acquired personal flotation devices (PFDs, 'life vests') for everyone in your care: the unexpected could happen during an evacuation (even a Cal Guard boat capsized in the 1986 flood). Even better is to make sure that you have equipped your PFDs with whistles, waterproof lights, and a few emergency rations (for starters; mine has a clipped-on locking folding knife that can cut through a kayak). An 'empty' clip-on water bottle holding plenty of packets of water purification treatments will also improve flotation (and survival). Beyond that, <u>if you have the skills, confidence and need</u>, it might be worth thinking—with safety coming first—about 'what floats,' including all boats, paddle-craft, and PFDs, that you might keep at your home. You might also proactively see whether a local boating or paddling club offers swift-water rescue training; I found that a two-day training program (in Appalachia) was very valuable.

A few other preparedness thoughts

Communications: If cell service remains up and working, do you have a way to keep a cellphone charged? Amazingly, some 'camping' wood-fired stoves with USB ports can do this; solar and hand-cranked chargers are also available. If only landline service is working, but is possibly overloaded, do you have a plan for how to keep current with those in your family and circle? If all electronic communications are out, do you know your neighbors well enough to keep some sort of information network operating? Do you or people you know in your area have CB, shortwave or ham radio?

Animals: Are you prepared to feed and care for your animals for at least six weeks? Animal supplies may have a lower priority for distribution than emergency food and gear for people, in an extreme crisis. During wildfire events, there have been good responses to provide emergency feed and relocation for displaced horses, but an extreme winter storm could be different, particularly regarding sourcing, access and transportation. If you must relocate, have you made arrangements to provide for your animals, with someone who will work with you to be sure that the necessary provisions have been secured?

Other items to stay on top of: Is your property insurance paid up and in force? If you are not in a flood zone, or lack flood insurance, has your insurance agent clarified for you whether damage from stormwater flowing across the surface of the land is covered by your policy (or, usually, is excluded as 'flood')? Can you prevent that surface water flow from happening, and keep it out of your home or structures? Have you cleaned out your roof gutters? Have you checked out your driveway or entry road for possible erosion sites? If there are storm drains or culverts along your road, are they clear? Have you lowered levels of any sizeable ponds while it is still safe downstream to do so? Are any private dam spillways or drains prepared? Are all potential problem trees and limbs dealt with, near your buildings, along your road or drive, or near stream channels that could become blocked and dammed by forest debris or brush?

Is everything you need stored where you can find it? Are your irreplaceable possessions either where you can grab them quickly, or else in the highest and driest part of your home, in a fireproof safe, in a waterproof wrap, and away from any overhanging or leaning trees? If you have a safe deposit box, is your bank out of the flood hazard one? Have you rehearsed different event scenarios and made notes on what to do? Have you identified potential problems with the routes you might try to travel, and ranked them from best to worst? Do you know who you can reach out to if you run into trouble? Have you backed up computer and other digital data (and video for insurance claims) and stored copies safely, including safely off-site? Have you charged all your devices and especially back-up battery packs?

Lists like these are starting-place tools for planning. Many more references and guidebooks are available to help you think through preparations for a period of self-reliant 'roughing it.' There are survival manuals, Red Cross, Boy Scouts and military manuals, and earthquake preparedness literature. Electric utilities are regularly distributing information and checklists to prepare for power shutoffs. All are valuable.

One of my favorite sources for books on 'roughing it' are the bookstores in visitor centers in state and federal parks and multi-agency centers (USFS /

BLM / NPS, etc.) where back-country activities are popular. Better camping and outdoor stores may also be good sources.

Californians who are earthquake-aware will have already made many of these same preparations for coping at home. Many who are wildfire-aware will have made preparations to relocate. Both kinds of preparations have some overlap with megastorm readiness. If you keep a wildfire 'go-bag' handy, why not add a 'winter essentials' bag for a possible departure during the cold, wet season? Established emergency shelters and relief preparations are generally scaled to handle wildfire- or earthquake-scale relocations (whereas a megastorm is predicted to be a much bigger event with different challenges). Human needs remain similar in most disasters… but the situations and challenges will differ, for example in scale of impacts and amount of isolation. Advance planning and preparation for a period of disruption or isolation can make all the difference. Because…

One idea that takes some getting used to is that help might not be on the way. The scale of a serious megastorm disaster could be so great, meaning severe impacts for hundreds of miles in all directions, that all emergency management and relief agencies, responders, and all levels of government will struggle to cope with it. Evacuating communities, serving areas where displaced persons are gathering, maintaining primary emergency transportation corridors, and trying to protect levees and dams and critical infrastructure are likely to be the focus of the most urgent attention. Relief services and supplies are likely to be unevenly distributed—concentrated where access is best or where the most people end up—until the crisis stabilizes. Smaller numbers of scattered folks, in more distant places, 'who chose to live out there**,' [inconveniently,] may amount to small blips on the emergency services radar. [** …as opposed to having chosen to live *on the floodplain*…]

Are you going to leave the area?

So, do you stay or go? This should be a decision you and yours have taken together and planned for long in advance. One simple scenario in the Foothills could be families living 'upcountry' with kids and grandkids living and working down in the Valley. If those descendants are anticipating an evacuation to higher ground, and if they inherited your smarts, they may ask to relocate with you early and in an orderly way. And when they ask how much food you think they should bring, the answer is always: "<u>All of it</u>." People arriving unprepared to shelter in hill country will be bringing avoidable potential problems, like food shortages, with them. So: bring all the food, meds, essential supplies including batteries, and fuel they can transport. Remember this author's magic (middling estimate for hill country) 'megastorm' number: a safe 126 meals per person.

Particularly if you have medical, or medical equipment, needs, or cannot be fully self-reliant, timely relocation may be your absolute best option. If you are getting out of Dodge, when do you go? To where, exactly? How much warning will you get? As I noted above, as of 2022, Pacific Atmospheric Rivers can be forecast out to about a week or a little more, and are 'officially rated' in the 72 hours before making landfall. So maybe it's been raining for a couple of weeks, and the rain is getting heavier, you've seen a bit of flooding, or a landslide, and the news tells you that it's going to continue and maybe get worse for another week. The news can't tell you whether it will go on for two more weeks, or three. There is a risk of thinking "It can't possibly get worse, no one has ever seen it worse than this." Well, no one alive today, anyway. Will you leave 'early' when it's easier, and risk feeling foolish later, or wait awhile and then risk being stuck where you are, or stranded somewhere along your evacuation route, perhaps in dire straits?

If you leave, you need a plan and a destination. Starting, for many people, with: where, exactly, are you going to park a car or RV? One or more millions of people on the road means hundreds of thousands of cars, campers, 5th-wheels and motorhomes looking for a high, dry spot.

The 1862 megastorm made a series of serious messes eastward pretty much all the way to the Rockies, including desert basin and river flooding, and far to the north and south, so if you are running from the storms, you may have a long drive with various challenges and a lot of company. It's hard to predict what road and traffic conditions might be, but they could be very different from what you are used to, with fewer options. First off, you might be trying to cross the Sierra (or more likely, go around the range) under storm conditions. The West has no real experience with hurricane-scale evacuations, particularly under sustained winter storm conditions, and you (and everyone else) may have to cross a lot of miles without gas stations or lodging. Air and rail service may also become difficult or unavailable at some point. Leaving is, eventually, not going to be a simple or easy choice, especially if you delay.

The attraction of RV's and motor homes is that you can take your shelter and some supplies, gear and amenities with you. The disadvantage is that they use a lot of fuel which is likely to become scarce in the West. A compromise, if you can haul everything you'll need*** for a few weeks, and you don't require assistance, is to drive your RV, maybe with like-minded friends and neighbors, to some high 'camping' ground (or parking area) nearby where you'll feel relatively safe and comfortable in your general home area. You could make a short list of destinations now. Many evacuation 'shelter' areas, in fairgrounds and some large parking lots, become, in large part, villages of RVs. Some accept horses and other animals. [***An RV may or may not have fuel reserves for generating adequate heat and electricity for an emergency relocation of several weeks. On-site hookups for services may be unavailable even in developed

RV parks under prevailing conditions, even if you can get a site. A clear-eyed assessment of your vehicle's energy or water capacity might lead you to relocate an RV to a designated shelter point, like fairgrounds, where there would ideally be warming shelters, potable water and waste disposal services, and emergency rations. How quickly space at such shelter points would fill is unknown. An acre will hold fewer than 100 RVs.] Normally, shelter-point information is posted promptly on the Internet… if you can connect. Start with county pages (Sheriff, Emergency Services). Responders should have good information if their tasks are not too urgent or the situation too chaotic.

On the other hand, for speed, distance, and fuel economy you may want to travel farther in a smaller, faster car and just accept whatever is available wherever you end up… which could be unpredictable. If you are leaving the area in a smaller vehicle not designed for 'camping,' think very carefully about what your extended needs might be under a variety of circumstances; try to have <u>everything</u> you might need in that car. Definitely take the best tent; for the PFDs you might have to flip a coin (they make ok pillows). Also, re-read thoughts on route research and planning earlier in this chapter.

In the past few years, hundreds of thousands of Californians and others in the West, but still only a small fraction of the population, have experienced local-area evacuations firsthand, mostly due to summer and fall wildfires; but also due to floods and to the flood risk from the spillway emergency at Lake Oroville in February of 2017. Others have seen what it's like and have their go-bags packed and their trucks, vans and RVs gassed up. Those experiences and preparations will be helpful if extreme winter storms hit California. What will be different is the weather, the road conditions, the unexpected emergence of areas that become impassable or inaccessible, the fewer and unfamiliar options for relocation, the numbers of people involved in relocation, possible scarcity of fuels, food, supplies, and everything, and the stress that the scope of a megastorm-scale emergency will put on public officials and agencies, and on private businesses. So: a really different experience.

Advance planning and preparation for a period of disruption or isolation can make all the difference. Preparation includes mental preparation. For many and perhaps most people, an experience like a megastorm sequence would be, and perhaps will be, the most challenging of their lives. Organizing and rehearsing periodically, even mentally, will make the adjustment to crisis mode, or better yet, coping mode, much easier when the time comes.

You may also want to become familiar with the Ready.gov, CERT, California Volunteers, and other programs described in a later chapter. Now, to sail us into the topic of community-level preparedness:

> No man is an island,
>
> Entire of itself.
>
> Each is a piece of the continent,
>
> A part of the main.
>
> If a clod be washed away by the sea,
>
> Europe is the less.
>
> As well as if a promontory were.
>
> As well as if a manor of thine own
>
> Or of thine friend's were.
>
> Each man's death diminishes me,
>
> For I am involved in mankind.
>
> Therefore, send not to know
>
> For whom the bell tolls,
>
> It tolls for thee.
>
> —John Donne

* * *

Further reading

Taylor, W. L., & R. W. Taylor. 2007. The Great California Flood of 1862. http://www.redlandsfortnightly.org/papers/Taylor06.htm

https://www.cnn.com/2022/01/15/us/winter-storm-preparation-groceries-wellness/index.html

Canned food guidance: https://extension.usu.edu/preserve-the-harvest/research/storing-canned-goods

Potable (safe drinking) water guidance [search site linked below on 'Emergency Water Purification' for a link to a .pdf file]: www.cnic.navy.mil

Preparedness learning activities for kids: https://kidsemergencysafety.com/?cid=em_PSPS_PSPSMonthlyNL_20220129_HelpChildrenLearnRes_email_na_na

https://kidsemergencysafety.com/grades-k-6

https://www.cnn.com/2022/07/29/weather/flooding-safety-preparedness-kentucky/index.html

Here's a selection of vintage emergency, survival and first aid manuals; check with government and Red Cross sources for additional and updated publications:

US Army Survival Manual. Reprint of Department of the Army Field Manual FM 21-76. Dorset Press, New York, 1992.

Expect the Unexpected. American Red Cross, Washington, D.C. 1986. Compact guide to emergency preparedness and what-to-do, with checklists. Prepared for Maxwell House Coffee]

Community First Aid & Safety. American Red Cross, Washington, D.C. StayWell, Boston, MA. 1993. 238 pp. [Training manual]

First Aid / CPR / AED for Schools and the Community. American Red Cross, Washington, D.C. StayWell, Boston, MA. 2006. 210 pp. [Training Manual]

Hostetler, Kristin. Don't Forget the Duct Tape. 2007 [2nd edition]. The Mountaineers Books, Seattle, WA. 109 pp. [Field repair solutions for outdoor gear]

14

Preparedness for Communities

Grass has many roots (us, again)

"Never doubt that a small group of thoughtful, committed citizens can change the world; indeed, it's the only thing that ever has."
—Margaret Mead

Personal safety and community safety are two sides of a coin. Once you have considered how to take care of yourself, family, and friends, consider how the community safety net, for example local congregations, service and benevolent organizations, and local leaders can anticipate and prepare to meet the needs of the entire community. A safe community is also one in which no-one feels desperate.

This is a topic that spans planning, preparation, training and practice, and is in line with the State Emergency Plan (SEP) at least as far as local responder and emergency management agencies are concerned. For small communities, neighborhoods, and local volunteer organizations, you may not want to wait for the creek to rise; it can't hurt to begin proactive discussions on possible needs, solutions, and contingency plans… years in advance. Organizers can also reach out to local agencies to learn more about plans, participation and coordination. Volunteer groups including local committees can contact California Volunteers, a state government office with responsibilities incorporated into the SEP, and see if they can offer information, guidance or support for community efforts. Your local CERT (Community Emergency Response Team) is another good group to connect with, to explore interests in extreme winter weather preparedness (same goes for your local fire chief). If there is no local CERT team organized to prepare for storm scenarios, you can start one, using online training and resources. Some CERT teams focus on supporting responders.

Once again, this is an area where actual disaster relief experts could bring useful insight, perspective and experience to you. For example, the Red Cross has established protocols for operations and for facilities assessments, and trains people to volunteer to assist and provide care at Red Cross run emergency shelters. It can be useful to learn about Red Cross Shelter operations—you can find and attend training sessions—and appropriate elements of their models could be adapted and applied elsewhere. I encourage communities to go well beyond the expectation that the Red Cross or the Cal Guard can meet all emergency shelter needs, for several reasons, including access and capacity. It may not be possible for Red Cross personnel to reach certain community shelters as extreme weather conditions develop. You may want to look at the 1986 medical evacuation incident I describe in the 'Lessons' chapter.

Regarding capacity, the Red Cross will use facilities allocated for that use. The number of displaced persons may greatly exceed local shelter capacity (which might be for example, 30–50–75 persons in a rural area shelter). Tuolumne County has completed work on two new facilities that could shelter 100–150 people (in total) according to the design concept; the county population was 55,620 in 2020, and flood-prone San Joaquin County is not getting any further away. Typical shelters are for 'small emergencies' but those are not the only scenarios waiting in the wings.

In the snap-evacuation of 188,000 people during the 2017 Oroville Dam spillways failures,

> "About twelve spontaneous shelters opened up in Chico. A spontaneous shelter is where a church, school, or other similar facility opens its doors to evacuees out of goodness. These shelters also required support, and the County gave it to them **as best as it could**." [A local Fire Marshal spontaneously checked all of these ad-hoc shelters for safety and other issues. Another large church opened its doors in response to a personal plea from a Sheriff's Deputy.] —Spillway Emergency

Envisioning both potential emergency needs and the limitations on feasible relief support, a community and its organizations can begin to enhance their own preparedness and resilience well in advance of an emergency, to provide more organized, orderly, and appropriate support. This includes coordination within and beyond the community. Local service organizations and churches, County OES and agencies, and Red Cross are worth connecting with, as are various volunteer organizations. Team Rubicon is one volunteer disaster response example; California Volunteers, a state office, is a good connection point for information on volunteer activities in the state.

In forested areas in the West, shelter operating plans and assumptions may tend to reflect an expectation of dry / summer wildfire evacuations rather than wet / winter storm relocations. A true megastorm will have a much greater scope of impacts, differently distributed. A lack of electricity or fuels and a need for space heating and drying of wet materials may not be factored into typical shelter planning, beyond incorporating a fueled generator with a limited fuel reserve. A lack of water, of waste disposal, and of an overland road network for receiving food, fuel and supplies, may not be anticipated. A healthy dialog with county officials, including a demonstration of compelling community interest, may help to remediate any evident deficiencies in facilities or wishful thinking in operational plans.

For those and other reasons, having multiple 'reserve' shelter options planned and prepared for in advance by local churches, benevolent organizations, food banks and charities, and citizen's groups could provide for expandable local shelter and support capacity to match the scope of an emergency, with enough flexibility to tailor the response to the actual situation and local needs. Pre-crisis coordinating discussions within the community and with local Red Cross and emergency officials could be useful in several ways.

A local grass roots planning committee, or just a bunch of proactive folks, could start the 'what if' process with a discussion and a few basic questions:

Where could we shelter our displaced neighbors, and how many of them?

What would their needs be, and how could we meet them?

What resources would be available if the community became isolated? (Run down the list of everything that would or could be needed… and that's a lot of things.)

Regarding the third question, various kinds of resource information might be deemed private or sensitive. Some might be volunteered. The SO, LEOs, Fire officials, CERT teams, and possibly county-designated local volunteer / NGO organizations or councils could find it easier to securely prepare resource inventories and in-residence personnel rosters (experienced community based responder teams may have a mental rolodex of such information, while also attempting to honor privacy concerns). An understanding of how Incident Command (IC) would be established or devolved in isolated communities, and at the county level, would help clarify where critical resource information should be available. Details of local IC protocols, at the 'who?' level, are not always clearly documented and are worthy of some dialog with your county officials. You may learn that who is designated for IC will depend on the nature of the situation. Tip: ask your local fire chief about these issues.

My assessment is that a small rural community, typically not affluent overall, is likely (under extreme weeks-long storm conditions, and depending on elevation, terrain and hydrology and the actual impacts and disruptions experienced) to have a substantial number of residents who would eventually need to, or elect to, relocate from their homes to some sort of sheltering facilities. A community could develop an estimate based on surveys with a scenario involving loss of roads and utilities. As a pure guess, I think 50–100 (–200) persons per 1000 would be a useful <u>first</u> estimate for rural / hill country areas (USGS, in one estimate [in a somewhat garbled section] estimates 14+% of those in flooded Valley areas would need emergency shelter); the percentage of persons relocating to shelters will depend upon many factors but is likely to increase over time if a disruption event drags on, as hardships persist or damage accumulates. Floods can strike rapidly; some hill country storm impacts may accumulate progressively. If that number seems high, consider what falling limbs and trees, surface water, mud or debris flows, unplowed snow, local road closures, and days or weeks without electricity, propane, heat, running water, an adequate pantry, or company will create for many households. Community shelter may also be the best choice for some residents with special needs, as the Red Cross is aware. If those 5–20% planning numbers still seem high, consider what the people trapped in the San Bernardino Mountains were in need of during and after the snowstorms of early 2023; many lives were lost there.

A substantial number of residents would presumably not have established food pantry reserves and could need to be provided with meals or food, as well as many other things. This need will be more pronounced in the hinterlands where wealth and income levels are relatively less, and a pantry could be a real or imagined extravagance (if you're from another part of California, please note that annual per capita income in this part of the Sierra, <u>before</u> Covid-19 hit, was just over $15,000; it remains well under $20,000 today. This may be fairly typical of 'ungentrified' rural settlements). Community-level planners ought to determine community area population and financial demographics and then employ proven processes to estimate likely levels of emergency need (shelter, food, other) among the population. Economic downturns might shift those numbers higher. State or federal planning frameworks might help with estimation.

I think it is helpful to keep in mind that one person will need 126 meals in a six-week period. If your mountain / foothills community of 2,000 only has on hand half of the food it would need in this scenario, and if you are isolated without resupply for that long, you are 126,000 meals short. This preparedness issue should be addressed at household and community levels.

It may not be possible to 'run to the store,' but even if your isolated community has a substantial grocery store or two, stores may only hold two days (this from a study in Nova Scotia) to seven days (this from calculating inventory turnover in stores across the USA) worth of food. The more proactive residents will have stocked up on retail groceries early in the event (or long before; please become one of <u>those</u> folks). There are plenty of photos online of empty store shelves during emergencies like hurricanes. Note that small communities have disproportionally smaller stores with less inventory.

You may next want to consider where food warehouses are located, and, even if your local roads are passable (many will not be), what about roads to and from warehouses and depots? Very briefly, many warehouses, depots, and major highways are on the floodplain of the Central Valley and other valleys or floodplains in the West. Even if you can reach a supermarket, the supply chain may be seriously disrupted, and you may have a lot of competition.

My point is that community and charitable organization food pantries and food banks, in addition to in-home pantries, could become the essential food supply safety net, if the community is made inaccessible and supplies cannot be delivered… and then everyone will be thankful that those circumstances were planned for. When part of a community suffers, in extremity, everyone is in trouble. Starvation, locally, and more widespread food rationing, were facts of life in the early 1862 megastorm. How would modern Americans react to rationing? In a perfect world a public agency would maintain small, distributed emergency warehouses among potentially isolated communities; while feasible (though an expense), that may seem impractical now… <u>but local organizations could begin that process</u>, especially with resiliency grant support. Even relatively inexpensive, weather-tight shipping containers could provide for a simple, rapid build-out of distributed storage facilities. It might take a tragic disaster and some pious hindsight, or a rapidly changing winter climate, to bring about official in-depth preparedness support at local-scale. Let's not, you and I, become that disaster.

Ideas, suggestions and details

Food banks may not be in the habit of building inventory reserves, especially with scarce resources, but I would recommend that that should become a standard policy—particularly for more remote communities, on high ground—as winter approaches each year. Fall-season donation cycles from people managing and restocking their own home pantries might be dovetailed with bolstering of community winter pantry inventories. Publicizing food drives between Labor Day and Thanksgiving each year, concurrently with families or households annually inventorying and renewing their in-home pantry items, could make for effective winter stockpiling campaigns. Rational stockpiling is not hoarding; it is prudently managing the inventory, flow and use of necessities.

The concept of community 'pantries' could be expanded towards more comprehensive shelter needs. For example, keeping a reserve of bleach or more specific chemicals for water treatment would be a logical step. Ideally local teams of pantry managers and future shelter hosts could determine which groups will coordinate and obtain and store which necessities.

If 5–20% of a local population requires emergency shelter, that would far exceed the officially designated constructed space currently envisioned by emergency planners (1% is closer to reality). For that reason, both community need and potential capacity, meaning the full array of public spaces, including community halls and schools, should be assessed. Additionally, better choices might be offered by churches, benevolent societies with halls, and servicemembers' organizations like the VFW. In conjunction with assessment, through consultation, a coordinated community care framework or plan may be agreed to at 'village scale.'

One consideration is that some such private halls may still have wood heat, and if not, they could be modified to receive a wood-burning appliance without undue red tape that could plague public buildings. Emergency planners I've spoken with have been surprised by the idea that shelters might someday not have electric power or fuels for heat, cooking or generators. Wood is the sole local fuel resource in many places and it is plentiful, and useable if cut and stored in advance. If insurance objections are a concern, then at minimum, pass-through hardware could be installed in advance in a wall or ceiling / roof, then mothballed, to simplify future temporary connection of a stove and stovepipe in an unheated emergency. Keep a carbon monoxide detector in reserve.

Heat is a human necessity in winter conditions, and for remote communities (you may have guessed that I live in one), firewood is a familiar heating fuel for many, but not all, households. Unlike in summer, winter relocators are likely to be chilled and it will be easy to become wet. Heated spaces will be vital. Boiling water to a safe condition may also be routine. Hot meals could be a lifeline for many. As community emergency shelters are evaluated, the ability to use wood for space heating, water heating and cooking should be given emphasis. Many people, especially those who buy their firewood, stock only enough for one winter, and run out of wood by spring. On a community level, as well as for proactive individuals, maintaining a reserve of additional firewood could become very important. In this county, at least one church organizes a community wood drive each year, to make sure that no one in need goes without. In a neighboring county, an organization called Wood Angels maintains a lot for processing and storing firewood for those in need. Not far away, some native tribes do this for their communities. Commercial firewood lots exist. Preparing and storing a reserve of firewood in and for remote communities in forested areas is a good community safeguard that fits nicely with the other resiliency elements described in this chapter.

It occurs to me that, after the next megastorm, these things will seem obvious. They don't, yet, broadly speaking.

You may also want to search online for information on 'rocket stoves' that can operate by burning twigs and very small branches not normally used for firewood. There are small, simple designs for these, including some that can be constructed from a few cinder blocks. For those sheltering in place without power, fuel, or any other heat source, a small outdoor twig-burner for boiling water, heating food and drink, and warming hands could make a real difference. You would want to have dry twigs or be able to dry damp ones.

I'd like to see a sleeping bag in every pot, so to speak, but that won't happen, so organizations that accept the eventual responsibility for providing emergency shelter and care would do well to build up some reserve of sleeping bags and/or bedding, and something like a soft pad, if not a Red Cross style cot, to provide a comfortable surface for sleeping or relaxing. "Never discard a yoga mat." Similarly, those organizations should give thought to how many people they could care for, and what their needs, including food, would be. Reserve pantries distributed across community organizations would be a robust support system.

Sanitation will be an issue to manage. Private septic systems using only gravity flow can be operated by 'bucket flushing' from any water source. Whether public septic systems would continue to accept piped waste is unknown and probably variable, depending in part on reliance on gravity flow as well as operating or holding conditions. Porta-potties aren't practical (availability, delivery, and servicing problems) under those conditions, but camping toilets could be acquired in advance. There are also traditional latrines in the worst-case situation. Tarps and lines would be useful there.

Community shelters would simplify communication, allow the monitoring of people who might be at risk for health or other conditions, and could conserve fuels and energy and things like labor for cooking. To provide remote care for stay-at-homes, some regimen of visits could be established. The issues would be how to fuel vehicles and how to travel the storm-beaten roads safely for many miles. Trees may be down, washouts frequent, snowplows not running. ATVs, snowmobiles, etc. will have their uses while fuel lasts. Besides horses, electric vehicle options might improve over time, for example becoming more rugged, more efficient, or having greater range, as technologies and designs are brought to market, and as long as charging can be done. Fueled and electric vehicles ought to conserve their range for trips of greatest need, including rescues and transport to shelters.

All such planning and preparation, including acquisitions and stockpiling, falls under the heading of increasing local resilience. Some mitigation grant programs extend to the level of 'resilient communities' and might be of interest to organizers and other readers (for example, search online for HGMP, BRIC, FEMA, or CDFA and various other state resilience and hazard mitigation grants). Some program pages are linked below. If Storm / Flood-Safe Councils ever form, they might tie into these efforts.

Communities may also want to discuss with their counties the nature of local administrative responsibilities should any community become isolated. Isolation of a community or district is perhaps best treated as an 'incident' under the State Emergency Management structure (SEM) and at that point an Incident Commander will be responsible for local administration of emergency response and relief activities, and communication with higher Emergency Operations Center (EOC) levels, under / within the state's Incident Command Structure (ICS). How that IC role is established and delegated locally is not fully detailed in the SEP; it is worth discussing now with county officials—the Sheriff, the county Office of Emergency Services, Supervisors—to see what they have to say, and determine whether the protocol is memorialized within the county's Emergency Operations Plan. This could be a good 'preparedness' topic in a local Town Hall meeting with officials, if follow-up seems useful.

Some Cal Fire officials in the field are sworn peace officers, but perhaps not as commonly in the more remote stations. The Governor has the power to commandeer all state employees, including peace officers working for many agencies, and many other resources in an extreme emergency. Local Incident Command (IC), working with or within Cal OES, and state and local officials and personnel, and Cal Guard, will need a coordinated response to any disaster. IC should have a clear picture, in advance, of what local resources can be drawn upon for relief and shelter services. For that reason, community volunteer organizations and any future Incident Commanders that could be activated locally should get to know each other and develop working relationships on an ongoing basis, now.

* * *

Further reading

Grant programs of possible value for increasing community resilience and preparedness:

https://www.fema.gov/grants

https://www.rd.usda.gov/programs-services/community-facilities-direct-loan-grant-program

https://www.calandtrusts.org/

https://www.cdfa.ca.gov/grants/

https://water.ca.gov/Work-With-Us

https://water.ca.gov/grants

https://water.ca.gov/Work-With-Us/Grants-And-Loans

https://water.ca.gov/Work-With-Us/Grants-And-Loans/
Small-Communities-Flood-Risk-Reduction:

https://www.caloes.ca.gov/wp-content/uploads/Preparedness/Documents/
CA-ESF-6-Mass-Care-and-Shelter-Annex_Final508.pdf

https://teamrubiconusa.org/

https://www.californiavolunteers.ca.gov

See also the book Spillway Emergency, on volunteer-based emergency shelter operations. Material for this chapter was also drawn from personal experiences and conversations.

15

Community-scale Roll-out

First experiences and TTEs from Tahoe / Reno and Ventura

English Idiom: "Get your feet wet;
Meaning: To try or start something. To begin gaining experience
in something."

This is a very abbreviated presentation of two real-world training experiences held about a decade ago. It will be of greatest interest to local organizers and emergency planners. Here, briefly:

In 2012–2014, the progress made by the 2011 USGS ARkStorm study led to efforts to continue the education and planning process at an area and community level, with two large exercises. One series of events was called the **ARkStorm@Tahoe** Project. Around 300 'stakeholders' participated in this effort. It could serve us now as a model for building awareness of extreme winter weather events in other communities, and for beginning to engage stakeholders to incorporate such events and challenges into their thinking, planning, training and protocols.

The full report is at University Nevada Reno [as I write this, links are not working to this report; you may need to contact the UNR Library for assistance]
https://www.unce.unr.edu/publications/files/nr/2014/sp1416.pdf

I <u>was</u> able to obtain it from ResearchGate at the link below:
https://www.researchgate.net/publication/275343147_ARkStormTahoe--Stakeholder_Perspectives_on_Vulnerabilities_and_Preparedness_for_an_Extreme_Storm_Event_in_the_Greater_Lake_Tahoe_Reno_and_Carson_City_Region

It's apparent from the report that this was a major undertaking, organized 'from the top down' by experts and key agencies and institutions. For example, the 2011 ARkStorm data were scaled down and redeveloped in greater detail specifically for the "greater Lake Tahoe, Reno and Carson City area." Inputs and participation in this project came from USGS, the National Weather Service, the U.S. Bureau of Reclamation, UC Davis, and the Desert Research Institute.

If you were not going to read this book, or if you are wondering what to read next, then I would urge you to read the "ARkStorm@Tahoe report." It's an excellent overview of AR-megastorm ('ARkStorm') impacts and the kinds of challenges that communities will face. It's more oriented to community preparedness and response than the larger 2011 USGS report.

During the same time period, in 2012, reported on in 2013, a similar but scaled-down initiative was carried out in Ventura County by local and federal agencies, and reported on by a team from the Ventura County Watershed Protection District. It was another step toward community-scale preparedness. Here are the title and abstract from their report:

> "ARkStorm II: A Hydraulic Modeling and Flood Inundation Mapping Effort on Santa Clara River for Emergency Planning Exercises by Local Responders in Ventura County, CA

> Abstract

> The ARKStorm II Emergency Planning and Response Exercise was a joint effort of Ventura County Public Works Agency (VCPWA), Federal Emergency Management Agency (FEMA), and United States Geological Survey (USGS). It is a FEMA RiskMAP pilot project designed to showcase how scientifically based watershed modeling of a large and plausible storm event can enhance disaster response and mitigation planning and foster public awareness. The inundation mapping for this project was developed using hydrological and hydraulic modeling based on data from two severe and rare storms on record for the Santa Clara River (SCR) watershed, namely the 1969 and 1986 extreme precipitation events. The rainfall data was provided by the USGS; these data represent the last two catastrophic flooding events that occurred in Ventura County, California. Using the rainfall data, hydrologic time series of flow (hydrographs) for each of the major tributaries of SCR were developed and used for hydraulic modeling. Real-time storm progression results from the hydraulic modeling were developed to mimic realistic expectations of where flooding is most likely to occur, the resulting flood depth, and what critical community facilities and public and private

infrastructure along the Santa Clara River are projected to be adversely impacted at specific time intervals during the storm event. For example, which transportation evacuation routes, bridges and underpasses, and designated community gathering places could become inaccessible due to flooding and flood-induced landslides at a predicted time interval (*e.g.*, 30 hours into the storm). With such information in hand, alternate routes and public gathering locations would need to be identified through coordinated emergency planning and response exercises by the participating responsible officials of the County of Ventura and Cities along the SCR, FEMA, and USGS. Flood plain maps showing the extent of inundated areas with simulated water depth, critical facilities and utilities flooded, and real photographs of the destroyed areas along the SCR in the 1969 and 1983 floods were prepared to dramatize the events and make it as realistic as possible during the course of the workshop exercise. The main objective of this exercise was to determine which course of actions the county and city emergency planners and engineers would need to take to be better prepared for responding to such a disastrous event. This paper will focus on the hydraulic modeling, flood plain mapping, and the day-long emergency planning and response exercise for this joint effort."

This initiative / event is reviewed on an online document, ARKSTORM / EXERCISE IN EMERGENCY RESPONSE, by the Ventura County Watershed Protection District, 2013, uploaded by the Ventura River Watershed Council.

ARkStorm II: A Hydraulic Modeling and Flood Inundation Mapping Effort on Santa Clara River for Emergency Planning Exercises by Local Responders in Ventura County, CA, by E. Zia Hosseinipour, Brian Trushinski, and Yunsheng Su. World Envirnomental and Water Resource Congress, [ASCE Library], 2013.
https://ascelibrary.org/doi/10.1061/9780784412947.164

ARKSTORM EXERCISE IN EMERGENCY RESPONSE, by the Ventura County Watershed Protection District, 2013.
http://venturawatershed.org/wp-content/uploads/2012/08/ArkStorm-01-23-2013-web.pdf

The Tabletop Exercise on October 25, 2012, included 77 local officials and 10 federal agency observers who also provided some presentations. Looking over the report, it appears to be a meaningful 'stress test' of local conditions, infrastructure, and agency responses. An emergency storm scenario was launched, with unexpected event 'injects,' to allow agencies to carry out simulated response operations in a somewhat unpredictable situation. A list of identified deficiencies and corrections needed is one outcome captured in the report. In my view, these 'rehearsal' exercises are what we need universally at the local area level. [Note: On page 3, the Ventura document perpetuates the misconception that a megastorm is a once-in-1000-years event; this error has propagated in part out of a misunderstanding of the 'k' in 'ARkStorm,' which I discuss later.]

* * *

Beyond these two exercises, the CA DWR CFF report and the various Cal OES plans (discussed elsewhere in this book) are large-scale planning frameworks for either water management and disaster mitigation planning, or large-scale disaster preparation and response planning. Meanwhile, if there have been other community-area-scale 'ARkStorm' TTEs or planning initiatives in California since 2012–2013, other than Tahoe / Reno or Ventura, I haven't been able to locate information on them. The State Emergency Plan calls for extensive training and exercises, including comprehensive Multi-Year Training and Exercise Plans (MYTEPs), but there are no explicit references online to incorporating megastorm-scale disaster scenarios. The scaling of extreme weather scenarios down to local landscapes and then carrying out community-level stress tests and simulation drills is an activity that has very high preparedness value, *and which could usefully be ramped up in California.*

16

State (and some Federal) Emergency Functions

An introduction

> *"Costello: Well then who's on first?*
> *Abbott: Yes.*
> *Costello: I mean the fellow's name.*
> *Abbott: Who.*
> *Costello: The guy on first.*
> *Abbott: Who.*
> *Costello: The first baseman.*
> *Abbott: Who.*
> *Costello: The guy playing...*
> *Abbott: Who is on first!"*
>
> *...*

The subject of state and federal plans and preparations for emergencies and disasters is a large and complex one, and is covered in greater depth in many official online documents. If you want to begin a deeper dive into local, state and federal agencies and frameworks, and auxiliary organizations, NGOs, and the National Guard, and planning documents, you will find plenty of information. Here I will just scratch the surface, with a focus on only the most relevant information, primarily for California. This is the logical place for me to present a <u>first look</u> at 'emergency officialdom' in the barest detail. This chapter begins to explain who does what.

The Governor's Office of Emergency Services (Cal OES) is the state agency directly responsible for emergency preparedness, mitigation, and response, also managing aspects of specific responsibilities assigned to other state agencies (for example, flood control and fighting under the CA Department of Water Resources, or DWR). The (non-statutory) master disaster document in California is the State Emergency Plan (SEP), along with sub-documents. Below are some key highlights on emergency response from the SEP.

Other important California emergency / hazard planning documents from Cal OES for interested readers of this book include the 2008 Base Plan (on state-federal cooperation), the 2018 State Hazards Mitigation Plan (SHMP), the 2018 Northern California Catastrophic Flood Response Plan (NCCFRP) (not released to the public), and, from CA DWR, California's Flood Future (2013), other flood mitigation planning documents, and the online overview of the DWR's Flood Operations Center. That's just the short list, with a focus on storm hazards. My concerns overall have been that (1) that the risks of megastorms and their impacts may have been underestimated in state (and local) planning and preparations, although this appears to be improving at the state level, and (2) that it's been hard to get a clear read on state and local agencies' postures, and details of planning and preparation, for the threat of extreme storms. After 2011 there were some mixed signals. I return to some viewpoints in Chapter 19.

* * *

The State Emergency Plan recognizes two sequences of events—response and proclamations (= legal authorizations)—around any emergency, and a set of actions during each stage. The 'calm before the storm,' between emergencies, is also accounted for. How emergencies occur and how they unfold, in addition to plans, frameworks, agreements and compacts, and even the state constitution, will affect how agencies including Cal OES react to them. These arrangements are many, somewhat intricate and convoluted, and beyond the scope of this brief overview.

Of greater interest to <u>this</u> book is: what's happening between disasters in California. The two key concepts are Mitigation and Preparedness. The SEP points to some mitigation grant programs that extend to the level of 'resilient communities' and which might be of interest to readers (for example, search online for HGMP, BRIC, FEMA and state resilience and hazard mitigation grants).

SEP section 8 covers Mitigation Programs, and points the reader to the Hazard Mitigation web page at www.caloes.ca.gov . This extremely important planning and action area is actually given its own separately released plan document under the SEP: the State of California's Enhanced Multi-Hazard Mitigation Plan (SHMP).

SEP section 9 covers Emergency Preparedness. "The State and its political subdivisions assigned emergency responsibilities in this plan will prepare appropriate supporting plans and related standard operating procedures that describe how emergency operations will be carried out."

Plans are important; so is preparedness training: the SEP says "training, tests and exercises are essential." While the SEP details the training obligations of emergency and responder departments, it is silent on how compliance is ensured. However, at least two counties (Sacramento, Los Angeles) have developed MYTEPs (Multi-Year Training and Exercise Plan for emergency response) and posted them online; I hope all counties are getting on board with that program (joint programs for natural-region sets of smaller counties could make sense). Cal OES also has an MYTEP for the state, with priorities set in part at the national level. Certification and credentialing programs are active. CA Department of Public Health also has an MYTEP program; of eight training scenarios addressed thus far, none have engaged with storm or flood effects.

Here are the types of training exercises envisioned by the SEP:

"Exercises range from seminars / workshops to full-scale demonstrations.

- Seminars / Workshops are low-stress, informal discussions in a group setting with little or no simulation, used to provide information and introduce people to policies, plans, and procedures.
- Drills / Tests are conducted on a regular basis to maintain the readiness of operational procedures, personnel, and equipment. Examples include tests of outdoor warning systems and the Emergency Alert System.
- Tabletop Exercises provide a convenient and low-cost method designed to evaluate policy, plans, procedures, and resolve coordination and responsibilities. Such exercises are a good way to see if policies and procedures exist to handle certain issues.
- Functional Exercises are designed to test and evaluate the capability of an individual function such as communications, public evacuation, or medical.
- Full-Scale Exercises simulate an actual emergency. They typically involve complete emergency management staff and are designed to evaluate the operational capability of the emergency management system."

[Author's note: Endorsed!]

* * *

Peace Officers and Law Enforcement

You may want to have an idea, in advance, who you will be dealing with directly in an emergency, in other words, who will be giving you instructions, warnings or guidance, and who may require or compel your cooperation. That is also outlined in the SEP.

In addition to local police and sheriff's offices, including their Reserves, many state agencies have peace officers who might be assigned to special duties during an emergency. Cal Fire has around 300 Law Enforcement Officers (LEOs) statewide. All University of California and California State University campuses have police departments. State Parks, Fish and Wildlife, Alcoholic Beverage Control, and many other agencies have LEOs. You may never have heard of some of the relevant state agencies with sworn peace officers, for example the Office of the Inspector General. In an emergency, LEOs not familiar to you may be issuing orders and compelling your cooperation.

The California Highway Patrol comprises a large force of peace officers. Under the SEP, they have primary responsibility in an emergency for managing overland transportation, including evacuations, according to routing established with Caltrans. CHP "**Secures** routes, **regulates** traffic flow, and **enforces** safety standards for evacuation and re-entry into evacuated areas in coordination with local agencies. Coordinates interstate highway movement on regulated routes with adjoining states." —SEP [For me, the subtext here is 'no nonsense,' even more so than usual; note particularly control over area re-entry.]

The issue of police powers and enforcement activities takes on a larger dimension during a major emergency. Quoting from the SEP:

> "Proclamation of a State of Emergency: The Governor proclaims a State of Emergency based on the formal request from the local governing body and the recommendation of Cal OES. If conditions and time warrant, the Governor drafts and signs a formal State of Emergency Proclamation. The Governor has expanded emergency powers during a proclaimed State of Emergency. The Governor:
>
> - **Has the right to exercise police power**, as deemed necessary, vested in the State Constitution and the laws of California within the designated area.
> - Is vested with **the power to use and commandeer public and private property and personnel**, to ensure all resources within California are available and dedicated to the emergency when requested.

- Can direct all State agencies to utilize and employ personnel, equipment, and facilities for the performance of any and all activities designed to prevent or alleviate actual and threatened damage due to the emergency, and can direct them to provide supplemental services and equipment to political subdivisions to restore any services in order to provide for the health and safety of the residents of the affected area.
- May make, amend, or rescind orders and regulations during an emergency and temporarily suspend any non-safety-related statutes, ordinances, regulations, or rules that impose restrictions on the emergency response activities.
- Can request federal assistance and resources.
- Can authorize funding under the CDAA when the magnitude and severity of an emergency is beyond a local government agency's capacity and capability to respond and recover.

Governor's Proclamation Without a Local Request: A request from the local governing body is not always necessary for the Governor to proclaim a State of Emergency. The Governor can proclaim a State of Emergency if the safety of persons and property in California are threatened by conditions of extreme peril or if the emergency conditions are beyond the emergency response capacity and capabilities of the local authorities."

* * *

What about the National Guard? Cal Guard (California Military Department, CMD) is in fact involved in many of the state's emergency responses, including recent floods and severe storms, and the 2017 Oroville evacuation. In the 1986 floods, the CMD was carrying out boat rescues among other tasks. Dating back to before the Gold Rush, there are now three branches of the Cal Guard: The first two are the state's Army National Guard and the Air National Guard, both of which are joint state-federal forces ordinarily under the Governor's command but which can be 'federalized' and placed under national command (and potentially sent overseas).

The third branch is the California State Guard (California Defense Force) which is a voluntary state military force under the sole command of the Governor through the Adjutant General. The CSG is particularly oriented toward emergency response and civilian protection. Their mission: "The CSG protects California and its citizens from natural and man-made disasters, including wildfires, floods, earthquakes, and pandemics. It was formed to provide California with a trained and organized force in the event of a state emergency. The CSG service members train and prepare for these emergencies." [This includes flood-fights on the front lines, for example in levee breaches.] In an evacuation, particularly a difficult one, the official personnel directing you (or rescuing you) may be CSG (or other Cal Guard) members, and you may be directed or transported to emergency tent shelters erected and operated by the CSG. [I was unable to find a number for the current emergency shelter tent capacity inventoried by Cal Guard, or anyone; however, it seems that a great number of tents are now deployed to shelter the unhoused population. Such shelter sites are often on low ground. Plans for evacuating already-sheltering populations need to factor in the time and capability needed to also relocate those tents.]

Cal Guard may be called on to carry out a wide range of tasks in an emergency, but one important role emerges during a large-scope disaster: if other branches of the federal military become involved in support functions, then Cal Guard is the connection through which the state and federal militaries can coordinate under the SEMS structure and as part of the response management of the Governor, Cal OES, and designated lead agencies. One other responsibility: "Can provide **limited mass care facilities**, along with **limited all weather shelter space** throughout California at CNG armories." It would be nice to know more details about capacity and areas served.

FEMA

People and even the media commonly expect to see the Federal Emergency Management Agency personnel out on the front lines of any disaster response (and may then voice disappointment at their absence); however, the stated initial orientation of FEMA in an emergency is to provide and coordinate behind-the-scenes financial and logistical support to the front-line responders—state and local agencies and NGOs—and their local mitigation, relief and rescue operations. FEMA presence becomes more visible with public contact during the relief-to-recovery transition phase. Also sometimes unnoticed are their ongoing hazard mitigation grant programs and readiness outreach programs.

* * *

A great amount of thought and effort has gone into official planning for California emergencies including storms and floods. The question we should ask is, "are those preparations adequate to respond to a disaster of the magnitude and scope of an 1862-scale megastorm?" For example, how many people are we really prepared to evacuate and shelter; is there detailed planning and provision for mass relocation? Is there a realistic timetable for preparations and for implementation of responses, such as evacuation? And this returns us to the topics of the preceding chapters on individual, community and local action: all efforts are prudent. You may find the section in the California SEP on volunteer activities to be relevant. More thoughts on this are presented elsewhere.

* * *

Further reading

https://www.caloes.ca.gov/wp-content/uploads/Preparedness/Documents/2017-SEP-Executive-Summary-ADA-Edits.pdf

www.caloes.ca.gov

https://calguard.ca.gov/

https://stateguard.cmd.ca.gov/public/

https://www.californiavolunteers.ca.gov

https://www.fema.gov/pdf/emergency/nrf/nrf-esf-06.pdf

DWR responsibilities including the Flood Operations Center
https://water.ca.gov/What-We-Do/Emergency-Response

17

Lessons and a Perspective

Some history, assessment and opinion

"I might say, indeed, that the recklessness of the state blunts the keener feelings and takes the edge from this calamity." —William H. Brewer, Journal entry, on a March 6, 1862 visit to flooded Sacramento

This chapter focuses on behavior: how weather behaves, how water behaves, how infrastructure behaves, and how people and their institutions behave. Chapter 18 on Risk Psychology will take a closer look at how human behavior mediates (or doesn't) among the other three. This is a fairly long, and important, I think, chapter about where we are and how we got here. I'm using past history to suggest future event possibilities to your imagination. Beyond 'weathering' a dangerous and destructive catastrophe larger than anything we have had to cope with in our time, the subsequent process of rebooting California would be formidable.

Knowledge: WWWD (What Would Water Do?)

Four thousand, six hundred years ago, the ancient Egyptians were able to build the Great Pyramid at Giza on a perfectly level bedrock foundation because… they knew that water flows downhill. They used water channels cut into the foundation rock to measure how level it was as they worked on perfecting it. Many ancient civilizations built canals and aqueducts; levees, not so much.

160 years ago, the native peoples of California, including the Mi-Wuk tribes, also knew that water flows downhill, and that when things got too stormy, they had to relocate to higher ground. Settlers scratched their heads; some built levees (one aspect of a complex, extended process of reconfiguring the river channels).

Europeans and their descendants, and other settlers recruited into the American Dream, have seemed to acquire an apparent imperviousness to this understanding of WWWD: 'Never in a million years did we expect a 100-year flood…' There were obvious advantages to settling along navigable waterways and river ports in the 19th century, but also, in a floodplain, there are obvious risks that clearly have been discounted. Pursuit of financial opportunity and 'civic growth' can, or did, arguably tip the scales away from a full consideration of risks. And government programs, from flood control to the National Flood Insurance Program, have kept a big thumb on the scales. The floodplains have been developed for occupation and use, creating a 'control, mitigation, protection and prevention' challenge from scratch.

Early landowners, developers and builders, and to some extent mortgage lenders, have for the most part taken their winnings off the table. And a lot of wealth, including the life savings of a lot of families, and plenty of public and private infrastructure, is now at risk on the ground.

See:

> Privatization of Gains, Socialization of Risks
> Musical Chairs
> Holding the Bag
> 'Greater Fool' Investment Theory

I'll acknowledge here that certain sentiments surfaced as I researched and wrote this chapter. And in this chapter, I'll incorporate a bit more opinion than usual. I reserve the right to adjust my opinions as my learning process continues… as any thinking person would do.

Meanwhile, how do we process this 1986 after-storm report, on the then-31-year-old Folsom Lake and Dam?

> "… the reservoir was continuing to swell, with **water running into the lake faster than it was designed to handle.** … [U.S. Bureau of Reclamation Chief Engineer Chuck] Abraham said he thought, for the first time ever, that Folsom Dam was in danger of overflowing… **'If that dam would have failed…'** said Doug Baldwin, a spokesperson for [USBR] **'it would have washed Sacramento away.'** " —Thom Akeman, in The Sacramento Bee, March 3, 1986.

Optimism Bias

What is 'Optimism Bias'? I cover that 'rosy outlook' in a following chapter. Here is a paragraph that might serve as an example, as regards flood control planning and infrastructure:

"Folsom Dam and its downstream levees were originally designed to accommodate a storm with a recurrence interval [estimated!] of 250 years, but flood events in 1955, 1963, and 1965 proved that 120-year (recurrence interval) flood protection was a more reasonable value. Peak flow conditions caused by the 1986 storms further tested the integrity of the LAR [Lower American River] conveyance system and showed that 120-year protection was also an overly optimistic estimate. The 1986 flood (3,794 m3/s) was defined as a 70-year recurrence interval event (Mount, 1995). Based on the reassessment of the design flood following the 1986 flood of record, the discharge rate expected from 100-year event doubled from 3,260 to 6,520 m3/s [which is 230,252 cfs, twice the original designed spillway capacity and LAR channel intended capacity]. The 1997 flood in Folsom had a 3-day volume identical to the 1986 flood of record, which resulted in reclassification of the dam's manageable return period event to about 70 years (James, 1999)." —Pinter *et al.*, 2018. ['XX0-year' figures here are, as usual, based on the traditional estimation methods.]

You may have spotted a trend above. This is an excellent example of how longer samples of data and recent events are invalidating earlier 20th century storm / flood estimates used in infrastructure design, which were generally already too low (at Folsom this became absolutely clear less than 40 years after it was designed). Notice too that Folsom Dam had two '1-in-70-year-events' (at the dam's control limit) 11 years apart; that breaks no rule of probability, but for those who extrapolate, it is not reassuring. (Recent improvements have increased both capacity, and flood control space, of this reservoir.) However, I don't think the flood protection downgrades can be attributed entirely to climate change, as the 1955, 1963, and 1965 storms were all mid-20th century, and resulted in a downward control capability estimate revision of more than 50% (in terms of recurrence interval). What might the role of optimism bias be?

Why would a developer in Marysville, Yuba County in 1972 build a 15-million-dollar (in then-money) shopping mall "in a hole?" The Peach Tree Mall really was situated roughly 10' lower than all of the surrounding land, which is flat and at low-elevation, and is only 1.2 miles from the confluence of the Yuba and Feather Rivers, two of Northern California's biggest, having water levels only about 20' lower 'in normal times.' "What could possibly go wrong?" The physical Peach Tree Mall sat 'dead' there for 35 years, since getting nailed by the storms and floods of 1986. For motivation, one could have driven there, taken pictures, and then driven almost anywhere else in the low Valley, held up the pictures, and used some imagination to visualize a megastorm… until early 2022:

> "A 400,000-square-foot eyesore is finally being torn down in a Yuba County community. Besides the blight, it also means goodbye to an ugly memory: the 1986 flood in Linda that left the Peach Tree Mall underwater. Excavators are now lined up to tear down the decay that has defined this building for decades." —CBS News Sacramento, January 27, 2022

Why? The State of California was held financially liable for the Linda levee failure; see 'Socialization of Risk.'

Recent new development northwest of downtown Sacramento sits at about (15'–) 20' elevation above sea level (ASL), half a mile from the Sacramento River, and adjacent to the American River, including the confluence of those two large rivers, behind levees that soar to a height of 20 additional feet. I am reminded that the American River reportedly rose 35' in Auburn, and possibly almost as much in Sacramento, in the then-existing leveed channel, in 1862 (with estimated flows of 317,700 cfs at Fair Oaks, more than two and a half times what the current Lower American River channel is rated for, relevant if Folsom Lake is full). Most of that area is in flood risk zone A99, meaning an otherwise-1%-annual-chance [as estimated by standard methods] flood zone protected by substantially completed federal flood control infrastructure. The lower American River channel, with levees, is intended to contain a flood flow of 115,000 cfs. There shouldn't be any problem, unless Folsom Dam can't limit outflow to 115,000 cfs. It has had to discharge 130,000 cfs on occasion, and the recently reconstructed auxiliary spillway there potentially allows the dam to accommodate even larger releases. Note that when both rivers are flooded, flows from the American River may have to travel three miles _up_ the Sacramento River (imagine a bulge of floodwater stalled along the Natomas levees) to reach the Sacramento Bypass.

> According to FEMA Region IX Director [now Cal OES Director] Nancy Ward, in 2011, **"It is entirely possible that flood control infrastructure and mitigation efforts could be overwhelmed by the USGS ARkStorm scenario,** and the report suggests ways forward to limit the damage that is sure to result."

Where is everybody?

When you read, for a Sacramento Valley county's Emergency Operations Center, "The _________ county EOC, located in the basement of the sheriff's headquarters…," you may start looking at flood zone or topographic maps.

The State Capitol in Sacramento sits 55.5 crow-fly miles from the entrance to San Pablo Bay, which is effectively at sea level, gateway to San Francisco Bay and the Pacific. The land area in and around much of Sacramento, at elevations of 10' to 30' above sea level (ASL), will drain very slowly westward along a slope of around 2–6 inches per mile (the Sacramento River bed there is also effectively at sea level). Almost all that land is behind levees (and below dams).

In my research, I've made lists of where, and at what elevation, many state and other agency offices and headquarters, including NGOs like the Red Cross, are located, in and around Sacramento. I won't include the lengthy list here; I do include a related list from USACE below. Most are in the area that USGS expects to flood if or when a megastorm flood overwhelms the levee systems there.

As just one important NGO example, one of the few primary American Red Cross warehouses of emergency supplies and equipment in the West is located in West Sacramento, an area of warehouses mostly located at elevations of 12–20' ASL, surrounded by the Sacramento River with a 40–41' ASL levee, the Sacramento Bypass flood control channel with a 33–35' ASL levee, the Yolo Bypass with a 30' ASL levee, and the Deep Water Ship Channel, which according to satellite data may lack continuous effective levees if the channel back-floods from the Delta or from a break along the Yolo Bypass, or if a flood flow gets past the lock gate complex at the Sacramento River, which reaches around 37' ASL, 4–5' lower than most of the river levee. The weir crest elevation feeding the Sacramento Bypass is given as 24.75' ASL; according to NOAA, on January 1, 1997, during a nine-day AR event, more than 10' of river water was pouring over the crest of the weir into the bypass (near the height of its 33–35' ASL levees). If all those numbers are making your eyes blur, the point is that West Sacramento is an area of modest levee protection, considered by one rating agency as having an extreme flood risk, and where Maendly, in a 2018 study, determined that some predictable floods could overtop even the higher Sacramento River levees… although the river proper there would first flood eastward, into downtown Sacramento.

Placing a warehouse of multi-state critical relief supplies there is… pretty optimistic. On that topic, a regional Red Cross warehouse is located in Yuba City at 60' ASL, about 3300' from the 73' levee on the Feather River, 4 miles from where the Peach Tree Mall was destroyed, along with more than $460,000,000 (before inflation) of local property, when the nearby Linda levee failed in the 1986 storm. Federally, Moffett Field is the Primary Distribution Center for FEMA's Initial Response Resources, a storage and staging point for emergency relief supplies for the states of the western continental USA; more than 100 pre-loaded truck-trailers sit next to the San Francisco Bay at an elevation of 8-11' ASL; Stevens Creek, draining 29 square miles, is at that elevation, 1.5 miles away; U.S. 101 access running northwest from there apparently reaches even lower single digit elevations along the bay within 2.5 miles.

This is a pattern, not just some cherry-picked anomalies. Low, flat ground is extremely attractive, until it isn't.

Back in Sacramento, I looked at those levees near downtown, on-site and using satellite mapping, and although most river levees in the area reach 40–41' ASL, the area of the Old Sacramento Waterfront near J and K streets along the Sacramento River have embankments that reach only about 33' ASL. River flows above the 33' stage could move eastward into downtown from that area. A number of state buildings are in that area. Two blocks away, I-5 dips to an elevation of perhaps 5' as it passes beneath the elevated Capitol Mall.

The 2018 study by Maendly also confirms the east embankment there as reaching 34' ASL, and shows the types of floods that would overtop those levees, specifically a flood flow of about 130–140% (or more) of the peak of the regulated flow of 1997. Per Maendly, flood control infrastructure like dams and bypasses 'regulated' or buffered the peak 1997 storm runoff flow into the Delta down to around only 40% of what it would have been otherwise. If future sustained storm runoff flows exceed reservoir or other flood control capability, then unregulated, out-of-control river flow becomes the problem for which, as yet, we lack detailed analysis, at least in public documents (see Cox, 2023). But in basic terms, the projected greater possible storm flows Maendly derived from the 1997 event (for example by multiplying those regulated flows by 140%) would be greatly exceeded by an unregulated peak flow in the range of 220% (using Maendly's numbers) of the 1997 (regulated) flood, which might occur in a more prolonged storm sequence with 1997 intensity, during which reservoirs would fill and would not be able to regain control capacity (see also RiskFactor.com mapping of such a scenario, which is evident in their results).

The few administrative facilities in higher locations around greater Sacramento include the headquarters of Cal OES, and the National Guard joint base, in Mather. At 60' ASL, the CA DWR Flood Operations Center in the Arden area, though near creeks, may be on high-enough ground to avoid flood impacts from the American River two to three miles away (Cal Expo flooding in 1986 is noted below); however, the neighborhood might become disrupted. I'll omit my own review of the many potential administrative facilities vulnerabilities around Sacramento (you are free to check those out yourself with a bit of mapping) and instead present a parallel assessment provided by the U.S. Army Corps of Engineers. The USACE authors are not unaware of nor unconcerned about the profound implications of disruption of the state government (though they do not emphasize emergency response functions here):

"Impacts to critical infrastructure from a flood event would have significant local, regional, and statewide impacts because Sacramento is the capitol of the State of California. The capitol and many State office buildings are located in downtown Sacramento, which could be flooded by up to five feet[*] of water during a flood event (http://www.safca.org/Images/Maps/AR_SR_FLOODDEPTHZONES.pdf). If critical elements of the State government were disabled due to a flood event, such as those related to emergency response systems, the Central Valley region and the State could be severely impacted. Impacts to State of California departments and agencies could become critical in nature for the entire state if the duration of flooding extends beyond a few days. State agencies provide payroll, retirement benefits, medical benefits, vehicle registration, criminal justice, and other activities that affect people throughout California. Flood recovery programs are run by State and local government agencies. Because these agencies could be located in areas impacted by flooding there is a potential for significant impacts on the distribution of disaster assistance. Although funding may be available, limited material and labor availability could slow implementation of needed repairs and recovery.

More generally, all businesses and government centers could be isolated from customers and employees. Significant numbers of people commute into downtown Sacramento to work at various Federal, State and local agencies and private businesses. The Sacramento District USACE offices are located in downtown Sacramento along with many other Federal and State facilities including the Secretary of State, California Department of Transportation, Water Resources Board, Attorney General's Office, Department of Consumer Affairs, and the Legislative Office Building. Local government facilities include police and sheriffs' offices, the City Library, and City and County of Sacramento administrative offices.

Another piece of critical infrastructure located in the Natomas Basin is the Sacramento International Airport, a major transportation hub for Sacramento and all of northern California. The airport can handle up to 29 flights per hour; in a typical month 800,000 passengers arrive or depart the airport. If a flood were to occur, passenger travel would be disrupted and those stranded at the airport would have to be evacuated to higher ground. Mail and freight transit through the airport would also be interrupted. Flooding of transportation routes, utilities and public services will also likely occur throughout the region and impacts would be felt in areas far beyond the actual flooding. Transportation facilities that could potentially be affected by flooding in the study areas include:

- Light rail lines in east and south Sacramento and downtown
- Regional transit bus routes and facilities throughout the City of Sacramento
- I-5
- I-80
- US 99
- US 50"

—from USACE's CVIFMS 2015 draft watershed plan for the Central Valley

[What flood scenario is being described above? Typically, agency and Corps flood scenarios don't get more extreme than so-called '100-year' or sometimes '200-year' estimated flood levels; generally, only flood maps invoke '500-year' levels (correctly thought of as flood <u>volumes</u>, arguably mis-named, rather than timetable-based events). Megastorm scenarios can be more extreme in all aspects, often including broader geographic scope (this USACE document has a focus on administrative ramifications of Central Valley flooding) and with flood and runoff <u>magnitude</u> estimates (not frequency estimates) reaching the levels comparable to the traditional so-called '500-year' flood magnitude estimates and locally becoming more extreme in places (USGS ARkStorm comparisons invoked runoff levels approaching what others would imagine to be nearing 5000-year levels in places). USGS predicted 10–20' of ARkStorm flooding depth in the Sacramento region (depending upon levee resilience, in which USGS had very limited confidence).]

Even if a particular site does not flood, an associated risk of chaotic disruption exists in areas or neighborhoods where services, roads and other infrastructure are compromised by flood and storm effects.

At this time, none of the three Cal OES regional administrative centers, nor the DWR headquarters, nor many other administrative facilities, are located on what might be called high ground, away from surface waters and potentially flood-impacted areas. For example, from 1991 into at least 2022, the Southern Regional Emergency Operations Center (SREOC) has been located in two trailers at the Joint Forces Training Base in Los Alamitos, Orange County, at an elevation of roughly 20' ASL, 1.5 miles across flat ground from the San Gabriel River, with a 1% annual flood risk using FEMA methods (but compare Sanders 2022 and USGS from 2011); Cal OES is now seeking funds to relocate it. I'm going to infer that, when siting much of the administrative and emergency management infrastructure around Sacramento and the state, the possible risk of extreme flooding has not until now been deemed to be a significant threat. That's striking. Or, the likelihood of having to pull up stakes and reconstitute a temporary EOC elsewhere (there are contingency plans for this, per Cal OES) is not seen as a significant problem deserving avoidance. Under what assumptions? During the 2017 Oroville Dam evacuation emergency, untrained staff had 3 hours to relocate the local EOC, which was in the path of the potential flood wave.

The state, through CDFA, in 2022 awarded $7 million for Resiliency Center (emergency functions) improvements to Cal Expo… a facility with a history of flooding (see below). This pattern and problem are not limited to greater Sacramento. When a brand new emergency shelter in the Sierra began shelter operations for the first time, in early 2023, floodwaters entered and closed the public buildings standing next door—not a good sign.

In an overview presentation on the unreleased Northern California Catastrophic Flood Response Plan, the following tabulations of at-risk critical facilities—just for 10 Sacramento Valley counties—tells a story of the pervasive problem of neglected risks.

Type of facility	Number	Number at risk	Percent at risk
Law Enforcement	172	50	29%
Fire Station	426	146	34%
Emergency (EOC)	71	24	34%
Health Care	850	372	44%
Hospital	44	17-37	39-84%
Long Term Care	269	110	41%
Correctional	36	18	50%
County Government	10	7	70%
Schools	2235	775	35%
Power Substations	597	244	41%
Wastewater Treatment	133	58	44%

Also, 346,063 dogs, 378,060 cats, 42,073 birds, and 24,296 horses. (— NCCFRP Overview presentation, *ca.* 2020, to the California Resiliency Alliance, a non-profit NGO)

Transportation routes and infrastructure (all are lifelines) on low ground in the Central Valley and elsewhere have been discussed earlier in this book, but here's a fresh take from Washington State on January 7, 2022:

"A 20-mile stretch of Interstate 5 is closed in both directions due to rising water from the Chehalis River, Trooper Will Finn with Washington State Patrol told CNN in a phone call.

"There is no viable route around I-5," Finn said. "We ask that folks delay travel at this time."

It is a primary interstate into Seattle from the south. There is no estimated time for reopening this stretch." — CNN

How on Earth can this all be solved?

"In many ways the solutions here are conceptually simple. Don't build any more stuff in the way of floods." —Oliver Wing, lead author of the 2022 paper, Inequitable patterns of U.S. flood risk in the Anthropocene, in Nature Climate Change, as quoted by NPR

There is a 1986 book called "Rivers of Fear," by Bob Teets and Shelby Young, West Virginia newspapermen who had previously published a book on 1985 West Virginia Floods. Rivers of Fear, published by C. R. Publications of Terra Alta, WV, is a compilation of contemporary 1986 articles from newspapers serving flood-stricken areas all over Central and Northern California.

I'm grateful to these authors for collecting and presenting these reports. It makes it simple for me to pick examples of what went wrong in the 'living memory' year 1986. And I'll do that to make two points. First, these are exactly the kinds of challenges and emergencies that people will have to face again, and in a megastorm, it won't be just tens of thousands of people affected, it could be millions, and the difficulties will be more extreme and will last much longer. And second, after more than a century and a half of effort and investment, these are still unsolved problems. I say this not to suggest blame, but rather to overcome complacency and align our thinking with our realities, including the nature of the problem.

"Let's all do our best!" —Widely heard Japanese exhortation

"It can't be helped." —Widely used Japanese capitulation

The lessons of 1986

In February of 1986, a 10-day atmospheric river event sequence produced major storm damage and flooding in Northern California.

> **"The government was so unprepared for such a disaster that no one knew how many people would be endangered, what parts of the city might be destroyed or how much water would be churning where."** —Sacramento Bee, 1986

The quote above refers to the fact that <u>if</u> the American River drainage, flowing through Folsom Lake and Dam, had received just one more inch of rain on February 19, 1986, U.S. Bureau of Reclamation Engineer Chuck Abraham would have ordered a levee to be broken, flooding unknown [!!] parts of greater Sacramento, to avert a worse catastrophe: the possible overflow or failure of the Folsom Dam (—story reported by the Sacramento Bee). Water was flowing into the Folsom Lake Reservoir "faster than it was designed to handle," and that was after a coffer dam broke upriver near Auburn and dumped another 100,000 acre-feet of water into the system. Many area rivers were above flood stage, officially meaning that

> "…water has risen to a sufficient level to cause sufficient inundation of areas that are not normally covered by water, causing an inconvenience or a threat to life and property."

You might not have known that there are people like Chuck who have to make decisions like these, Pretty Damn Quick.

Folsom Dam ended up releasing 15,000 cfs more water than the downstream American River Channel was designed to handle. (Another, later consequence was that the starting reservoir capacity allocated to flood control was increased by 50%, from the overly optimistic 400,000 (in the original operating design) to 600,000 acre-feet, while seasonal water storage was potentially reduced by up to 200,000 acre feet).

Levees failed in many places.

> "The giant Sacramento River threatened to break through its levee along the Golden State Highway [US 99], a breach that would have flooded the 15,000 people who live in South Natomas, **washed out Interstates 80 and 5**, closed Sacramento Metropolitan Airport and inundated the new Kings Arena."

—The Sacramento Bee [The population in South Natomas in early 2022 has reached <u>30,402</u> according to niche.com]

Radio station KMYC in Marysville, carrying the Emergency Broadcast System signal, flooded and went off the air. Workers at the station, located on flat ground about a mile from the Yuba River, had to be evacuated by boat. EBS was switched to a more distant station. Storm winds blew down a transmitter tower near Candlestick Park, taking some iconic San Francisco radio stations off the air. Winds were clocked at 100 mph at Pt. Reyes and Mt. Tamalpais.

Sections of I-5 were underwater for two weeks [two weeks of highway interruption might be an 'inconvenience' in planning circles, but prolonged unavailability of key transportation lifelines might seriously worsen a disaster]. Half the lanes of U.S. 99 were closed by a bridge collapse at Bear Creek. Road bridges were also destroyed or made unusable at Rio Dell, Taylorsville, and Camanche (after the dam overflowed for the first time ever).

A railroad bridge over the Bear River was destroyed, and erosion took out the rail line in Blairsden.

250 horses were trapped when the stables at the state fairgrounds (Cal Expo) flooded to 6'. One horse died. Horse owners filed a class action suit against God [just kidding; against the state.]

Observations quoted: <u>After getting 20" of rain</u>, the flood in Napa "… **took all by surprise [when] … the first indications of trouble lapped at area doorsteps…**" [Ahem.]

10" to 30" of rainfall in the 10-day storm was typical around Northern California; part of Plumas County reported 55". Calaveras Big Trees SP, at around 4700' elevation, got 33.2" in 10 days.

Flooding: many square miles. Evacuations: many tens of thousands, or more. Losses: great, especially to residents of small low-elevation homes. Road damage: extensive. Agricultural damage: significant.

One tragedy out of many: I relate this incident because it shows what a modern storm emergency here can be like: In the same kind of terrain in Santa Cruz County where people were killed and disabled by mudslides in the storms of 1982, more people were killed and disabled in the storms of 1986. In an area not many miles from Silicon Valley (people make the commute every day) a woman suffered a paralyzing spinal cord injury when a tree fell through her canyon house. Her husband called 911 but it took rescuers 11 hours to reach them. She was carried on a backboard over another landslide to where a jeep waited to take her to a hilltop. A helicopter came but because of weather, could not make the pick-up. She was then hand-carried for 3.5 miles to a point where the road had washed out. Firemen used ropes and pulleys to get her across the washout and into an ambulance which took her to Watsonville Hospital. It was determined that she needed immediate emergency transport to a specialized medical facility in San Jose. But all the highways had been closed by landslides, and the medical helicopter was unable to fly in the weather. It took another 24 hours before she reached the spinal injury center. It will be hard for many of us to imagine that we, in our own home, could go through an experience like that in modern California, especially in a rustic 'suburb' of a global technology hub. But many of our lifelines become stretched thin in such extreme circumstances and complex terrain.

Repeating this: sometimes the helicopters can't fly.

The lessons of 1997

At the end of 1996, a 9-day atmospheric river event sequence produced major storm damage and flooding in Northern California. Levees broke; 23,000 homes and 2000 businesses were damaged or destroyed. If you read the official weather summary below, you'll see that this event was attributed to 'a series of storms;' more commonly now this event is described as a series of atmospheric rivers. Twenty-five years ago, atmospheric rivers delivering storm-pulses of precipitation were not yet well understood; in fact, scientists were focused on the much higher jet stream, rather than the <u>visible</u> very wet plumes of air funneling just above the ocean surface.

> "Heavy Precipitation Event
> Southwest Oregon, Northern California, and Western Nevada
> December 26, 1996 - January 3, 1997
>
> General Summary
>
> A cool winter storm brought valley rain and several feet of mountain snow to southwest Oregon, northern California, and western Nevada on December 21 and 22, 1996. This system only set the stage for what would become one of the most historical flood events to affect the region in recent times. Beginning Christmas Eve, the overall weather pattern began to shift from a polar air mass toward a warmer and wetter tropical regime with promises of a noteworthy precipitation event. Not only would the relentless precipitation through early January 1997 bring widespread flooding, but **the snow pack from the pre-Christmas storm would significantly melt to only exacerbate problems** from the excessive amounts of runoff.

Over northern California, damage reports due to the high water were widespread while **reservoirs released large amounts of water to make room for increasing inflows**. More than 100,000 people had to be evacuated as flood waters threatened homes and businesses. The state's agriculture industry suffered severe losses as numerous dairy farms, orchards, and vineyards were affected. Across the San Francisco North Bay counties, the rivers and creeks overflowed their banks, inundating agricultural lands and some cities. In particular, the town of Guerneville was hit hard as flood waters from the Russian River rushed across the area. Inland across the Sacramento and San Joaquin Valleys, several levee breaks were reported. A large levee break occurred on the Feather River above the community of Linda, an area that was also affected by the widespread flooding and another levee break back in February 1986. In Sutter County, an aggressive flood fight took place following a levee break in the Sutter Bypass, saving the town of Meridian. Farther south, Yosemite National Park was closed as flood waters from the Merced River shut down all three major roads. A number of people were stranded in the park's lodge for several days until flood waters receded. Transportation was hampered by the excessive amount of precipitation and melting snow. **Major highways, including Interstate 5, Interstate 80, and U.S. Highway 50 were all closed at some point during the event**.

Across the eastern Sierra Nevada and portions of western Nevada [this is normally a fairly dry area], the series of storms caused an estimated $1 billion in damages. Numerous homes and businesses suffered extensive damage, while the transportation system experienced widespread issues. Casinos in Reno were using sandbags to protect their properties, allowing several to remain open to gamblers. However, four of the major casinos needed to close during the peak of the flooding due to extensive damage. **Major highways were closed due to the flooding or subsequent mudslides, including Interstate 80 both east and west of Reno, U.S. Highway 395 to the north and south of Reno, and the Mount Rose Highway (Nevada State Highway 431). Flood waters from the Walker River destroyed several miles of Highway 395 through the narrow Walker River canyon. The Reno-Tahoe International Airport (RNO) was completely shut down to** air traffic as flood waters submerged runways and portions of the terminal building."

...

"As noted several times, runoff from the Sierra Nevada basins that drain into the central valley of California was **compounded by rain at the higher elevations and contributions from melting snow.** The final New Year's Day storm **certainly put the Sacramento-Feather River flood control system to the test, balancing local runoff and reservoir releases required to maintain the integrity of the system itself.** A NOAA / NESDIS satellite image clearly shows the extent of flooding along the Sacramento-Feather River systems and the tremendous amount of water in the bypass system that empties through the Sacramento Delta into San Francisco Bay. As shown in the table below, **weir overflow was enormous, with water depths as much as 10 feet spilling over the crests of the weir structures into the bypass. Unfortunately, the high flows overstressed some levees, with breaches reported on the Feather, Cosumnes, Mokelumne, and Tuolumne Rivers.**"

...

"Leading up to the December 26, 1996 through January 3, 1997 significant precipitation event, the major reservoirs were able to reduce their storages based on the latest weather forecasts, scheduled operations, and downstream conditions. **When the series of storms began to affect the region, these flood control projects had essentially regained their respective flood reservation space.** [So: To what extent, at what times, should encroachments on flood control space be avoided? In what ways should weather forecasts affect management for adequate flood control capacity?] As the strongest of the storms in the series pummeled the area around New Year's Day, these reservoirs quickly filled near capacity requiring an increase in downstream releases. This series of storms set new records for instantaneous peak flows, one-day flows, and three-day flows into Shasta Lake and Lake Oroville. The three-day flow into Folsom Lake was only slightly exceeded by the February 1986 flood event."

...

"Weather Synopsis

The series of storms that affected the region between December 26, 1996 and January 3, 1997 was a classic instance of the weather pattern classified as the "pineapple express". **The flooding during this significant precipitation event was not attributable to a single storm, but rather a series of successive storms** that affected the region spanning a period just over a week. Collectively, these storms resulted in increased runoff until a final New Year's Day storm pushed rivers and flood projects beyond their natural or designed capacities." —NOAA storm summary [The weather maps in this NOAA report show a low-altitude atmospheric river (fused from two Pacific sources), although the term was not yet in use; they are called "moisture plumes" here. More attention was paid in 1997 to the jet stream.]

Average six-day rainfall for the Feather, American and Stanislaus River basins was 21.53", 15.71", and 14.97", respectively. Peak basin-wide precipitation intensities on January 1, 1997, in inches per hour, averaged over six-hour segments, were 0.43", 0.33", and 0.35" per hour, respectively. The peak precipitation intensity recorded at Blue Canyon on the American River was 0.78 inches per hour on a sustained (average) basis for six hours. When sustained for hours, these are very high precipitation levels (we saw similar sustained levels in the Sierra in October of 2021, in a Cat5 AR storm; even higher levels are predicted for the coming decades).

The NOAA storm report excerpted above has links to much more detailed information, as well as links to home movies of the flood flows at five Sacramento area bridges or weirs. The movies of the 1997 New Year's Day storm and flood might be most useful (considering that in some ways the 1997 storm was like the 1986 storm used in the second half of the ARkStorm simulation) if we try to visualize "What would this flood look like if the extreme 1969 storm (the first half of the ARkStorm simulation) or the 1986 storm had happened instead during Christmas week of 1996, back to back with the New Year's flood of '97?"

The lessons of 2017—a new twist

The book "Spillway Emergency" by William Sager and Wayne Wilson, residents and retired members of a local fire agency near Lake Oroville, makes for compelling reading, if you are into weather, infrastructure, and emergency management. That book, Koskinas *et al.*, 2019, and DWR statements are my main sources for information excerpted and paraphrased below. The strong AR storms in February 2017 did considerable damage to my farm and the local area, including closing our state highway for two months.

I describe the Oroville events primarily because they were a flood event, even though the 2017 situation is usually remembered as an infrastructure failure. Both are relevant to our understanding. The descriptions below are abbreviated.

In February 2017, with the lake 'storage pool' full (so the starting <u>flood control pool capacity</u> above 'storage' was at only the minimum amount specified by regulations), and then receiving high inflows (much higher than forecast) for several days, the failure of the main spillway on February 7, which was being used to release water and regain flood-control capacity, and then the emergency spillway (an uncontrolled concrete overflow weir atop a dirt hillside) a few days later, was an emergency.

Many other things happened, and didn't happen, but eventually water started flowing uncontrollably over the top of the second, emergency spillway, which soon began to deteriorate, potentially seriously, beneath the weir. Meanwhile, 188,000 people were evacuated on short notice.

From Sager & Wilson:

> "We have no way of knowing the thought process when the weir [of the emergency spillway, above the dirt hillside] was being designed and built, but in people's minds it is an easy leap to thinking, 'It will never happen,' or 'A thousand years is a long time.' … it was supposed to handle [overflow of] 328,000 CFS, but it never got close to a tenth of that when it appeared to start failing." [Note: If this dam is ever faced with its calculated Maximum Probable / Possible Flood, the overflow will be much, <u>much</u> higher than 328,000 cfs; see Koskinas *et al.*, 2019.]

When this overflow-caused damage at the weir atop the emergency spillway became obvious, there was an immediate concern that at least one section of the weir might fail, allowing the upper 30' of water in the lake to drain very rapidly and uncontrollably. The lake surface, when full, covers 25 square miles, so that's a lot of water. At that point the best of the bad options was to restart the main spillway and let it continue to be destroyed by the outflowing water. This caused other serious problems described by the authors, one of which—think energy vulnerability—was the near-flooding of the Hyatt Powerhouse there. Another was the threat of erosion at a transmission tower, which, if lost, would have required stopping the release of water through the turbine channels. And if the main spillway deterioration had progressed back to the release gate mechanisms, damaging those gates, the level of the huge lake could have dropped 87' very rapidly. Almost half a cubic mile of water would have started flowing downhill as fast as it could.

Later, engineers modeled a flood scenario in which a 900' section of the weir lost its 30' of height; the study showed that a 30' drop in the lake level would have flooded more than 570 square miles downriver, to depths up to 30' [unstudied areas further downriver would also have flooded; the additional contributing effects of flows in or from other rivers were not studied].

The infrastructure, and its operations, both came under scrutiny. With respect to the dam and spillway construction and maintenance, and safety program, an independent forensic team prepared a report (summarized by I. A. Alvi and communicated by the Association of State Dam Safety Officials; for brevity I present only a few key highlights):

> **"The incident was fundamentally the result of a long-term systemic failure to recognize and properly address the deficiencies and warning signs which preceded the incident**, and there was no one root cause. This systemic failure involved practices of the owner, its Federal and state regulators, its consultants, and general industry practices in the United States. Therefore, the incident could not reasonably be "blamed" mainly on any one individual, group, or organization.
>
> . . .
>
> **Numerous human factors, including organizational and industry factors, contributed to the physical factors not being recognized and properly addressed, and to the decision-making during the incident:**
>
> - The principal designer of the spillways appears to have been a relatively inexperienced engineer and, despite the very large size of the dam and spillways, the design of the service spillway did not fully meet the spillway design best practices of the era
>
> - The owner [CA DWR] was generally **overconfident** regarding the integrity of its civil infrastructure
>
> - The owner took a reactive rather than proactive approach to dealing with civil infrastructure risks; this was fostered by **inherent pressures to control costs and deliver water and power without interruption**

- The owner, both regulators, and the many consultants paid insufficient attention to the spillways, as compared to the main dam

- The owner's dam safety program was not sufficiently mature, lacked clear executive-level accountability, and was excessively reliant on regulators and regulatory processes to identify risks

- The owner lacked sufficient staffing resources and technical expertise; this was influenced by **governmental and organizational bureaucratic constraints and insularity of the owner's organization**

- The owner's information management system for its dams was inadequate, resulting in important information sometimes not being in the right hands at the right times

- There were strained relationships within the owner's organization, particularly between its Operations & Maintenance (O&M) and Engineering Divisions, which inhibited effective communication and collaboration within the organization

- The dam industry in the United States lacked effective and efficient organization and dissemination of technical best practices information for dam engineering and dam safety throughout the industry, resulting in insufficient technical expertise of many engineers and geologists involved in the Oroville Dam project.; these engineers and geologists "didn't know what they didn't know"

Lessons Learned: As detailed in this forensic report, there were numerous lessons learned from this incident for the owner, its regulators, its consultants, and the dam industry in the United States. Most broadly, the independent forensic team concluded that:

"Although the practice of dam safety has certainly improved since the 1970s, the fact that this incident happened to the owner of the tallest dam in the United States, under regulation of a federal agency, with repeated evaluation by reputable outside consultants, in a state with a leading dam safety regulatory program, is a wake-up call for everyone involved in dam safety." "

Operations: After the event, an engineering review recommended that the Oroville reservoir and dam management protocol be modified to maintain a schedule of lower winter lake levels, to provide a larger reserved buffer capacity (*i.e.*, the top layer of the lake, normally, called the Flood [Control] Pool) than what had been established in the original 1970 Water Control Manual (WCM). [This echoes the corresponding post-1986 revision of operating capacity rules for Folsom Dam.] Those prudent changes were incorporated into the Flood Operations Plan adopted for Lake Oroville by CA DWR in 2018–19. As of late 2021, USACE had not yet released an updated Water Control Manual for operations at Oroville.

Reservoirs are designed and operated based on selected assumptions and tradeoffs, beginning, for federal projects, with 'purposes' defined by Congress (with help from lobbyists, who represent the larger financial would-be stakeholders), and an attempt to 'balance' those purposes, which may conflict. Overly high reservoir levels might be optimistically and/or methodologically miscalculated to be operationally safe, or might be reached 'unavoidably' due to weather that is just too unpredictable or 'too hard to imagine' (or beyond a calculated risk / reward point). It's also true that reservoirs sell water ($1.1 billion to the CA SWP in 2015, per CA DWR); whatever they can store and sell has a monetary value, and a usefulness which might otherwise be 'wasted.' Flood control responsibilities, on the other hand, while mandated, and while obviating the public and private costs of flooding, generate no agency revenue. Water managers are also exposed to the pressures of customer demand, and drought 'down south' is seemingly a more prevalent concern (there) than flooding 'up north.' This may be true about drought across the West. One hopes that flood control lessons travel rapidly and compellingly, putting any excessive optimism under scrutiny.

More reminders from the atmosphere: The Category 5 AR Storm of October 23–25, 2021

This was effectively a 36-hour AR storm event; on my land at the 3000' level this area received 8.6" of rain in under 30 hours. This would be like one 'pulse' in a sequence of AR storms like an 1862-scale event. Fortunately the land was bone-dry (a drought emergency was declared two days earlier). Items below are from media outlets NPR / AP and KCRA:

7% of PG&E's 5.5 million customers lost power, as did some of SMUD's customers in 31 areas. Flooding brought down power poles.

Landslides, rockslides and mudslides closed U.S. 50, State Routes 70, 16 and 20. Explosives were used to clear U.S. 50. Other roads over a wide area were closed by flooding, including SRs 70, 99 and 113, and U.S. 50. Flash floods were expected on SRs 36, 70, and 89.

Flooding or hazard risks (*e.g.*, debris flows) caused evacuations "across Northern California" and in Santa Barbara County. A number of rescues including "swift moving water" rescues were performed.

10:22 p.m.: Sacramento fire officials say they are helping "an unknown amount of homeless people" out of waist-high water <u>after sump pumps near Pell Drive and Pell Circle stopped working due to a nearby power outage</u>. [A preview of potential / future issues with lifeline infrastructure interdependencies; imagine cascades of such systems failures…]

Two large trucks on the Richmond-San Rafael bridge were overturned by winds.

Perspective

Sacramento's mayor called the 2021 storm a "200-year" event. (♪ *Don't Worry, Be Happy Now…*)

Four weeks later, after a series of AR storms pounded British Columbia, "British Columbia Premier John Horgan called it a once in a 500 years event." [—Daily Mail]

Rx for anxiety: take two or more zeros and relax…

Months later,

> "Over the weekend, French President Emmanuel Macron
> thanked the more than 1,200 firefighters battling the wildfires
> in extreme heat. He also acknowledged this year's fire season
> was <u>one of a kind</u>…" —NPR, 18 July 2022

If you can spot patterns, you will notice how often political leaders recite these same simple incantations to, arguably, ward off any repetition, or unrest, or fallout, at least during their tenures in office. Compare also how often the immunizing word "unprecedented" is used.

> "It was during this <u>unprecedented</u> weather system that
> DWR discovered damage to Oroville's main spillway on
> February 7, 2017, during routine visual inspections." —CA
> DWR, 2017 Oroville Spillways Incident Background

(That said, it's at least possible that some well-intentioned communicators are using 'unprecedented' as a code word to flag climate change impacts.)

The hits just keep coming

The extended but mostly moderate 22-day sequence of atmospheric river storms beginning on December 26, 2022, dropped 29 cubic miles of water on California (more followed later) and caused $1 billion in initial damages, according to news reports. If you experienced it, and wonder about 1862, imagine storms sometimes twice as intense, the sequence continuing for 45 days… and melting the Sierra snowpack in the process. One memorable 2023 newsreel interview quote, from a storm-tossed young woman in sandals in Capitola:

> "I've lived here for three years and I've never seen anything like it."

Weeks later, days of heavy snows blanketed most of California down to low elevations, causing a humanitarian crisis with fatalities in the San Bernardino Mountains. Facebook posts from further north, in the Central Sierra, which at mid-elevations received somewhat less snow than in San Bernardino Co., included many reports of distress and hardships while roads and long driveways were impassable; a medical rescue in Sheep Ranch was even more challenging than the one described above from the Watsonville area. Now, just a week into March, more ARs, warm ones this time, are producing intense precipitation (up to 13.4" of 24-hour rain in Pacifica on March 10, reported) which is melting the snowpack up to mid-elevations, creating flood impacts downriver, especially in the Tulare Basin and southern San Joaquin Valley, while increasing snow loads and structural damage at the high elevations. Most of the work on this book was done during a serious drought; now as this project wraps up, Californians are getting a fresh reminder of what wet-winter storm impacts, and extended AR sequences, are like.

* * *

How's our infrastructure looking? (Or: are problems just rare flukes?)

> "During the fall and winter of 2017-18, California residents lived through a devastating series of disasters. After years of drought, devastating wildfires ravaged thousands of homes from Northern to Southern California; deluge rain events after the fires led to catastrophic floods, mudslides and

debris flows that washed away bare soil, houses and cars and closed stretches of Highway 101, crippling transportation routes. Over this time, the state received five Major Disaster Declarations, three Emergency Declarations and 23 Fire Management Assistance Declarations—a combination never experienced before. Sixty-five Californians lost their lives and thousands of homes, numerous roads, communication towers, phone and electricity distribution lines, fleet vehicles and parks either were destroyed or sustained damages that are still being tallied and remedied. **Against a backdrop of aging infrastructure that some describe as "crumbling" these extreme events offer a first-row seat to the fragility of our infrastructure systems** and they give us a glimpse of the future in a changing climate. For people to be safe, our communities must be prepared. **Our infrastructure must be resilient and sustainable to withstand these growing threats, particularly worsening extreme events**.

"Yet, as noted in the 2017 report by the Union of Concerned Scientists—Built to Last: Challenges and Opportunities for Climate-Smart Infrastructure in California—California's infrastructure is not. **Our infrastructure is aging and deteriorating and, despite recently increasing investment, still requires better upkeep and modernization. Lack of emergency action plans for high-hazard infrastructure, a long backlog of deferred maintenance projects and billion-dollar gaps in spending on infrastructure upkeep plague the state of infrastructure in the fifth largest economy in the world.** These truths provide a stark backdrop to the rapidly growing need of investing in new infrastructure and preparing for the accelerating impacts of climate change."

...

"Focusing solely on the status of the physical assets, in 2012, the ASCE [American Society of Civil Engineers] completed the state's second comprehensive infrastructure assessment. Even at that time, ASCE gave barely passing grades to levees / flood management (D), urban runoff (D+), wastewater (C+), and drinking water (supply) (C). These grades are roughly similar to those ASCE gave in its initial California Infrastructure Report Card in 2006, indicating little, if any, progress in improving the overall condition of California's water infrastructure over the previous six years. Regarding water supply, ASCE called out a few key issues, including aging infrastructure nearing or exceeding the end of its useful life; the vulnerability of the Sacramento-San Joaquin Delta as the "vital link" in the state's conveyance system for water depended upon by millions of Californians; continued population growth; seismic and security risks; and the unique problems posed by small water systems. Funding was an issue across all four areas of water infrastructure, with a total of $18.6 billion per year required to raise each grade by one letter."

"The 2017 ASCE's nationwide report card included a number of updated facts for California's water infrastructure, suggesting that the challenges have in no way decreased and the investment need is considerable (Box 3.1). **The condition of the Delta** and specifically its vulnerability to earthquakes was noted as well in the **levees / flood control** portion of the ASCE report card, which stated that **catastrophic levee failure there could lead to a "mega-disaster" on the scale of Hurricane Katrina**. With respect to flood management specifically in the Central Valley, the Department of Water Resources (DWR) issued its System Status Report of the State Plan of Flood Control (SPFC) in 2017. In it, the Department evaluated the condition of the SPFC's urban and nonurban levees, channels, and flood control structures. **Approximately half the levees were assessed as not meeting acceptable design criteria for a variety of characteristics (*e.g.*, freeboard, stability, seepage), while a similar proportion of SFPC channels were found to be potentially inadequate in terms of capacity.**"

—CA CSIWG report to the State Legislature, 2018.

I could say more about the California Climate-Safe Infrastructure Working Group (CSIWG), its 2018 report to the state legislature, and the AB 2800 bill (2016; Quirk) that launched the CSIWG initiative, but to keep this book manageable I'll refer you to the free online report. I do want to note the phrase "**worsening** extreme events" above, and also this definition from the CSIWG report: "Climate-safe infrastructure is defined as infrastructure that is sustainable, adaptive and that meets design criteria that aim for resilience in the face of shocks and stresses caused by **current and future climate**." Unlike some initiatives including CA4_CCA (the state's latest climate change assessment), <u>this view encompasses existing risks, including possible historical misperceptions of those risks</u>, and thus smoothly transcends the narrow focus on 'climate change' that limits other state initiatives like CA4_CCA. I think Civil Engineers tend to get it.

A few more notable highlights from this and other sources:

Flood control infrastructure adequacy (Sacramento River Watershed)

> "The problems that have been identified by this watershed assessment process are:
> - A **high risk of flooding** threatens public safety, as well as property and critical infrastructure throughout the study area,
> - The consequences of flooding in the study area **would be catastrophic,**
> - Systemwide residual **flood risks will remain** after implementation of current projects in high risk areas…"
> —USACE, CVIFMS draft plan, 2015 [making clear to us that flooding remains a serious problem in the Sacramento Valley, and that even the round of infrastructure projects then in the works won't solve it.]

Dams

California has 678 (or 833, from a second source) dams rated as 'high hazard dams,' meaning loss of life would be a consequence of a failure. Fairly recently, 32% of the state-regulated dams did not have an Emergency Action Plan. The Associated Press, on May 5, 2022, reported an in-house analysis that found "more than 2200 high-hazard dams in poor or unsatisfactory condition across the US;" while they did not provide the full analysis, some examples from California were given.

Levees

You might have imagined that all Valley levees were built to prevent floods, but that's not entirely true. Neither were they built to modern standards, nor even to endure…

> "The existing levee system was designed and built at the turn of the last century [that would be 1900] before modern construction methods were employed. These levees were constructed close to the river, using naturally occurring riverside deposits as their foundation, **to increase flow velocities which would flush out hydraulic mining debris; at the time, mining debris deposition that** [sic] **causing widespread deposition was occurring across the valley floor and, causing disruption**

of economic uses of the river. This debris is essentially gone now but the high velocities associated with flood flows are [sic] **have been eroding the levees since construction, compromising the existing flood risk management system.**

Levee failures within the existing system can be caused by a variety of mechanisms, including:

- Seepage of floodwater through (through-seepage) and under (under-seepage) the levee,
- Continuing erosion of the levees and river banks,
- Lack of stability of the levees, and
- Overtopping of levees during events that exceed the facilities design, much of which was completed in the mid-1900s.

Evaluations conducted by the State and documented in the CVFPP and the Flood Control System Status Report (December 2011) indicate that **approximately half of 300 miles of urban levees do not meet current design criteria for freeboard (height above the recorded high-water mark of a structure), stability or seepage. Approximately 60 percent of about 1,230 miles of nonurban levees have high potential of failure from under-seepage, through-seepage, structural instability or erosion** (Figure 1-1). It is important to note that in non-USACE documents, level of protection (LOP) is often used to describe a level of performance but due to USACE regulations, is not used in USACE documents.

In addition to structural concerns, the early estimate is that **approximately 500 miles of channels on SPFC lands have potentially inadequate capacities to convey the design flows.** There is currently on-going work at DWR with additional modeling to determine the true amount.

The SPFC was designed to pass **the known flood of record**, which at the time of Congressional authorization **was the 1909 flood**. During construction of the system, a new flood of record occurred in 1927, which was incorporated into the overall system design. After completion of the Federal system in the 1950s, a new flood of record occurred in 1986, followed by the slightly smaller flood of January 1997. The floods of 1986 and 1997 delivered much more water to the leveed reaches than they were designed to carry, resulting in levee failures (see History of Flooding section). On the American River, the four biggest floods occurred after completion of Folsom Dam and the SRFCP." —USACE, CVIFMS draft plan, 2015

I must point out here that even though the 1862 flood was clearly much bigger than anything later, the design for the federally funded SPFC levee project in the Central Valley required only that the system be able to handle the smaller 1909 flood… which by 1927 was deemed to be an inadequate standard. 1862 was not and is still not a 'flood of record' because, let's imagine it now, our pioneers and settlers were too busy trying to survive it to be able to measure (record) it sufficiently. The roots of turning a blind eye to 1862 reach at least this far back in time. Even quite recently (2018), California's <u>future</u> Delta levee adequacy has been evaluated in a state-sponsored report using a 1970's concept, based on even older data, of a 'hundred-year flood.'

Bridges (State Highway System and local routes)

Then: 74.9% on SHS are in good condition, 21.8% are in fair condition and 3.3% are in poor condition.—Data from **2018** Caltrans TAMP report

Now: 54.1% on SHS are in good condition, 42.4% are in fair condition and 3.5% are in poor condition.—Data from **2022** Draft Caltrans TAMP report

The trend above is not positive. From Infobridge, the database of the NBI (National Bridge Inventory), U.S. DOT, I can see that various bridges our local communities depend upon are in 'fair' or 'poor' condition, with 15% 'poor' currently the situation on and around SR 49 from Placerville through Jamestown. See Sources below if you want to check individual bridges in your area.

Culverts (State Highway System)

"There are about 205,000 culverts along state highways. Statewide, 65% of all culverts are considered to be in "good" condition, 23.5% are in fair condition, and 11.5% are in poor condition. The more than 23,000 culverts in poor condition need to be replaced or rehabilitated. Culverts may be exposed to scour from coastal storms, wildfires, mudslides, **and extreme precipitation events resulting in roadway overtopping, etc.**" —Data from 2018 TAMP report; in 2022 only 10% were known to be in poor condition, per Draft TAMP update; these are just the culverts on the State Highway System, not counting local roads. If just 10% of the 'poor' SHS culverts (~1% of all culverts) failed in an extreme storm sequence, the estimated direct repair cost would be roughly 2.3 billion dollars; the resulting costs from secondary damage and transportation interruptions and detours are not included. Note that USGS in 2011 considered only <u>landslide</u> damages to roadways from the ARkStorm, predicting that those highway repairs would cost $2.5 billion. *An underestimate?*

Note: Per NPR, June 30th, 2022, inflation sharply curtailed the scope of public infrastructure maintenance in 2022.

California's acquired perspective on hazards, circa 2018

The State Hazard Mitigation Plan was released in 2018, and Annex 3—LIFELINES INFRASTRUCTURE AND HAZARD MITIGATION PLANNING presents a series of principles (or 'lessons learned' from specific examples of actual disasters that are presented), indicating that some very fundamental concepts may now be receiving more advance attention going forward [I've **emphasized** some that reflect particular themes in this book]. These include:

- "In both the emergency water system and the transportation system, the **importance of redundancy is demonstrated**.
- To ensure lifeline redundancy, the backup system should be independent. This means that the backup system is either not subjected to or is resistant to the same loading conditions.
- When independent redundant systems are infeasible, isolating failures to the main system can improve overall system performance.
- **Some transportation corridors do not have simple alternate routes, particularly when dealing with difficult topography**.
- **The cost of armoring certain lifelines against closure should be weighed against the repeat costs of closure. If possible, cost benefit analysis of mitigation decisions should include not only life and property loss, but also lifeline repairs or lifeline outage consequences**.
- Sewer and storm water systems, along with household and solid waste systems, are essential for societal function and require lifelines consideration because of their spatially distributed nature.
- Combined storm / sewer systems can result in small but chronic failures that affect the health of the environment and citizens.
- Debris after a disaster can hinder rescue and recover. Addressing post-disaster debris in pre-disaster planning efforts can enhance post-event response.

- **Levees can and do fail under less than peak loads due to adverse foundation soil conditions.**
- Redundancy is often too costly or infeasible to ensure with levee systems.
- In coastal, tidal, and delta regions, sea-level rise will increase the hazard to existing levees and make protecting low-lying areas with levees an increasingly risky proposition.
- **The interconnectedness / interdependence of lifelines can result in cascading or multiple service failures.**
- **Communication is often the most critical service during a disaster. Without it society cannot function.**
- **Major transportation corridors, because they cover large spatial areas, are susceptible to a range of failures which all result in diminished capacity.**
- To have backup systems function as true redundant systems, the design must ensure that they are not subject to the same loading as the primary systems.
- Critical nodes that require active input are not reliable when that input is severed. A passive system, in this case a nuclear power plant that can cool down without being connected to the grid, presents a more reliable node.
- **Interdependence of electricity and gasoline distribution was highlighted in this disaster.** Simple redundant measures (*e.g.*, manual pumps) could have alleviated some of the electricity-caused gasoline shortage."

The following final three principles are derived from consideration of two particular infrastructure failures including the 2017 Oroville Dam spillways emergency:

"Principles Identified (SERVICE LIFE AND AGING INFRASTRUCTURE):
- **Aging of infrastructure is often not considered until a failure occurs. And when these "old age" failures occur they can be catastrophic.**
- Prior code-based designs may not be sufficient for aging infrastructure.
- Backup components (*e.g.*, emergency spillways) should be functional in a crisis and not subject to the same weaknesses as the main components."

* * *

We aren't perfect, nor can we be, but I believe that we must do better.

* * *

Further reading

Teets, Bob and Shelby Young. 1986. Rivers of Fear: The Great California
Flood of 1986. C.R. Publications, Inc., Terra Alta, WV. 128 p.

Sager, William, and Wayne Wilson. 2018. Spillway Emergency: The Story of the Failure of
the Oroville Dam Spillway and the Evacuation of Oroville. 205 p. Kindle Edition (Amazon).

Pinter, Nicholas, *et al.* 2018. Flooding in the Sacramento Region. Pp. 236-245 IN
Geology of Sacramento, California, United States of America; Cities of the World
Series. A paper released as part of the XIII IAEG Congress and AEG Annual meeting
held in San Francisco, 17-21 September 2018. https://aeg.memberclicks.net/assets/
docs/Cities%20of%20the%20World%20-%20Sacramento%20-%202018.pdf

https://cnrfc.noaa.gov/storm_summaries/jan1997storms.php#:~:text=Not%20only%20
would%20the%20relentless%20precipitation%20through%20early,exacerbate%20
problems%20from%20the%20excessive%20amounts%20of%20runoff.

https://cnrfc.noaa.gov/images/storm_summaries/jan1997/misc/precipitation_totals.html

https://www.air-worldwide.com/publications/air-currents/2017/imagining-the-
worst-what-if-the-oroville-dams-auxiliary-spillway-failed-catastrophically/

https://water.ca.gov/Programs/State-Water-Project/SWP-Facilities/Oroville/
Oroville-Spillways/Background#:~:text=The%20Feather%20River%20
watershed%20above%20the%20Oroville%20reservoir,on%20February%20
7%2C%202017%2C%20during%20routine%20visual%20inspections.

https://water.ca.gov/-/media/DWR-Website/Web-Pages/Programs/State-Water-Project/
Oroville/Misc/Lake_Oroville_2018-2019_FloodOps_Plan_011819_ay_19.pdf

http://www.friendsoftheriver.org/wp-content/uploads/2016/01/
Oroville-Dam-joint-intervention.pdf

https://mdpi-res.com/d_attachment/geosciences/geosciences-09-00037/
article_deploy/geosciences-09-00037.pdf

Alvi, I. A. [undated]. Case Study: Oroville Dam (California, 2017). https://
damfailures.org/case-study/oroville-dam-california-2017/

Koskinas, Aristotelis *et al.* [8 authors]. 2019. Insights into the Oroville Dam 2017 Spillway
Incident. Geosciences 2019, 9(1), 37 (24 pp.). https://www.mdpi.com/2076-3263/9/1/37

https://www.climate.gov/media/8040

Griggs, Gary B., and Lance Paris. Flood control failure: San Lorenzo River, California.
Environmental Management volume 6, pages 407–419 (1982). https://www.researchgate.
net/publication/225837977_Flood_control_failure_San_Lorenzo_River_California

Cox, Christopher. The Trillion-Gallon Question [Extreme weather is threatening California's dams. What happens if they fail?] New York Times, June 22, 2023. https://www.nytimes.com/2023/06/22/magazine/california-dams.html?smid=nytcore-ios-share&referringSource=articleShare

A useful site for area and property flood risks, a more comprehensive approach that the FEMA/NFIP mapping through 2021, and using different, more inclusive methodology that integrates changing climate effects: https://floodfactor.com/about

https://www.npr.org/2020/10/18/918725965/undisclosed-most-homebuyers-and-renters-arent-warned-about-flood-or-wildfire-ris

https://www.npr.org/2022/07/18/1111985667/a-blistering-heat-wave-has-sparked-massive-wildfires-throughout-europe

https://www.npr.org/2021/06/23/1009062465/more-than-half-of-u-s-buildings-are-in-places-prone-to-disaster-study-finds

https://www.npr.org/2021/10/14/1046106672/floods-threaten-to-shut-down-a-quarter-of-u-s-roads-and-critical-buildings

https://www.cbsnews.com/sacramento/news/old-peach-tree-mall-building-demolished/

18

On the Psychology of Risk

"What accounts for the blithe dismissal of potentially cataclysmic threats? … I have witnessed time and again—in myself and in others—a powerful impulse to believe what we hope to be the case." —Mitt Romney, The Atlantic, July 4, 2022

"Risks can be absent from the agenda of decision-makers in society for various reasons." —Jana Fromm

"But even more surprising than our findings themselves was the reaction to our study in 2010. Many officials simply refused to accept it." —Lucy Jones, head of the USGS MHDP team that produced the ARkStorm study

"Complacency: self-satisfaction especially when accompanied by unawareness of actual dangers or deficiencies." —Merriam-Webster Dictionary

"I'm not really worried about some future flood," said Alex Navas, 48. As he spoke, Navas trimmed a hedge by the house he moved into three years ago. "It's like all the warnings about a huge earthquake coming—but who really knows when that will be?" —quoted by the Los Angeles Times, October 31, 2022

'Psychologist' is on the long list of things that I am not. Yet the psychological dimension of preparing for a catastrophe, and then dealing with one in real time, is profound, and will strongly impact how this book is interpreted; it will also impact one's prospects for success / survival and for reducing hardship. So, I really can't ignore it. Instead, I will paraphrase or quote brief passages from other sources that I think will help to introduce and begin to illuminate the topic of risk perception and risk management or neglect. One particularly important factor discussed below is <u>optimism bias</u>. Another is <u>risk neglect</u>. These are issues that affect us as individuals and as a society and its institutions.

> Risk: "The possibility of meeting danger or suffering harm, loss, etc." This only captures part of the concept of risk as it is interpreted in scientific research—the probability of an event happening. An equally important part of risk is the outcome and the negative consequences associated with this outcome. These two parts constitute the core of many definitions of risks—an estimation of the likelihood of an event happening and the possible outcome of that event. [—paraphrased from Fromm, 2005]

Why would people tend to minimize or be in denial about an unfamiliar risk that is deemed to be plausible, or even inevitable? Quoting from the very informative 2005 thesis by Jana Fromm, titled "Risk Denial and Neglect: Studies in Risk Perception:"

> "The present thesis studies societal and individual attention to risks and focuses especially on the issue of neglect. Some risks are ignored simply because they are new and unknown. **Neglecting risks, on the other hand, implies that there is a certain degree of knowledge about the risk. Despite this knowledge, the necessary precautions to avoid the risk, or mitigate the consequences, are neglected.**"

A first psychological issue, suggested above, is <u>availability bias</u> (unfamiliarity): events that can be more easily brought to mind or imagined are judged to be more likely than events that could not easily be imagined because we haven't seen them and/or don't hear about them. Most modern people have visual images of earthquake, hurricane, and terrorism events, thanks to news and entertainment media, but many Californians do not have a comparable experience of extreme storms on this landscape. The relevant storm / flood risk scenario is effectively an unknown for many residents and is not a source of dread or a motivator for action. A dread risk elicits visceral feelings of terror, whereas an unknown risk is new and hard to evaluate. The more a person dreads a situation, the higher its perceived risk and the more that person wants the risk reduced.

Here's one visual experience you can borrow: I highly recommend the 2015 Norwegian film 'The Wave' by Roar Uthaug. The middle section of the film will give you plenty to process: the lack of a compelling sense of dread, and people's cognitive-response conflicts even when protocols have been established for an immediate short-notice flood evacuation, and the snap risk calculations and decisions, or indecisions, that everyone from official agency staff to individual civilians have to make in almost no time at all. Many documentaries and dramatizations capture risk denial and immediate cognitive conflicts very clearly.

The USGS 2011 ARkStorm report included this observation from a study team participant in the CalEMA agency (which since 2013 has been reincorporated into the Governor's Office of Emergency Services, or Cal OES):

> "Finally, a concern of CalEMA is the level of complacency about evacuation in California (D. Owens, CalEMA, 2010, personal commun.). In contrast to the Gulf States, the residents of California are not routinely faced with flooding and evacuation warnings and orders. **Tendencies to ignore official warnings and wait until the last minute to evacuate will put more people at risk. Changing passive perceptions toward flooding evacuations is a challenge for emergency managers because people's risk attitudes and beliefs is what makes evacuation a reality.**"

It seems to me that as many of our citizens become less familiar with nature, our collective impression of it has become benign, even 'fluffy.' Watching documentaries of people flocking to waterways to see tsunamis, or to the craters of active volcanoes, or chasing tornadoes, or reading about people planning a family holiday trip to experience a blizzard, or perhaps going out on a levee or bridge or wharf to see if it might fail… or just ignoring evacuation orders… indicates to me that hardship, unfortunately, may be the only effective teacher. Ask Pliny the Elder (see below).

Elsewhere in this book I've flagged the pattern of elected leaders routinely explaining catastrophic events as 'once-in-200-years' events or 'one-of-a-kind' events, in conjunction with the increasingly pervasive use of the word 'unprecedented' by officials offering a conceptual framework for how they evaluate such events. This pattern of downplaying or 'exceptionalizing' catastrophes has some insidious social aspects in addition to the immediately self-serving ones: people (and agencies and legislatures) may silence the alarms in their minds about the prospects of future, recurring catastrophes and the need for preparedness; officials immunize themselves with context suggesting that there is no problem with, or accountability for, 'unprecedented' risks having been neglected (or continuing to be), nor with failing to use adequate research and a bit of imagination to obtain a realistic picture of the possibility of extreme natural disasters which could otherwise be anticipated and perhaps mitigated or at least prepared for.

Many people I know in the Foothills keep a 'go-bag' of clothing and medications ready and in easy reach during wildfire season. They have also done some planning for a possible evacuation occurring with little warning: they have a list of what special items should go in a vehicle (animals, personal records, family history, computers and devices, chargers) and a destination in mind for a temporary stay. That used to be about a once-in-a-lifetime event, at worst, but many of us have now gone through a fire evacuation at least once in just a few recent years; it has become familiar. No one around here, or generally in the parts of the West where vegetation is abundant, thinks that planning ahead for fire evacuation is strange. Wildfire return intervals (re-occurrences) span a range of years, with 40 years being in the ballpark for some forest types (although that interval is apparently getting shorter). A 40-year average return interval has been predicted for mid-sized AR-megastorms late in this century (Swain *et al.*, 2018; Huang & Swain, 2022).

People in the American West are less familiar with the possibility of sheltering in place, or relocating, during an extreme winter storm event. A few road closures, a few trees down, and losing power for a week, is about the worst many of us have experienced in recent decades, with more impacts at higher elevations in non-flood years. Some folks do go on trips or visits when a strong storm is in the forecast, or when the grid fails. It may be human nature to not want to believe that something much more serious will happen here from time to time. We may feel silly preparing for an event that is unlikely to happen this year or next. We may be afraid that 'friends' will make fun of us.

Preparing may make a calamity feel 'too real,' and call forth an unwelcome sense of dread. A sense of dread can be a motivator to action, but in extreme cases, it can instead be paralyzing. Many people have an aversion to considering anything that might lead them to experience a sense of dread. If you are one of those people, it's unlikely that you are still reading this book! I can only hope that you have folks in your life who will read it for you and begin to take appropriate actions. *"This book makes a great gift!"*

How do we grasp an event that is both seriously dangerous and relatively uncommon? Our minds have difficulty with this. The odds of winning a big lottery are around 1 in 300,000,000, and many people gladly buy tickets. The odds of having to experience and survive a megastorm in California may now be around 1 in 70 to 80 each year, yet people may be unmotivated or even reluctant to stock up on food and supplies, or to make or even consider just-in-case <u>lifesaving</u> preparations.

As an extreme example of an extreme risk event, a major asteroid impact on Earth seems to be very rare: sub-extinction-level events are perhaps one-in-one-hundred-million-year events. Yet NASA spends money to spot and track dangerous asteroids and also spends to develop plans and systems that might protect Earth 'in the event of…' In fact, as I write this, on November 23rd, 2021, a spacecraft has been launched from Vandenberg SFB in California, and it is on its way to impact an asteroid and alter its trajectory [update: successful, in 2022]:

money spent on a first time ever practice run, to get our game on in case a killer asteroid ever does show up. Taking this as 'the parable of the rock and the rocket,' the lesson is that when the outcome could be extremely bad—like the loss of all you hold precious—even rare but plausible hazards must be taken seriously.

> "The absent / exempt error is yet another cognitive explanation to optimistic bias—if a negative event has not happen[ed] so far, it is perceived as less likely to happen in the future ... In the estimation of future risk, extrapolations are made from prior experiences ..." —Fromm, 2005 [See use of the word 'unprecedented' commented above and elsewhere in this book.]

Two other interrelated psychological behaviors strongly affect the outcomes of risk assessments: optimism bias and risk neglect. Optimism (or optimistic) bias is a concept that is frequently cited in research on risk and is another individual-level factor, sometimes reinforced collectively and even manifesting institutionally, that influences risk perception. Optimism bias includes a person's tendency to believe that a negative event is less likely to occur to him / her than other people, and the person's perception that s/he is more adept at averting injury should a negative event occur.

> "Fortune favors the bold!" —Pliny the Elder, among his last words, commanding his ship to sail towards the vicinity of Pompei, while Vesuvius was in full eruption.

> "I knew what could happen out there. But you don't believe it will happen to you." —Kelsey, volcano tour guide, survivor of the 2019 mass-casualty eruption of White Island, NZ; *The Volcano: Rescue from Whakaari* (documentary film).

Institutionally, optimism bias may be fostered by expediency, cost control pressures and institutional culture including peer pressure to conform or 'achieve.' What consequences can arise from optimism bias at the institutional level? From the forensic report on the spillway failures at the Oroville Dam, owned by CA DWR, in 2017:

> "The owner was generally overconfident regarding the integrity of its civil infrastructure."

Risk neglect is a companion to optimism bias. According to Fromm, a continuum of limited response (or no response) to risk may span ignorance-

<u>neglect-tolerance</u>. Neglect, "to give little attention to," is neither ignorance of risk nor tolerance of it. Rather it occupies a sort of comfortable semi-blind spot in which known risk remains unevaluated and 'out of mind' and consequently is not an influence on choices or actions. And, I'll offer the view that optimism bias from individual to institutional (collections of individuals) levels, especially when shared and reinforced by peers, furnishes much of the comfort that could foster any risk neglect that may exist.

Some personal thoughts: Looking 'institutionally' at patterns of land development, of issues with flood zone estimation and peak stream-flow estimates, of what scenarios are deemed plausible for design and engineering purposes, of potentially undersized flood control infrastructure… of minimum standards and cost-cutting trade-offs and low-bid contracts… of malls built in holes and emergency spillways made of dirt and electrical grids running overhead through forests… of frozen O-rings on rocket booster engines… of structural collapses… it seems to me that optimism bias / risk neglect may be pervasive (and often profitable, or career-enhancing, in the short term). We live in a world in which expenditures on robustness, resilience, redundancy and risk reduction are constrained by both external (political, financial or business considerations) and psychological factors. In parallel, the perceived near-term rewards for accomplishment outweigh those for precaution.

Our culture warns us against raising possibly false alarms from an early age: crying 'wolf,' Chicken Little; don't rock the boat. It takes a terrorist attack to persuade agencies to attempt to retrain adults to 'See Something, Say Something.' Cassandras, Nervous Nellies, Worrywarts—we could have used more before September 11, 2001.

"Kid, when you think you see a wolf, cry wolf; when in doubt, shout!"

> "Not only are there different levels in the relation between the individual and the risk, there are also different levels of actual neglect. On the first level, which is quite close to that of ignorance, the individual refuses to hear, think or reflect about the risk—he or she actively chooses to stay ignorant. The difference between this level and that of ignorance is this active choice of refusing information—information that is available. On the second level, the individual has some knowledge about the risk but denies it. This is associated with optimistic bias, where the individual has information about a risk but does not acknowledge that the risk applies to him / her. Optimistic bias is also related to the third level of neglect, a selective search for information. This bias in selection may either focus on information about the risk that is relevant to the own person or be biased in the sense that only information supporting the belief that the risk is low or irrelevant, regardless of whom it potentially affects.

"So far I have only discussed neglect in relation to the individual—but risks can also be neglected on a societal level. Risks can be absent from the agenda of decision-makers in society for various reasons. One reason might be that the issue has not at all been taken into consideration. Another possibility is that, after careful consideration, it was decided not to give the issue priority. It is only in the first case that the term "neglect" is adequate. … if an accident happens and the related risks only then get attention this would be an obvious case of neglect. The necessary safeguards to prevent a negative event from happening have not been taken even though knowledge about the risk existed. A neglected risk is not any hazard that turns out to be dangerous once it has become a reality, but one where reasonable safeguards have been ignored." —Fromm, 2005

Somewhere on the risk neglect continuum is risk denial, invoked for whatever reason. That has become particularly evident during the recent Covid-19 pandemic; it has long been a persistent mitigation hurdle even while climate changes become increasingly extreme. *Denial as a habit or a creed has lately morphed into a political behavior.*

Circling back to some earlier remarks, it may be hard to separate risk neglect from issues of risk perception, which might involve unconscious selection biases. After years spent reading about natural hazards including storm and flood threats in the West, I've concluded that perceptions here have tended to highlight earthquake, wildfire, and drought, while filtering down (or 'lowlighting') the storm and flood risks (especially prior to 2022-23). USGS in 2011 anticipated this filtering, which persists in many camps; they released a warning video to try to overcome this blind spot. With hindsight, seven years later, Lucy Jones, chief scientist of the USGS MHDP team that produced the ARkStorm study and report, reflected on the reception the study report received; some themes will be familiar from the paragraphs above:

"Which brings us back to the psychological dimension. As disaster scientists, we knew that floods cause less emotional distress than earthquakes, so we shouldn't have been too surprised. But I thought that when we presented the evidence, cities would say, "We need to change our priorities." Instead, the data was largely rejected because it didn't conform to the emotional responses of the emergency managers—people who, like all of us, are more afraid of the unseen. Scientists might say they were acting on confirmation bias, critical of data that didn't match their point of view.

> "This inability to accept the possibility of extreme flooding events increases the risk for people across the United States, and indeed the world." [In fairness, there were other hurdles. Public officials even today all rely on the more optimistic (and, unfortunately, misleading) assessments provided by all involved federal agencies including FEMA, and by the state and other agencies that employ the same 'standard' estimation methods; the USGS MHDP team in 2011 elected not to confront this technical conflict directly, thus they did not overcome it. In Chapter 20 I comment further on why the 'ARkStorm message' was dismissed.]

For a good dramatization of this pervasive psychological phenomenon, there is the Polish dramatic series, 'High Water,' by Jan Holoubek, about the official response to the developing 1997 floods in Central Europe; the series was presented by Netflix (2022). It can also help you visualize extreme urban flooding. Twenty-four years later, the similar-scale 2021 floods in Europe (fatalities: 243) prompted the following *deja-vu* remarks:

> "The weather models did a good job predicting the extreme [2021] flood event in Western Europe, too. It wasn't that the meteorologists didn't know it was coming. You can have conversations about why that knowledge didn't translate to the right kind of evacuation or preparation. But it was not a mystery. It wasn't like it came out of the blue. So what's interesting is that the weather models do capture these events in advance." —Daniel Swain, interviewed for Grist, July 23, 2021.

Here's one suggestive example of priority-altering view-filtering from a Cal OES 2022 budget request for facility relocation:

> "The transitional Southern coordination facility will provide the space necessary for the Region to respond in support of catastrophic **earthquakes**, as well as **wildfire** sieges such as those faced by California in 2017, 2018 and 2020…" [Unmentioned is the fact that this important facility is currently located in a FEMA 1% AEP floodplain; will it relocate to higher ground?]

To some extent this could arise from the human tendency to "re-fight the last war in the next war," planning to repeat familiar actions once taken against old threats, or threats most vividly remembered or cinematically amplified, whereas the ability to imagine 'new' (or very old) threats and how a future or uncommon threat might require a different response is a rarer ability and, it seems to me, is often underappreciated and underutilized, even mocked. Indelibly, I watched a company, the biggest employer in its rural county, with 1200 employees, fail in the face of new threats because "we always done it that way" was the watchword in that community.

Some other concepts of related psychological tendencies have also been developed within the field of risk perception and management; I've provided some references below if you are interested. These concepts include social action theory, protection motivation theory, risk compensation theory, and habituated action theory, if you want to go deeper. Per these theories, people who take risks feel adequately shielded from harmful consequences because they overestimate the effectiveness of protective systems or equipment (levees, Emergency Broadcast System, some extreme 'nanny state' fantasy), underestimate their personal susceptibility to harm ("I seem to be great at this…"), or are lured into a false sense of security because of repeated high-risk behavior without an adverse incident ("Hey, y'all, watch this!"). Understanding the subtle ways in which sociological and psychological forces interact to encourage or suppress risk-taking behavior could aid significantly in creating messaging and programs to make communities and workplaces safer.

The role of imagination

Preparedness at all levels, even with an imminent threat, may be compromised by risk denial or neglect, or by misperception or flawed assessment of a threat, or perhaps other issues (see next chapter). A future review of the individual and official storm responses and tragedy that unfolded in March 2023 in the San Bernardino Mountains could provide a painful lesson that the public and their agencies will take to heart, at least for a while.

Failure of imagination is another specific factor deserving more attention:

> "This is **an unrivaled, unparalleled weather event not experienced in several decades**," Kris Mattarochia, a meteorologist with the National Weather Service in Hanford, said during a briefing in Fresno. "There will be high water and areas that are usually not impacted. So everyone needs to be ready. … Combined with snow melt, the Kings River, along with smaller streams like Mill Creek, will be **pushed to limits which are unimaginable.**"

> "We want everyone to know that this is not a normal situation. This is something that is **completely outside the realm of even possibilities that we can imagine as meteorologists**," he said." Los Angeles Times, March 10, 2023

<u>Speaking frankly</u>: 'Never, ever' thinking can be deadly, more so at higher levels of responsibility. The implicit absolution in such 'unimaginable' statements is the insidious icing on that lethal cake. "Could not imagine…" is a poor, even disqualifying, defensive skirt to hide behind, especially in events that history has recorded before. In my considered opinion.

We might at first equate imagination with frivolous fantasy, but imagination as a survival skill is the ability to see and figure out how to connect all the available dots of information, and then look over the horizon for the next dot(s) in the series. This is skilled extrapolation. In this sense, imagination is like a muscle in the brain; if we let that muscle become flabby or lazy, our ability to predict and prepare for unfamiliar events or changing circumstances, and to respond to complex emergencies in real time, becomes degraded.

> "No training scenario imagined this." —attributed to Masao Yoshida, plant manager at the coastal Fukushima-Daiichi Nuclear Plant, located 10 meters above sea level, after the earthquake and tsunami on March 11, 2011, destroyed virtually all control and response capabilities (and ultimately, the six nuclear reactors, three of which exploded); see the official Yoshida Testimony to the Japanese government.

> "…I think historically there's been a little bit of a lack of imagination regarding what different levels of warming actually mean… I think we've had, from a broader societal standpoint, kind of a failure of imagination in the sense that there hasn't been enough conversation about what it really means to warm a degree or two degrees or five degrees, god forbid. I don't think people really understand—and I think this is even true of some scientists, even some climate scientists, honestly. People who are climate scientists might study the carbon cycle or might study large-scale dynamics or paleoclimate. I think a lot specifically about the extreme climate, these transient huge bursts of severe weather that can occur. And we're adding a lot of extra energy to the system." —Daniel Swain, on the pace of 'new' weather, interviewed for Grist, July 23, 2021.

This facet of the imagination is more highly regarded when we acknowledge it as foresight. Now, consider the following:

> " 'Nobody saw this coming. Period.' —Maui County Police Chief," reported by CNN, 12 August 2023

Temperament

If you 'dodge a bullet,' do you say, 'I'll never risk that again!' or do you think, 'Looks like I'll be pretty good at dodging.' How a person actually reacts to risks involves psychological tendencies as noted above, but may ultimately boil down to personal temperament. Decisions and actions are filtered through trade-off calculations: on the one hand, spending some time on pre-stocking an emergency pantry, making sure you have any gear you might need for 'roughing it,' and giving some thought to planning, preparation and problem-solving, may seem like good insurance, and a small price to pay when the stakes may be your life, your wealth, and the protection of friends and family. On the other hand, someday finding yourself in a difficult situation and just 'winging it' as you scramble to find what you need to pull through it may seem like a small price to pay for all those years of a more carefree existence. These are traits rooted in temperament, personality, and outlook, among other things… including experiences.

For example, some people hate change, and trouble usually means change, and avoiding trouble may also require change, thus there is an aversion to dealing with risk. A friend pointed out that persons who are temperamentally inclined toward passive acceptance of events and circumstances may find reinforcement for their innate tendencies in their interpretations of various philosophical, spiritual or religious traditions. So, I'll point out that most persons who were foundational figures to the world's most widely followed religious and spiritual traditions were persons of action. Even Buddhism, which has something to say about acceptance, does not promote passivity, but rather intentionality. The Buddhists at Tassajara fight wildfires.

Finally, regarding psychology, during and after a megastorm: <u>Resilience</u>: Making good clear-headed decisions and avoiding shock and discouragement are crucial to coping with an ongoing crisis. And during the recovery period, "There is no question that people living in the direct vicinity of high-profile disasters suffer mentally as well as physically. Hurricane Katrina, for example, was followed by an increase in psychiatric disorders, substance abuse, and domestic violence among people living in the areas affected." [—source now offline]

"But public health officials say that, in the aftermath of an extreme weather event like a hurricane, the toll of long-term psychological injuries builds in the months and years that follow, outpacing more immediate injuries and swamping the health care system long after emergency workers go home and shelters shut down." —Vestal, 2017 [Anyone willing to consider the psychological impact of forced flood evacuation, loss of loved ones, and the destruction of homes and communities *should really, really read this brief online article*.]

Mental preparedness can mitigate some psychological distress. Actual preparedness includes and reinforces mental preparedness, while intentionally mitigating future harms. Resilience is a survival trait not only during a catastrophic event but especially during a prolonged aftermath.

* * *

Further reading

Fromm, Jana. Risk Denial and Neglect: Studies in Risk Perception. Dissertation for the Degree of Doctor of Philosophy, Ph.D; Stockholm School of Economics, 2005
Distributed by:
EFI, The Economic Research Institute
Stockholm School of Economics
P O Box 6501, SE 1-113 83 Stockholm, Sweden
www.hhs.se/efi
https://ex.hhs.se/dissertations/377299-FULLTEXT01.pdf

Risk Perception: Theories, Strategies, And Next Steps, by The
Campbell Institute, National Safety Council. (2014)
https://www.thecampbellinstitute.org/wp-content/uploads/2017/05/
Campbell-Institute-Risk-Perception-WP.pdf
[or]
https://www.nsc.org/Portals/0/Documents/
CambpellInstituteandAwardDocuments/WP-Risk%20Perception.pdf
https://en.wikipedia.org/wiki/Risk_perception

https://www.nsc.org/Portals/0/Documents/
CambpellInstituteandAwardDocuments/WP-Risk%20Perception.pdf

https://understandinguncertainty.org/node/109

Neal, A., M.A. Griffin, & P.M. Hart. The impact of organizational climate on safety climate and individual behavior, by Safety Science, 34, 99–109. (2000) https://understandinguncertainty.org/node/109

Weinstein, N. Why it won't happen to me: Perceptions of risk factors and susceptibility, by Health Psychology, 3, 431–457. (1984)

Smith, Hayley *et al.* 'Unrivaled, unparalleled' storm hits California; evacuations, flood fears heightened. Los Angeles Times, 10 March 2023

Vestal, Christine. 'Katrina brain': The invisible long-term toll of megastorms. Politico, 10/12/2017. https://www.politico.com/agenda/story/2017/10/12/psychological-toll-natural-disasters-000547/

Teirstein, Zoya. Is climate change happening faster than expected? A climate scientist explains. Grist, July 23, 2021. https://grist.org/science/is-climate-change-happening-faster-than-expected-a-climate-scientist-explains/

Kadota, Ryusho. 2016. A Reading of the Yoshida Testimony: What Actually Happened Onsite at Fukushima. Kindle Edition

19

What I Would I Like to See

The author's suggestions, and advocacy, with a nod to USGS

"The future belongs to those who believe in the beauty of their dreams." —*Eleanor Roosevelt*

In this chapter I lay out a number of proposals in some detail, and it may be welcome reading if you are looking for more constructive positivity at this point, or feeling motivated to channel some energy into activism to work for improved public safety. I do want to keep this narrative moving toward the positive, starting with our thinking. Here I'll outline topics I've given some thought and ink to. I'll go into some detail in this 'advocacy white paper' because I think the only good long-term way forward through the anticipated reality of more extreme weather and recurring megastorms on the West Coast is for us, as a society, to rethink resilience from top to bottom, taking a much broader view than simple pantry-stocking or flood insurance. These aren't the only possible proposals, and I've no investment in believing they are the best possible solutions; we all should be thinking about better ways forward.

These admittedly ambitious ideas assume the likely odds of having a big and destructive megastorm in California are increasingly approaching ~2% per year (and possibly more), and that the impacts could be as significant as what is described by USGS and in the additional reports collected for this book. Such expected events would be ignored at our collective peril. If these proposals seem like a lot to tackle (yes, they are), try reading this chapter as a 'what if' exercise: *What if we commit to minimizing the losses, disruptions, dangers and other impacts of plausible extreme winter weather events on the West Coast?*

I'm not implying that none of the steps or preparations proposed here are being done or considered yet; they may be, to greater or lesser extent, perhaps on paper or out of the public eye. I'm just surveying things that I think are important elements of improved contributions to public safety. Some current implementations may be uneven. While California is referred to specifically in these proposals, they can be applied generally in other states and provinces.

All ideas here are intended to be constructive. Exploring ways to improve is not a criticism; encouragement and perhaps impetus are intended. (And institutionally and professionally, a willingness to improve and progress resilience must not imply an admission of prior failure.) For an example of how a constructive critique is prepared, see the California State Auditor's 2023 assessment of the forecast methods and protocols being used by the CA Department of Water Resources (cited below).

One last comment. It's not my intention to tell professionals how to do their jobs… but some suggestions here may seem to skirt that line. I have the greatest respect for expertise, competence, and commitment: things that we expect from our trusted public officials. However, issues can arise from old or poor data, incomplete knowledge, unfamiliarity, one's perceptions or misperceptions, reliance on experience or strategies that may not apply, psychological tendencies discussed earlier (see 'unimaginable'), structural and institutional constraints, and other factors; hence, this book. When a disaster scenario is accepted as plausible, and when it's accepted that such a 'worst case' <u>might not really be rare</u>, then these suggestions and others may have an effect.

After a catastrophe, much will seem obvious.

Common context, better data and hazard predictions, developing and applying benchmark expectations: official adoption of the appropriate weather scenarios for planning frameworks

Researchers Huang & Swain (2022) published the first installment in an 'ARkStorm 2.0 project' series of papers, a development I had hoped for; they presented a method even more elegant than what I envisioned for representing the entire range of possible events both in terms of impact magnitudes and probabilities (I discuss this in the final chapter). I'm delighted to see the USGS team's work being reanimated and extended, and I look forward to these future contributions. From work like theirs it is becoming possible to re-estimate megastorm recurrence intervals and magnitudes, now and in coming decades, and (at least provisionally) to adopt one or more appropriate standard extreme-storm scenarios, plus assessments of expected impacts, for official planning purposes. It's reported that ARkStorm 2.0 will include a full hydrology workup of a model storm, which was curtailed in the earlier USGS-led project.

The state should follow the best science and take a formal position on the actual potential for megastorm events (now and in coming decades), and on any uncertainty around those estimates, and require that all official agency or state-supported planning and study scenarios extend to, or include assessment of, at least one example of the impacts of a standard-model megastorm-scale event. [A defined model event with a target recurrence probability could be standardized for planning and assessment purposes, drawing from the ARkStorm and ARkStorm 2.0 work.] The state should further disseminate its estimates for events (frequency, magnitude, impacts) across all areas and levels of in-state government, and encourage their incorporation into local planning. Median estimates (*e.g.*, 50% of models) do not go far enough for public safety considerations; 80% might.

Toward that end, the state should be a leading advocate for reconciliation, by a qualified consortium or team, of two divergent long-term weather event recurrence interval or probability estimation ('forecasting') approaches: the long-standard 'historical / observational' approach that uses (and extrapolates from) only small samples of recorded weather, and the 'model / simulation' approach that reconstructs digital representations of climates, including future climates, and then generates large numbers of years of simulations of possible weather for any time period and climate conditions. These two approaches agree on recent-past weather but give divergent forecast results for rare and extreme events, for various reasons which are not that complicated. Earlier I discussed some of the shortcomings of the 'historical / observational' approach used by NFIP/FEMA, USACE, USGS, and other end-user agencies including state water agencies and emergency managers at all levels of government. Because the results from the two approaches overlap, the differences arising from limitations of methods, including assumptions, can—surely—be resolved with some insight and effort.

Needed improvements to precipitation event frequency and intensity estimation, and consequent flooding depths and extents, are also flagged by the First Street Foundation (2023). Specific improvements to now-standard methods, for example by including pluvial flooding impacts, and accounting for climate trends, should become standard. Revisions to accepted estimates should affect planning estimates for evacuations, infrastructure vulnerabilities, etc. The improved forecasts and probability / frequency estimates, ideally a synthetic consensus, should become the new standard, while anticipating further updates. The era of using arguably inadequate tools to do a vital job should end (thoughts echoed in Chapters 3, 18 and 20).

Of course, nothing is stopping the federal agencies from kick-starting this methods-reconciliation consensus process on their own or via a consortium. Failing that, the state should inform all parties that only studies which include a best-available synthetic understanding of all storm recurrence intervals and magnitudes, and which extend the range of events analyzed to include megastorm-scale events and their potential impacts, will be useful for state purposes. The state would regard external studies more highly, and give them more weight in planning, if that extended range of accepted scenario criteria, including a 'standard model megastorm event,' were applied. Studies, plans and proposals that look ahead only via an obsolete '1-in-100-years' estimate of an event are inadequate, and unhelpful or worse if they create the impression of having addressed actual near-term risk assessment needs.

I would like to see all emergency managers (starting with Cal OES and counties' OES) and storm / flood impact mitigation project planners (starting with CA DWR and USACE) in California apply the results of those accepted revised forecasts and impact studies, ones including model megastorm-scale events, to guide planning for such events, and infrastructure design and planning, and to clearly explain how their plans address the greater evaluated risks. (In a general way, at the framework level, Cal OES has begun this process for one 10-county area in the NCCFRP document.)

When adopted, this would effectively replace all the popular old '100-years-' or 1% AEP-based assessment limits with a defined extreme storm event (with or without a recurrence interval estimate). There should also be clarity, especially if a 'standard megastorm' is not included, on what levels of estimated risk over what time horizon are within the scope of any response and mitigation planning action agenda. Ideally, as proposed here, this would be determined at the state level, but if not, it should be an explicit part of agency reports and proposals including local plans. Limitations regarding the scale of events or the assumed rarity of events should be made explicit, to document the degree of preparation that is within, or beyond, any planning framework that is developed.

[The potential for some resistance to adoption of revised weather, risk and impact estimates (and methods) might be imagined within some institutions invested, literally or figuratively, in the lower, rosier traditional estimates, or in their legacy work. Ultimately, this becomes a personnel matter.]

One important aspect of improving weather forecasting, in conjunction with improving estimates of frequency and magnitude of extreme weather, including establishing the range of upper-end uncertainties, is to enable the safe implementation of Forecast Informed Reservoir Operations at more (or all) large California reservoirs. Executed properly, this FIRO approach will increase the flood-control capacity in reservoirs as storms approach, and carefully retain more water in storage when storms are absent from the forecast. Forecast accuracy is essential; the huge underestimation of inflows at Lake Oroville in February 2017 would not allow for safe FIRO; a realistic handle on possible extreme weather patterns could then add back guidance for an additional, acceptable margin of safety. The State Auditor's report cited below documents the broad uncertainty around CA DWR's current runoff forecast estimates.

Related to this is the need to reassess control capability for all California flood control infrastructure, primarily dams and levees, for a 'standard model megastorm' scenario having a target recurrence interval (possibly a composite of an ensemble of selected simulations from the ARkStorm 2.0 project): generate the expected hydrology including a margin of uncertainty, identify vulnerabilities, develop, prioritize, and schedule (and fund) any redesign and reconstruction work, meanwhile modifying the operating regulations at those reservoir locations to maintain safe practices under the more extreme conditions.

Preparedness, training, rehearsal, assessment

I'd like the state to promote public awareness of and preparedness for extreme weather and flood risks *up to megastorm scale.*

I'd like to see readiness, response and relief training programs that would reach all levels of agencies, and include volunteers and the engaged public, employing hydrological-area-wide multijurisdictional tabletop exercises, drills, and stress tests, at intervals in a five- to ten-year range, rotating around the state. Independent assessment of problems encountered and an agreed approach to address any identified problems could be a part of this program. Among agencies and lead NGOs, MYTEPs involving extreme weather scenarios should be carried out on a repeating five-year, or not more than ten-year, basis in each county or multi-county area. I'd like to see a certification process for local response planning and training for storm emergencies, with training program review by the state with outside consultation, with public comment. I'd like to see a similar periodic 'stress-test' process for assessment of extreme-weather preparedness for local agencies, lead NGOs including the Red Cross, Cal Guard, and FEMA, covering staffing, inventories, warehousing, replenishment, logistics and transport under those conditions. Issue identification, correction and reassessment should be part of the program design.

I believe that emergency management agencies and officials, and infrastructure owner / operators, across California, consistent with the SEP framework, should periodically (ideally not longer than every 10 years, possibly on an alternating five-year schedule with big earthquake drills) carry out statewide or regional table-top exercises and on-the-ground drills to stress-test <u>all</u> of the emergency response preparedness in the state simultaneously—at EOCs and in the field—by simulating the predicted behavior of a unique modeled megastorm system before one actually arrives (also thereafter). Similarly, or concurrently, infrastructure resilience and vulnerability could be reassessed, with an emphasis on 'what if' triggers of failure cascades. The benefit of a statewide exercise is to give Emergency Operations Centers and the full SEMS and Incident Command Structure exposure to a scope of crisis management involving all levels of the ICS when the entire state is impacted.

Building on the ARkStorm approach, or later refinements like ARkStorm 2.0, scientists and technical experts should, for each exercise, present a unique (pick a simulation), detailed storm scenario with defined preconditioning, snowpack, wind, precipitation and rain-on-snow inputs over the landscape, down to local scale. Standard hydrological models and proposed flood control routings would then provide the expected streamflow and floodplain behavior of the storm runoff, much as the flows of 'mathematically upscaled historical storms' were modeled for the 2015 Central Valley Hydrology Study and the 2018-reported Bay / Delta component for the CA4_CCA report (Maendly, 2018). Note that the extreme-storm runoff flow analyses <u>should be independent of any return-interval, flow-frequency, or AEP considerations</u> (though a linkage to a recurrence estimate based on simulations or a synthetic method might be available). For now, megastorms are real things having uncertain (or not yet universally accepted) recurrence frequencies within an unhelpfully changing climate.

An all-levels of government MYTEP framework for coordinated extreme storm response training should be put in place as soon as is practicable. In a TTE or drill, emergency managers and infrastructure operators would use the expert storm scenario and details, then activate and assess responses, and attempt to agree on the evolving, realistic status of communities, activities (like relocation), facilities, and lifeline infrastructure on (ideally) a daily basis, paying particular attention to shortfalls and complications, interdependencies, chokepoints, and likely cascades of failures (a comprehensive and objective catalog of existing vulnerabilities would be essential); each update would be used by all participants to establish the new and evolving conditions and challenges they would face as the situation progresses. Managers running the exercise would periodically inject unexpected events or resolve uncertain consequences during the course of the simulated event. Almost no-one has weeks or months to spend on such a training exercise, so a choice would be made on how much to accelerate the events in the simulation. Spending 2–7 days on such a drill every (5–) 10 years could be very productive (compare this to reservist military training).

Finally, a detailed after-TTE-action report identifying crucial vulnerabilities, including insufficient redundancies, should be prepared, followed by a summary of consequences to the population, to the economy and its sectors, and to finances at all levels. At least some components of this review should be provided by independent outside experts. Such reports would serve as 'mini-ARkStorm reports' focused on impacts and informed by outcomes of simulations, and including recommendations or action points.

Yes, this level of training would be a big undertaking for California (for the world's sixth-largest economy... or, fifth? fourth?). But remember, the 2008 "Shake-Out" exercise involved millions of people in a drill simulating a major earthquake in Southern California. Japan holds a nationwide earthquake drill every September 1, the anniversary of the 1923 Great Kanto earthquake "which left more than 100,000 people dead in and around Tokyo." We justify big exercises like that with the knowledge that major earthquakes are recurring and inevitable.

A megastorm, another recurring and inevitable threat, is likely to be much more challenging, potentially deadlier, less familiar, and more expensive, affecting many more people directly, than a coastal earthquake. By some computer models megastorms may be or will soon become more frequent in CA than major earthquakes are. Unlike an earthquake, a storm sequence is also going to have a run-up period with advance warning, and direct impacts will unfold, progress, and persist over days and weeks, rather than in seconds or minutes; some repairs to lifelines during persistent storms or flooding might not be possible as rapidly as for seismic damage. Major storm and flood TTEs must focus as much on planning and preparedness in a run-up period as they will on emergency response and on relief operations. Because a different range of mindsets and action tempos are involved, compared to (for example) an earthquake, a storm / flood event rehearsal is not a generic emergency training; it deserves its own priority and place in any schedule. Reinforcing the concept that storm and flood response must begin before the impacts arrive is important.

Promote volunteerism; train volunteers, emphasizing local service. Assess NGO staffing needs in catastrophic scenarios, starting with the American Red Cross. I'm aware of present-day concerns.

The alternative to meeting this planning and training challenge would be, in the aftermath of the storms, to offer "We did not imagine that we would have to face such an unprecedented situation."

More on planning, especially evacuation and shelter; communication

I have concerns about the status of our official evacuation planning, based on research and conversations, and reflected in this recently quoted advice from a California DWR manager, referring to anticipated mid-2023 flooding threats in the San Joaquin Valley:

> "Be aware of your flood risks… Be prepared by **planning out evacuation routes**…" said Jeremy Arrich, manager of the division of flood management with the DWR—Los Angeles Times, April 11, 2023

Why, exactly, should Jane Citizen, and thousands like her, have the primary responsibility for figuring this out by herself (and, collectively among us, thousands of times) when considerable experience with hydrology, forecasting, engineering, topography and terrain features, road conditions, traffic control, and any non-public emergency plans, threat assessments, and/or potential real-time developments would be necessary for competently selecting a reliable evacuation route plan? After the county sheriffs, Caltrans has this responsibility, perhaps shared in the event with CHP, according to California's SEP, but that might be interpreted as the task of coming up with solutions 'on the fly,' as a <u>response</u> to a situation, rather than as an advance planning assignment.

I emphasize this point in part because I've seen, a few years back, botched, 'fend for yourself' wildfire evacuation in my patch, and yes, I shudder (wildfire evacuation planning and prep was a part of my own duties, five decades ago). If this sort of possibility bothers you, you do have a voice.

In parallel with providing evacuation plans (and public access to them), the plans for redeployment of public sector and medical personnel to destination locations should be thoroughly developed and made public in general terms. The public will also feel a need to know what provisions are being made for security of their property (if it survives) in areas under evacuation orders.

I would like to see, for the plausible lowland flooding event(s), establishment of a set of reliable evacuation routes to an adequate number of designated relocation areas, with route signage (for Sacramento-region counties as a minimum example here). Neighborhoods should be familiar with their own routes, marked memorably with color-coded signage designations like "Apple, Blueberry, Cantaloupe, Dewberry," etc.; easily visible in storm conditions. Similar schemes could be replicated wherever dense populations in at-risk areas must someday relocate to pre-established sheltering sites. Of course, those sites must be determined (soon), and ultimately prepared for service in conjunction with local authorities. At-risk neighborhoods should be familiarized with their designated destinations in advance (soon). Routes should be pre-hardened and well defended by state and county road crews; residents should be advised routinely that conditions on the ground might require Caltrans and CHP to divert to alternate routing with appropriate portable signage [Note to legislative analysts: budget for programmable electronic signs].

Proposals: On a three-year rolling basis, on staggered, publicized spring dates, neighborhoods could have voluntary sheriff- (SO) and CHP-coordinated evacuation drills to drive their designated route and see their pre-planned destination (*first, we need destinations; see below*). It would be nice to arrange a picnic and entertainment for participants arriving at those sites; food trucks, music and a bouncy-castle would not be over the top (cheap, as public safety goes), in addition to checklists, guidelines, preparedness kits and literature, and examples of tenting grounds and RV arrangements. It might also preview an indication of what actual traffic congestion would look like under more difficult and stressful conditions; that experience could help SOs, CHP, Caltrans, OES agencies, potentially Cal Guard and those transporting non-mobile populations, and other planners, who should also be evaluating any weather vulnerabilities along the routes and flagging them up for Caltrans or local public works.

And here we've arrived at the key issue of… where would more than a million people from the Central Valley floodplain—as an example, among other floodplains in the state—relocate to for an indefinite period of weeks?

Several planning documents, for example the NCCFRP, assess the *'from'* side of catastrophic flood evacuations, but <u>none that I've seen describe the *'to'* side</u>. Add in the assumption, per USGS and CC4_CCA, of road network closures in multiple directions (as I edit this today, in March 2023, a section of U.S. 99 is closed in both directions due to flooding). A state-led panel or team, with local partners from involved jurisdictions and possible FEMA and DOD input, should assess where that displaced population can be directed or escorted, and safely and effectively sheltered, and what would be required (below, a planning process for counties is suggested). Because we have useable hard structures to shelter only a fraction of that population, at a bare minimum that means acres and acres of well-drained, gently sloping, preferably porous-surfaced (*e.g.*, with crushed gravel) land with good access, parking, RV and tent areas, with services and access needed for relief operations. After assessing what is already available and its suitability, the remaining need can be defined and geolocated.

At a guess (and as a proposal), undeveloped land in the low foothills above floodplains would need to be acquired and prepared. This would not be extremely expensive, as infrastructure projects go; however, it could easily seem like an extravagance, 'a folly,'… until the day when this relocation capability is needed to avert a mass casualty event. A dual land-use solution would make sense, and the first one that comes to mind is a design for solar PVE farms that could also provide some structural shelter from the elements (while providing a cost-recovery income stream, more in-state power generation, and at least some emergency power at microgrid scale). Similar dual-purpose 'solar canopy' structures exist over many parking lots today. A state-led initiative in this direction, perhaps funding a design competition among university teams, would be appropriate.

Some proposals for consideration:

- Cal OES should revisit the NCCFRP to advance it from the framework level (of operational concepts) down into detailed planning. The state's THIRA document has, as one planning capability target, defining the sequence and scope of tasks needed in any threat scenario; I'd take that literally to mean 'well or fully defined.' [Arguments against detailed planning usually invoke the anticipated need for flexibility in response to unpredictable events, but really, WWWD?: (1) existing and recalibrated flood maps, plus (2) recent and emerging extreme storm models with hydrological data, plus (3) ongoing flood control (including levees) exceedance or failure assessments, provide a very clear, likely and reasonably predictable master planning scenario, which is especially useful if each river drainage is modeled for its worst plausible case.] THIRA (2019) and NCCFRP (2018) as well as USGS (2011) provide enough detail to allow a reasonable catastrophic flood event model scenario to be described at this time; more so if the continuing ARkStorm 2.0 project delivers full single-event hydrology (which, in a single simulation, may describe near-maximal impacts in some areas but only sub-maximal impacts elsewhere; better yet would be to collate maximum local impacts up to at least an estimated 0.5% AEP level from across the 800 available simulations; see Chapter 20). Of course, storm impacts other than flooding must also receive their due.

- Cal OES and partners should repeat this process for all significant floodplains, beyond just the Delta plan (since enlarged to the NCCFRP) mandated by the legislature in the Sacramento-San Joaquin Delta Emergency Preparedness Act of 2008.

- Then evaluate threats off the floodplains.

- General catastrophic event response planning including a version of the NCCFRP and future plans should be public information. The recent (July, 2023; link below) online posting of an NCCFRP fact sheet with general details is a welcome step.

- Cal OES should notify each county, including SO, OES and HHS offices, about the expected size and needs of populations that will relocate from or to each area, and the routes they are expected or likely to travel, and any anticipated problems. Right now, we have a rough outline of the 'from' *but not the 'to.'* Emphasize that the scope of the impacts renders past experience inadequate for 'winging it' through an adequate response. A best scientific estimate of the yearly potential for such an event should also be communicated, as well as notes on possible complicating factors such as loss of grid power or fuels.

- The state could invite or instruct county and local officials to take a year to work with those estimates, and develop a detailed response plan, including all mass care and shelter (ESF-6) functions, then (I'll suggest) present those plans at a meeting of all counties within a feasible (perhaps hydrological) incident command / management area. Issues, gaps, conflicts and objections should be identified and addressed at such meetings. Refine and repeat.

Finally, to encourage early and smoother, orderly evacuations, destination relocation areas should be opened for use whenever an evacuation warning (prior to an order) is considered likely and imminent. This brings us to the topic of response posture.

Posture

Before impacts of forecasted, high-confidence extreme weather events arrive, the state should lean proactively toward a regional or statewide activation of its emergency response (SEMS), perhaps by emergency proclamation, to allow smoother coordination of the ready response across counties and agencies, and to avoid some possible escalation delays.

California's complete SEP describes, in different passages, either proactive or reactive stances at defined points in a progressing weather event. A reader can find guidance and interpretations in either direction. Provided are indications of a general sequence of escalation steps, somewhat elastically linked to progressive developments on the ground. This may reflect an anticipated need for a flexible response; however, a possible downside would be any latitude for interpretations that could miss opportunities for preemptive or timely actions and deployments.

I ultimately decided not to attempt to sort out those issues, memorialized in state documents, for you; I'm not sure it can be done clearly or precisely at this time. I'll just present an example of possible concern. The state's active, defined Response Phase 2 (or 2a) may, or may not, begin with <u>the onset of severe flooding</u>. One possible interpretation of those passages could lead to a late start for launching an evacuation (in Pajaro, CA, in March, 2023, an anticipated levee failure caused flooding that trapped hundreds of people, many of whom had to be rescued by Cal Guard). Now imagine a massive evacuation over a vast area. I'll suggest that such SEP and subsidiary document language be made more consistent and explicit, leaning toward early action. In a crisis, ambiguity is unlikely to help.

I stress the great value in having a response posture that is proactive rather than reactive (the word 'response' implies a reaction, but emergency managers <u>do</u>, and frontline responders may, take action in response to the <u>threat</u>, not the later consequence, in the run-up to a weather event). So, how quickly is a response escalated in a developing situation? I think this deserves some attention. In some state planning documents, we can read that increased support can be provided 'once local capabilities are overwhelmed.' A local official told me that their agency can request support from the state level "once our [local] resources are exhausted." Taken literally, that is a reactive response posture that could prove tardy and costly. While in reality emergency managers might anticipate and trigger an escalation of uninterrupted support (Cal OES is also, in some passages, tasked to meet <u>anticipated</u> needs of counties and Operational Areas, or OAs), why not put clear language in all EOPs that encourages that prudent, forward-leaning approach?

How might any 'wait, wait' guidance play out in reality? Here is a simplified, possibly relevant timeline for the actual February / March 2023 snow emergency in the San Bernardino Mountains, as taken from news reporting (citations below):

- February 23: an NWS alert warns " "Travel will be VERY DIFFICULT TO IMPOSSIBLE due to the extremely heavy snow and extremely high winds expected," the weather service notice said, emphasizing the danger in capital letters."
- February 24: Blizzard starts at about 4 a.m. Late that day residents begin to report that they are snowbound and unprepared. "Several thousand requests" for help begin to arrive at the county emergency hotline.
- February 28: San Bernardino Co. Sheriff's Department sends out message for people to text or call 911 if trapped inside the home.
- March 1: State of Emergency declared by Governor; Cal Fire deployment ordered, some units are ready on site on March 3.
- March 2: California National Guard crews arrive midafternoon, reporting to Cal Fire; air assets placed on standby.
- March 3: "Officials admit being unprepared for epic mountain blizzard, leaving many trapped and desperate." —Los Angeles Times headline, March 4, 2023
- March 4 on: contact and rescues accelerate.
- March 7: A resident is quoted: "More resources" would be helpful for mountain communities... "I know local authorities are doing their best, but **the resources were too slim, and they waited a little too long to deploy more resources**," she said.
- Reported fatalities: 13. Officials are reluctant to attribute them to the storm event

I think this incident (count the days), taken at face value without benefit of an insider perspective, may offer a good case for establishing a more forward-leaning posture toward emergency response escalation, within the SEMS / IC structure. If escalation depends (in part) upon upward requests from local officials, are the correct incentives for proactive triggers in place? Would anything lead to a reluctance to ask for help? Are avoidable delays a potential protocol issue?

There are different ways in which state action can be initiated, for example the multiple paths toward issuance of an emergency proclamation. Any ideal emergency response protocol would rely upon a short chain of activation steps designed with robustness, redundancy or delegation of authority as needed, and a bias toward timeliness / urgency, and against delay. Rectify any possible shortcomings. Avoid any scenario in which county sheriffs and officials attempt, for longer than absolutely necessary, to independently address in-county needs during a developing multi-county catastrophe (such as a megastorm), without coordination or resolution of potential conflicts or gaps.

Also, develop additional response strategies for 'no-warning' evacuation scenarios, such as in rapid levee collapses, onset of dam issues, and fast-moving wildfires, potentially coinciding with compromised communications and/or transportation. [While checking final proofs of this book, Lahaina, Maui, Hawaii has burned to the ground, with great loss of life, and some official statements. As with any tragedy, I hope that a complete review of warnings and responses will provide more lessons that will be communicated widely and taken to heart.]

Relief and responder agencies in early 2023 were doing post-impact 'wellness checks' with residents who became isolated by storm impacts in California. It could arguably be more effective to apply the same energies and resources to doing advance 'preparedness checks' before an event, to communicate the need for preparedness and to log, for follow-up, potential problems that could develop for residents who identify concerns or issues.

Paying for preparedness: rather than call budget surpluses a 'rainy day fund,' why not earmark at least a part of them for a 'Big One' reserve fund? That could improve public and legislative understanding and support for reserves of financial resilience to catastrophe. The state can't print money; would it be creditworthy after a large disaster?

Planning and preparation, by level

Individual, family and friends—check. Neighborhood and community—check. Earlier chapters covered many of the issues.
Town, City, County—check. These are the front lines; see notes above. Get discussions started. Disaster preparedness and pre-planning, in writing, in public documents, in advance. Explain roles of Sheriff's Office, other LEO, County OES and HHS, other responders, and officials in Incident Command and Emergency Management authority. Regular (biennial?) drills, TTEs and 'stress-tests,' under unique scenarios, including LEOs, responders, volunteers, and transport, shelter, care and medical staff and facilities, scaled to reflect local realities and anticipated impacts from other jurisdictions. Pre-assessment and designation of shelter options under winter and flood conditions including community isolation. Pre-assessment of population needs, including arriving displaced populations, and how those needs will be met. Communication >> public awareness of local plans and designated shelter providers. Rehearse SEMS-based umbrella coordination of volunteer organization efforts, CERT teams, Red Cross, etc. Provision for administrative support for potentially isolated

communities, including provisions for LEO, emergency services, and road network, bridge and infrastructure maintenance and repair or rapid replacement; also support 'local council' coordination addressing needs and shelter services. Support local relief, resiliency and preparedness initiatives and instigate them in communities where appropriate. Take advantage of state and federal agency programs for training and preparedness. The public may confirm a clear and documented approach to local Incident Command and administration at county or more local levels; get details. Why the focus on a clear IC protocol?

> "As the school district's police chief at the time, Arredondo was the de facto incident commander at the scene, state investigators and law enforcement analysts said.
>
> Arredondo has said he did not consider himself to be the incident commander." —CNN news report, "Uvalde Under Scrutiny," August 5, 2022

State—check. The SEP master plan provides many of these preparedness elements under the SEMS umbrella. The state has a role in:

- state and local level training and preparedness, including monitoring compliance;
- ensuring a uniform policy of rebroadcasting weather alerts and warnings over county-level alert networks;
- identifying and prioritizing infrastructure and manpower needs, and working with counties to identify and prioritize improvements (roads and services hardening, prepositioning of supplies, materiel, equipment, personnel) for communities, especially those at most at risk of isolation or deprivation;
- providing funding for hardening lifeline infrastructure and for emergency services; pursuing federal funding initiatives for infrastructure hardening and resilience / preparedness;
- maintaining active cooperation structure with FEMA, DOD, USACE, Reclamation, USGS, NWS and other agencies;
- promoting public awareness about hazards and planning, including sources for formal alert information and the likely necessary / recommended public responses, via annual mailings and television broadcasts, a master web site, PSAs for broadcasters, YouTube videos, and other media;
- taking the lead role in promoting and ensuring local-scale evacuation and relocation pre-planning; evaluate routes with Caltrans; determine which destination counties can absorb what numbers of displaced persons; make those plans public; identify predicted needs of refugee-impacted communities and prepare and provide for those needs.

If you interact with state officials, you can communicate your need and desire for clear information about their actual plans and preparedness for a catastrophic winter storm emergency. In particular, Cal OES, Caltrans, and CHP could release details of storm and flood evacuation master plans, and from OES, a public version (hopefully expanded) of the currently restricted Northern California Catastrophic Flood Response Plan. Are other area Flood Response Plans in the works?

Federal—check. Support all the above, from state levels on down. Find ways to help the most disadvantaged populations prepare and survive. As part of the NEMS structure, designate an appropriate agency to lead other agencies to produce an independent, detailed 'after-action' report following each regional or statewide 'tabletop stress-test exercise' and include recommendations. Also issue an improved version of the impacts section of an ARkStorm-style report every 10 years after new census data and weather data are available. Specifically include a greater focus on the human dimension of the event, and advise state and county authorities on any federal estimate of the numerical range of displaced persons they could expect to be taking in, and what levels of need and care would be anticipated for quantified sub-populations. Ensure that detailed coordination plans are memorialized, for example building on the 2008 Base Plan, and participate in rehearsals. Review adequacy of flood control infrastructure under ARkStorm-scale conditions and flag vulnerabilities and probable events; help design and fund corrections and improvements. Review methods for estimating magnitude-specific flood return intervals and uncertainties in view of geologic and USGS-led 2011 storm history and modeling; seriously evaluate amending estimation methods, for example by including ranges of predictions determined by simulation methods under appropriate climate assumptions.

Proposals, by focus area

Administration, public services

Re-assess the flood risk to administrative and emergency management and operations facilities using megastorm-scale assumptions, preferably with additional fine-scale flood routing and mapping. Based on risk and practical considerations, prioritize and initiate the phase-out and relocation of the most vulnerable government / public service facilities, including emergency services and management, law enforcement (including jails; prisoner relocation ties up huge amounts of resources), fire and ambulance, hospitals and long term care facilities, and emergency shelters to sites which are secure from storm and flood damage, and from fire. In cases where relocation distances would be too great, consider phasing in elevated structures or complexes which might safely remain dry and self-sufficient (a 'tall order') during area flooding. A 20–30-year timetable? Make sure residential and inpatient care facilities have ready evacuation plans and capabilities; at destinations (*which are still needed*) these populations will have special needs. To serve existing floodplains communities, consider any best options for creating flood-secure facilities, vs the possibility that such communities may be entirely evacuated, facilities staff and all, under megastorm conditions (a fundamental planning requirement). Draft plans for how local service providers would continue service to a population that is displaced (see also ICS below).

Draft clear plans for how administrative responsibilities and public services will be addressed in the event that any communities become isolated, with or without embedded administrative and/or LEO personnel. Clarify role and on-site specifics of an Incident Command Structure (ICS) under circumstances of local isolation as well as during relocation.

Longer term—and here's a big idea to chew on—consider the desirability of (1) having the administrative capital of the world's sixth-largest economy (fifth? fourth?) remain on a floodplain behind aging levees, at the confluence of two major rivers, below dams, in an era when extreme storms and floods will become larger and more frequent; or (2) alternatively, as agency headquarters and administrative office structures approach the end of their useful lifespans, consider building their replacement structures within a new CAL GOV campus located on higher ground, where threats are minimal and access and services can be maintained. One possibility might be the area south of U.S. 50 between Clarksville and Sprekelsville, very roughly bracketing the 1000' elevation level, less than 30 miles from downtown Sacramento. Other options exist to the west. Seem daunting? Indonesia is currently relocating their national capital to a safer island. In my lifetime, Brazil and Germany have also moved their capitals.

Development and settlement

Pause or halt all new development in flood-prone areas, at least until a genuinely comprehensive cost-benefit analysis of the practice, including public costs of all losses or subsidies, and all human costs, are prepared and debated. Someone will ultimately take losses on any speculative land investments; unfortunately, without action it may be our living and future taxpayers. If we accept that land speculation is involved, are financial safety nets appropriate? Would lottery tickets be appropriate compensation?

Begin / continue a difficult local and national conversation about how to move forward in the face of millions of residents, dwellings, and businesses that have been situated in flood-prone (and disaster-prone) areas. Assess the public and/or private costs of establishing truly adequate levees, and subsidizing property losses and relief efforts, vs the costs of other alternatives including relocation. In the interim, if housing in flood-prone areas becomes less desirable, and relatively more affordable, the existing trend for the flood-threatened population to be people of limited means would presumably accelerate, further complicating evacuations and posing a net decline to public safety; meanwhile, housing stock in such areas is likely to deteriorate. This will affect many different calculations, from flood control investment to evacuation logistics to recovery prospects. We ought not to neglect the present and potential demographics of flood risks. Bear in mind that after a flood, affected and threatened properties are very likely to be even less desirable.

Disclose actual flood risks and uncertainties to homebuyers, residents, and businesses, in an effective manner. Do not rely solely upon traditional AEP/ACE estimates which are arguably underestimates.

If you own property on, or live on, low ground, even as a renter, I would recommend that you consider obtaining and maintaining all of the flood insurance coverage that makes sense, even if the coverage is capped at less than the value of your property, and even if you are not in a traditionally-defined NFIP SFHA 1.0% or 0.2% AEP flood zone but have reason to foresee possible flooding. Remember, your standard homeowner's policy excludes flood damage, and might define a flood as <u>any ground-surface flow of water</u> (these determinations and exclusions can be complex, even in flood insurance policy coverage; consult with your agent). And for you, and your kids and grandkids, if they listen to you… when you or they are contemplating a move to a new home, you may want to consider two words: "high ground." This is not advice; you have your own lifestyle and investment priorities. I'm just offering my awareness of a factor which I believe is worth some careful thought.

Transportation

Designate essential transportation corridors, especially those running north-south, and those that connect reliably to the full interstate highway and rail systems; improve and harden those road and rail links to provide unimpeded access to all 'high ground' areas under storm and flood conditions. Evacuation route connectors between floodplains and higher destinations, for example, should also be prioritized for improvements and 'hardening.' For example, flood maps show possible flooding vulnerabilities on many routes heading east from the Central Valley to the Foothills; this is probably a more widespread general issue. Some of these routes were flooded in 2023 even without levee failures.

All the above would become the major transportation network during a megastorm flood; the rail network will involve similar considerations. Secondary roads into potentially isolated communities also deserve prioritized improvements (or, alternatively perhaps, greater overall investment in community resilience and intermittent self-sufficiency).

Because of how the coastline, valleys and mountains tend to run in California, several major highways have long stretches with a north-south orientation. I-5 and U.S. 99, major transport routes, are considered to be (or are known to be) vulnerable to flooding in places, as are portions of roads along the coast ranges and eastern California. If the Sierra pass routes are closed, including I-80, and if I-5 closes south of Dunsmuir or elsewhere toward or into Oregon, then overland supply routes would have to enter California from the southeast.

Choices for stormproof long-distance north-south routes include elevating and improving I-5 and U.S. 99 wherever flood risks exist, and making similar improvements plus eliminating landslide and erosion risks for long-distance highways in the hills to the east and west. If the floodplains highways are not elevated, then the hill-country routes could be the only long-haul north-south arteries, and improvements should be prioritized, especially low-foothills routes like SR 49.

Southern California has a somewhat different geography and terrain, but similar principles and considerations will apply.

Two remaining areas that need attention are road connections around Bakersfield where storm and flood may prevent access to U.S. 99 and I-5, and conditions east of the mountains that could cause other route closures including out-of-state closures, both for the southeast and for I-80 (if otherwise open).

Any <u>new</u> road and bridge (re)construction, of any size, should be winter-hardened and correctly situated, with priority going to hardening of the essential road network, including east-west routes and lifeline routes to relocation sites and to isolated communities. *The best available hazard assessments, not only the NOAA Atlas 14, should be employed in planning.* State agencies including Caltrans should work with DOD and Cal Guard to estimate the number of possible failures of existing bridges, in their current condition, on essential routes under extreme model storm conditions (which are likely to exceed original design assumptions and requirements), prioritize their improvement, inventory the available number and capacities of portable bridges (Bailey bridges), determine how many should be acquired, and where they should be stored, prepositioned or deployed (by Caltrans and in military inventories) to address most likely needs. Use the same approach to forecast where, even after prioritized improvements, temporary roadbuilding capabilities under winter conditions may be needed in a present-day event to secure an essential road network.

For all roadways, implement a program for managing and/or removing stream-adjacent vegetation to some distance upstream of smaller bridges and culverts (especially those with small channel cross-sections, low clearance, or with posts or pilings spaced at short intervals), to minimize storm-caused debris flow and damming. Even so, trees and logs may travel great distances in floods. Annually remove any accumulated debris lodged at the upstream side of those structures. Initiate a state or USACE engineering review of solutions (unless some are known) to protect bridges and culverts from debris accumulation, for example to determine whether any physical debris traps upstream of smaller or older bridges or culverts on vital roads are feasible. Traps must be accessible for maintenance. Implement a statewide standard based on those recommendations.

In isolated areas, develop a coordinated state and local storm-response plan (for example, based on AR Cat4 and Cat5 forecasts) to embed road crew (and utility, including propane delivery) personnel and equipment at or near local road maintenance facilities (for example), and plan for the pre-positioning of equipment with adequate fuels and materials where the community need for road or utility repair and maintenance will likely be greatest.

Determine what civilian and commercial air travel facilities will be impacted by extreme flooding and establish the roles which non-civilian facilities can play. For any future airport improvements, long-term flood-proofing would be required.

Evaluate impacts of water levels and currents on port facilities and functions, and shipping; determine technical solutions (if any) to identified problems.

Identify vulnerabilities to the rail network and determine what alternatives will be required to compensate for specific failures.

Energy

I would want state or other (interstate) agencies periodically to produce a comprehensive report on what part of our energy supply and infrastructure is at risk under some standard megastorm-scale scenario(s) supported by modeled hydrology data, and what energy shortfalls are likely, to provide planners and the public with a realistic projection of what to expect, as well as a list of priorities for improving resilience and maintaining supply and distribution of hydrocarbon fuels and electricity. Having read some related assessment reports, I have to add that optimistic assessments are not suitable for public safety planning; even 'median estimates' mean that 50% of outcomes will be worse than anticipated. If details of vulnerabilities are deemed sensitive, then realistic expert bottom-line predictions by area would be adequate for public preparedness.

Harden (including flood-proofing) all physical plant and infrastructure. Phase out of facilities at risk of flooding; opportunistically shift electrical production (fueled, legacy hydroelectric, or solar) and distribution facilities to high ground in a phased replacement scheme. Design solar installations that do not require flat low land. Avoid scheduling maintenance during winter on elements of hydroelectric / flood-control facilities that could reduce options for water flow management. Maintain a distributed inventory of critical equipment, for example transmission towers vulnerable to wind or erosion, pumps, etc. Apply megastorm impact assessments modeled along the lines of the CA4_CCA assessments to preparedness planning.

California's Fourth Climate Change Assessment and sub-reports (2018) represent a very similar 'parallel' assessment initiative being undertaken by California's energy and resource agencies; it is limited by strictly focusing on future climate change impacts rather than existing needs. To a simplistic first approximation, the 30–80-year CA4_CCA impacts-timeline assessment for identified vulnerabilities to energy infrastructure could be compressed down into a single hypothetical month, to simulate the immediate challenges of a megastorm in a present-day winter (or a future one incorporating weather trends; sea level rise impacts are a special case but overlap somewhat with storm surge impacts). Going forward, the state should jointly assess <u>both</u> existing risk and risks expected to increase due to climate change. As argued above, both present- and future-risk assessment scenarios should extend to include megastorm-scale events; a 'standard model megastorm' could be defined for that purpose. The assessment should be comprehensive, statewide, beginning with high-risk zones.

One such zone is the Delta, the nexus for Northern California natural gas distribution. Develop a plan to relocate gas and other pipelines to safer areas, or engineer and build 'invulnerable' pipelines and crossings there.

To support resilience, integrate into preparedness planning the assessment of the role of and options for mitigation of household-scale energy needs, including on-site electricity production by end-users, favoring available renewables to augment or supplant hydrocarbon-fuel-limited generators, and newer storage technologies and designs, from portable units that accept charging inputs from portable solar PVE panels, to EVs with V2G or V2H connections. Consider all ways to improve resilience at household scale in addition to community scale (*e.g.*, with microgrids).

Other infrastructure

Assess all other lifeline infrastructure, including water systems, for storm and flood vulnerabilities; prioritize and correct issues; have implementable backup plans for all eventualities. Note the example of the Los Angeles Aqueduct failure report cited in Chapter 6.

[Note on general resilience costs: Infrastructure improvements on these scales have very substantial costs (billions, spread over decades), which, however, are much less than the full cost of a major destructive storm sequence (one or more trillions). On the positive side, investment and initiatives would provide major gains in employment, income and economic activity (with taxable returns). If some of those gains could be directed to further improving resilience at a personal level, or beyond, through a supportive tax policy, then the safety enhancements would ripple further outward.]

Supply chain

Legislate or order a prohibition on construction permitting / licensing of warehousing in low-lying or flood-risk areas including FEMA/NFIP 0.2% risk zones, for any facilities that will store and distribute food, medical items, critical equipment and parts, basic 'emergency' construction and structure-protection materials, and all materials including relief supplies that may be deemed essential under a state of emergency or during reconstruction. Phase in re-zoning to higher defensible ground and offer relocation incentives. Repurpose low-lying buildings for activities deemed non-critical. Promote a departure from 'just in time' acquisition of essential items every year in the months leading up to winter, favoring Q3 and Q4 increased local and end-user inventories, from the consumer level up; allow some tax relief to offset costs of transient inventory increases; this option could become flexibly responsive in future if developing Pacific Ocean or other conditions begin to provide more reliable 'lead time' predictive forecasts for a winter megastorm season. As forecasting improves, there may be enough lead time to permit a federal role via the Defense Production Act to increase and position stocks of critical supplies and equipment.

If a catastrophic flood occurs sooner rather than later, rescind the permits for any warehouse that becomes flooded, unless or until non-critical uses are proposed for the facility.

Insurance

Some questions about NFIP flood insurance deserve some thought:

- Why are there coverage caps on NFIP policies? On life insurance; one pays accordingly for the desired coverage. Does the Federal Government want to limit the size of its flood risk exposure? What would that suggest about the magnitude of this risk, nationally? As property values rise and coverage does not, how do lenders manage their increased exposure to loss?

- Should properties behind levees continue to be treated as though they are outside the 1% AEP zone, thus paying less for flood insurance?

- Within the 1% AEP (or so-called '100-year') flood zone boundaries there are some properties with shorter average flood recurrence intervals, such as 20- or 30-year flood recurrences. Should all properties within the 1% boundary be assessed as having a 1% annual-chance risk? Is finer-scale risk assessment appropriate? Within a zone, should a property that, based on history, is frequently flooded and has had multiple successive damage claims receive the same coverage and policy terms as one that will only rarely flood?

- Should there be a lifetime cap on flood insurance payouts for individual properties, as there is for some medical and long term care policy coverages?

- After some frequency of repeated flood insurance claim payments, should relinquishment of the property to a public open space or wetlands designation be a condition of payment of a final claim?

More generally, with homeowners' insurance, what happens if more insurers continue to exit more markets due to increasing climate hazards?

Review the general coverage situation and have the State Insurance Commissioner and the NFIP decide on the best appropriate short- and long-term remedies for insufficient flood or damage coverage. Reach out to property owners to (re)educate or incentivize them. Address the flood insurance needs of renters, beginning with education and awareness. Set realistic fair premiums (this is now underway at FEMA/NFIP, as of 2021).

Educate policyholders about any coverage exclusions for flowing surface water, and about correction of any potential hazard situations such as channels becoming dammed by debris, or debris being swept into structures, or flood damage to live electric lines, etc. With respect to hazard mitigation and loss prevention, consider expanded approaches. Similar to the Fire Safe Councils campaign, consider creating and promoting proactive local Storm / Flood Safe Council programs aimed at addressing on-site and neighborhood flow, drainage and vegetation issues and interacting with authorities and funders regarding larger concerns. Local councils, especially with grant support, could (as one example) use crews to potentially extend water-channel vegetation removal efforts, upstream of road crossings, in conjunction with what Caltrans and counties are willing or able to do.

Educate homeowners' policy holders about any coverage exclusions for earth movement including subsidence, landslides, and rock, (mud?,) and debris flows, which may be numerous during extreme storm conditions; develop coverage remedies. [As climate changes, the costs of insuring against damage from natural hazards could become prohibitive. Some hard truths may be emerging.]

Establish a conceptual framework for the evolution of floodplain insurance vs risk exposure and mitigation, and the potential costs to the public including liability exposure. The costs of emergency services and recovery funding should not be ignored. Convene an expert body to advise the legislature on floodplain management options and comprehensive costs.

Require prescription drug plans to cover personal medication reserves needed for emergency preparedness.

Communications

Ensure that local officials are transmitting state and federal warnings and emergency alerts including weather alerts and advisories, in a consistent and uniform manner statewide, and not on a discretionary basis. Resident participation in official alert services is elective; determine which serious emergencies should also require 'push notification' of alerts to all local phones (cell phones present, but with non-local numbers, should also be hit). Ensure that any agencies with public contact responsibilities during an emergency, for example Sheriff's Offices and county OES, feature clear and distinct icons for emergency alerts and information, located high up on each official home page such that they can be seen and accessed on any device as soon as that page opens.

Require that official agency sites, rather than social media feeds, be the primary access for official and emergency information (and support that, as discussed below). Social media companies, which have business and other agendas, which may act in unpredictable, arbitrary and capricious ways, which are not regulated utilities, are not 'journals of record,' and which many people avoid for various reasons including privacy issues, owner agendas and disinformation problems, may have a <u>secondary</u> role in amplifying emergency information mirrored from agency sites. If that point is unclear, consider this March 2023 notice from the National Weather Service:

> "Twitter announced on 3/29/23 that it will begin limiting automated tweets. Should this implementation occur, the automated warning graphics shared on this account may not be posted. Have multiple ways to receive weather information and alerts." [Short version from NWS: Don't rely on Twitter for NWS warnings.]

This policy fiasco came into effect on April 14, 2023, per NWS offices all across the USA:

> "April 14 | Twitter is currently restricting @ NWSacramento's automated Tweets for the following products as they are issued:
> - Tornado Warnings
> - Severe Thunderstorm Warnings
> - Flash Flood Warnings
> - Special Weather Statements

> "Twitter is now limiting automated tweets and as a result this account can no longer post all watches/warnings/advisories as they are issued. We will continue to provide general updates, but ensure that you have multiple means for receiving weather information & alerts. [NWS Hanford] [Automated tsunami warnings, which can be very urgent, were also now blocked by Twitter.]

> "A Broken Twitter Means Broken Disaster Response." — Lede from November 19, 2022 article by Molly Taft, re-upped by interviewee Dr. Samantha Montano, July 2, 2023, after new access limits were enacted.

Social media accounts have become popular for official business in part because of their reach, but also because the applications make it simple to post information, and then capture a link to paste into an agency web page, without special skills. The state or even FEMA could develop a secure site and application to allow the same ease of content posting and link recapture onto county SO and OES pages, with social media companies then being the secondary sites for further dissemination of emergency and safety information. Also,

Evaluate effectiveness of a master statewide one-stop website and graphical interface for <u>all</u> current emergency notices including extreme forecasts, alerts, warnings, and orders, plus incident status updates and road closures. Flag 'push' notifications to devices in urgent emergencies.

Supporting resilience and preparedness

Provide a capped ($100 per annum?) state tax credit or deduction for, or eliminate the sales tax on, certain personal emergency equipment, for example backup battery packs for cell phones and other communications devices. Review what sort of equipment should be on a sales-tax carve-out for emergency gear and supplies, for example water purification solutions, reflective thermal blankets, etc. Enhance programs, including grant programs from CDFA and other agencies, leading to increased citizen and community preparedness as outlined in earlier chapters.

Additional guidance from USGS

In the 2011 ARkStorm report, the study teams provided several extensive lists of actions that were recommended to be taken in order to improve preparedness and resilience at all levels. I've opted to leave them out of this streamlined presentation, but they are available to you in the original USGS ARkStorm report, in a more scattered form, online at no cost. If you are serious about improving resilience and preparedness at the state / society level, it's worth reading this advice from USGS and experts. See also the more general 'lessons learned principles' presented by Cal OES in the 2018 SHMP, which I provided in an earlier chapter.

Storm, flood, weather: technical matters, and communicating them

I'd like hydrologists and meteorologists [the upcoming generation?] to propose a new classification system for storm- / flood-event magnitude, and flood zones, that is free of probabilistic / time-based labeling. Let accountants apply 'true' probabilities in a transparent way for fiscal purposes, but use different terminology in the public arena. There are numerous problems with the accepted traditional approach, the most obvious of which are persistent public confusion and the fact that the estimated event probabilities, even when not inaccurate, keep shifting from decade to decade. There is no clear fix for that except to apply a completely new naming convention, reflecting magnitudes and impacts, which should be applied to storms, runoff, floods and flood zones. Wean the public from the illusion of a scientifically validated reprieve.

I'd like to see improvement including standardization of graphical weather forecast and weather hazard warning images, to provide clear, balanced, intuitive and familiar weather messaging. Elements that should be present in standard 'strong weather graphics' include, (1) for longer range projections of 10–15 days, both magnitude and probability information* including 'most likely event magnitude' and 'most extreme event magnitude having an estimated probability of [say] 10+%,' and (2), for short-range forecasts of 3–5 days, a multi-day time sequence of expected impacts and their likely and possible severities. If there is a specific threat, for example flooding, a pointer (for online materials) should link to a more detailed description of the threat, such as at-risk maps with possible timelines. In my view, NWS is leading the field with their graphics, which might yet be further improved. In this field, attention should be paid to both details and consistency of (1) 'magnitude color scheme choices,' (2) top vs bottom / left vs right position of most- and least-extreme categories, (3) most straightforward and clear placement of graphical elements, and (4) consistent standard layouts that will become familiar. If there is broad acceptance of one source of messaging, like NWS, then federal and state recommendations to media to use standard imaging would be helpful. Ad hoc, gee-whiz 'novelty' graphics from multiple sources (media) can be unhelpful.

[* If models indicate a 20% chance of disaster and an 80% chance of good times in the forecast, that is exactly what the messaging should portray. Agencies should not unnecessarily either soothe or alarm. Provide a best-effort, good-faith, clear picture of the information and allow people to evaluate it for themselves. In this example, further guidance might consist of 'Given this range of possibilities, some initial forethought, planning and preparation is advisable.' Protocols scripting the appropriate guidance for defined situations could be established, if they have not been already. I think NWS does this fairly well.]

I'd like to see work on existing interactive, graphical 'weather and climate' websites, including future-oriented projects, aimed at public awareness and education, continue toward improvement of their products, including the expansion of the range of scenarios depicted to extend to megastorm-scale events. For as long as communicators rely on established 'X00-year' event labels, which are based on megastorm-free observational data mostly from the 20th century, megastorms—even when included in representations—will have to be represented as exceptions ('probability-free' or 'having independent odds' or 'unpredictable' events). I can imagine the conceptual struggle that may ensue. If a more synthetic estimation approach is adopted, as recommended above, this 'anomaly' issue goes away.

My preference would be a richer sort of interactive mapping site where storm flows and floods, infrastructure vulnerabilities and likely points of failure (compare www.riskfactor.com), and other impacts (population relocation, *e.g.*) could be mapped and explored by the public as well as by emergency responders. There could be layers showing estimated likelihoods of flooding extents, attributed to particular methods, for specific events and types of events. This would assist all users to move toward a planning and preparation mode, and would facilitate communication at and across all levels. I'll say again here that remaining locked into the 'X00-year' event naming scheme runs a significant risk of miscommunicating actual storm and flood risks, in part because of the progressive obsolescence of online (or other) data.

An early example of an approach to more accessible data is online as Cal-Adapt ("2.0"). Several projected climate-change impacts can be explored using different input assumptions and output filters. In my opinion it's a decent early step toward showing us what we might want and expect in future; however, it doesn't quite show me what I want to know. So, here's my general critique in support of what I'd want to see from that site or a similar site in future. First, add modeled extreme weather events including megastorms, without getting stymied by probabilities. Second (upstream), instead of showing <u>average</u> monthly or yearly stream flows, which are mostly useful to water managers who are worried about drought (or dam operators worried about storage and sales), show <u>peak</u> flow levels and volume / duration conditions, and their potential to exceed dam and channel regulation (flood control), and which create a predicted flood risk to various zones on the floodplain. It would be useful to be able to see specifics of the <u>existing</u> calculations (if made public) identifying which storms would lead to unregulated flows through reservoirs, and where such events would fall within 'reconciled' likelihood estimates. Third, I'll make a similar argument for extreme precipitation projections (presently on an isolated page with no information on consequences); link that to runoff behaviors and impacts, again considering durations; defined events can now be assigned probability estimates by simulation methods (Huang and Swain, 2022). Finally (downstream), have a page that will report anticipated flood <u>behaviors</u>, in other words, <u>put some consequences into the available views</u>.

Some clever soul could provide an application with a tweakable hydrograph, for adjustable precipitation and with defined base flow and runoff efficiencies, that would then flow that water through a digital model of one or more actual watersheds and any local infrastructure. More modeling and computer power in future might be able to do this on the fly.

As a specific need, fine-scale flood mapping pertaining to defined events will be a great help to individuals seeking to assess flood risks. As of late 2022, the RiskFactor product from the First Street Foundation comes close to providing this sort of tool at very fine scale. Both free and fee-based products are offered. RiskFactor / FloodFactor mapping is still linked to probability estimates (the flip side of '100-year' type approaches), but as it is a tool intended for comprehending exposure to financial risk to property, that's a reasonable choice. Significantly, it redisplays adjusted fine-scale flooding estimates calculated for today, 15, and 30 years (the 'mortgage brackets') into the future, as the climate shifts. It also accounts for pluvial flooding effects. Their methods are not entirely disclosed, for example it's not clear whether historical megastorms or future modeled, simulated extreme events and their probabilities are directly included (personal communication); they also acknowledge that the effects of flood control reservoirs are also not explicitly accounted for; however, for the big, uncommon storms, one can deduce from maps showing dams in uncontrolled flow that flood control capacities have been exceeded in their 1% storm models. I have found this tool very helpful in visualizing possible stream and river runoff flow, in hill country, on infrastructure, such as roads, bridges, and powerplants, although it was intended to be a property-parcel risk assessment tool. Some of the extreme flows predicted for mountain and foothills rivers are really eye-opening.

If we consider what the new (RiskFactor; see also Maendly, 2018) methods are predicting about 1% AEP (or so-called '100-year') events, together with what computer simulations (Swain & colleagues) are showing about megastorms currently having estimated 1.4% annual probabilities (equivalent to 1-in-70-years events), it appears that these two definitional concepts are now converging and possibly overlapping; thus the RiskFactor 1% AEP flood mapping is highly relevant to the theme of this book. Finally, their online products are simple to use if you scroll the maps, and may surpass the FEMA map products both in future-based accuracy, richness of detail, and in ease of use.

For another example of what is possible today in fine-scale flood mapping, see the 2022 paper by Brett F. Sanders and colleagues at UCI.

I'd also like all future online and (other flood) maps to have <u>flood depth / duration estimates</u> (as in the USGS ARkStorm rough maps, but finer; RiskFactor gives peak estimated depths but only to 3' depth, so the rest must be calculated from topographic data) available as optional layers in the graphical display. Additional layers could estimate the numbers of 'exposed to flooding' or displaced persons, even their demographics, and damage to structures and the losses to property, in current dollars, for each square mile (or county, or basin) displayed. Ease of use and display clarity is important. At this point it's clear that displays with and without levee integrity would be needed in some areas. All these suggestions aim toward public awareness.

Finally, and generally, any issues around the meaning and uncertainty of estimates, particularly frequency and magnitude estimates, and what the reasonable ranges around such estimates might be, should be explained in a way that a 3.0 GPA high-schooler can understand and apply to their evaluations of the information, with options for deeper detail on demand.

Other current and emerging examples of interactive flood-forecast mapping for sea level rise with or without storm effects can also be found online.

For the more attentive and proactive members of the public, I'd like CA DWR, Cal OES, and/or USACE to consider how to provide, as a permanent graphical or look-up reference, some guidance incorporating easily-accessible information (a range of estimates) on how long it could take California's various rivers to reach flood stage at particular communities or river crossings, for a range of different model storms including extreme storms with typical storm centering. I realize that estimates are specific to different scenarios, including run-up conditions such as base flows and stages, but giving the public an enduring awareness of <u>how much of a range of flood warning time they might receive, including for roads</u>, in various scenarios including the most extreme storms, has great public safety value, for example in supporting more effective and orderly evacuations (similar information is already available online, with some searching and detail-delving, for dam failures—the 'extreme case'—in California). So, while I appreciate the complexities and difficulties of the task, I hope for a messaging shift towards "the approaching storms are still a week out, but the public needs to keep an eye on their progress; when a storm like this gets underway over [California], under current conditions, evacuation orders could follow within [say] 12 to 24 hours, and low-lying roads could become impassable by then." The 'surprise' element of evacuation planning should be minimized, while not promoting undue alarm. This would address concerns voiced by CalEMS, per USGS (2011).

Hurricane forecasts generally achieve this; AR sequence advisories should achieve the same long view (adapting to the 72-hour window imposed by the CW3E ranking scheme) with reference to guidance as proposed in the paragraph above.

For actual storm events in progress, there should be a readily accessible web page of best estimates and forecasts of river and flood behavior, looking further ahead than flood and evacuation warnings do. To some extent NOAA and NWS already do a good job of this, if you know which web sites to check (Twitter feeds have become degraded); bring this information forward into one primary state situation / advisory home page including linked affected-area OES pages. Some emergency services (OES) agencies post some of these links. Best clear-eyed expert predictions could be disseminated to media and local alert networks as soon as potential impacts are anticipated, for example when incoming Cat4 or Cat5 AR storms are identified (3 to 5 days before riverine / fluvial flooding would be expected). I'd also like to see provided to the Valley and floodplains populations a summary of how evacuation orders will be triggered, what pre-evacuation order alert or warning protocols will look like (and at what intervals), and, as suggested above, how much time under warnings or orders any affected area could rely upon having, as built into prudent protocols and realistic plans, in which to complete an evacuation. This assumes that actions, at least warnings and advisories, will be taken <u>before</u> levee failures.

All roads crossing low ground where water may flow or accumulate should have depth gage posts in place, to alert drivers to the degree of hazard present (reflective color coding could help); this could be especially vital during storm and flood evacuations. I'd personally like bridges to be marked with stage gages that anyone could look up online to determine flow rates based on empirical records or calculated results. The number of working USGS-networked stream gages in areas like the Sierra is small. USGS / NOAA could potentially add 'virtual gages' to their data displays, including predictive displays, for ungaged reaches of streams, especially those with road crossings on upper reaches (which all deserve flood forecasts). There are people, including local emergency managers, LEOs, and responders, who may depend upon being able to track flows, stages, and rise rates at various river crossings, and on various reaches, based on field reports from their personnel.

The state should ensure standardized weather event forecast messaging statewide, and rebroadcasting of specific alerts in an affected area over county alert networks in affected areas. As for local EOS messaging, some counties—Monterey Co. provides good recent examples—proactively alert their residents that they are about to become isolated, or alert them to stock up to 2 weeks of emergency supplies for an immediate event. Others may tell the media where they hope to provide sandbags. Some official systems may limit a first notification to an evacuation warning, rather than preview a watch or other advisory. Some offices rely more on advising media outlets than on direct outreach. State guidance can help ensure consistent, thorough and proactive preparatory messaging.

If my emphasis on standard, uniform public advisory protocols seems great, consider that in March, 2009, CalEMS (now Cal OES) departed from long-agreed protocols and declined to disseminate an earthquake forecast warning transmitted (by prior agreement) by the California Earthquake Prediction Evaluation Council (Jones, 2018). Does the 'cry wolf' parable distort our trade-off calculations?

Regarding the diverse suggestions above, I appreciate that handing the public easily understood information on flooding risks, as I advocate above, could have impacts—economic, demographic, political, etc.—but that is not a compelling reason to refrain from fully educating the public and progressing toward any eventual adjustments favoring risk reduction.

* * *

In conclusion: These are big ideas, because these are big issues. We have a lot of work ahead of us. Saying that the state will be devastated only once every 100 or so years, or more often, and shrugging, just doesn't cut it. Neither does closing our eyes, nor simply accepting 'fate.' If you don't favor these proposals… why not? Good answers are welcome. So are more and better ideas.

Just about every one of us can find some way to contribute, at least to our own personal or family safety. And take the message upwards, to the people in the administrations and agencies who have the responsibility for public safety, from the local level on up. How do we collectively meet our responsibilities 'in the middle' between citizen and government?

* * *

Further reading

https://files.resources.ca.gov/docs/climate/ab2800/AB2800_
Climate-SafeInfrastructure_FinalWithAppendices.pdf

Parks, Grant. California State Auditor. 2022-106: Department of Water Resources; Its Forecasts Do Not Adequately Account for Climate Change and Its Reasons for Some Reservoir Releases Are Unclear. May 25, 2023. https://www.auditor.ca.gov/reports/2022-106/index.html

Kay, Robert, Kif Scheuer, Brenda Dix, Maya Bruguera, Angela Wong, Julia Kim
(ICF and Local Government Commission). 2018. Overcoming Organizational
Barriers to Implementing Local Government Adaptation Strategies. California's
Fourth Climate Change Assessment, California Natural Resources Agency.
Publication number: CCCA4-CNRA2018-005. https://www.energy.ca.gov/sites/
default/files/2019-12/Governance_CCCA4-CNRA-2018-005_ada.pdf

Inspiring infrastructure commitments:
(1) Rebuilding the Oroville Dam spillways
https://www.youtube.com/watch?v=ekUROM87vTA

(2) Relocating Jakarta:
https://www.npr.org/2022/01/26/1075720551/jakarta-indonesia-sinking-into-java-sea-new-capital

Cal OES, July 2023. Northern California Catastrophic Flood Response Plan (NCCFRP, 2018) Fact Sheet. https://www.caloes.ca.gov/wp-content/uploads/Preparedness/Documents/CalOES_FactSheet_NCCFRP_v2023_06_22-final.pdf

https://www.cnn.com/interactive/2022/08/us/uvalde-shooting-key-figures/

https://www.sbsun.com/2023/03/07/from-local-to-state-authorities-how-has-the-multi-agency-response-to-blizzard-23-worked/

https://abc7.com/san-bernardino-mountains-snow-national-guard-county/12904034/

https://www.ocregister.com/2023/02/23/major-road-closures-avoided-so-far-in-chilly-snowy-storm/

https://gizmodo.com/twitter-broken-disaster-response-elon-musk-climate-1849802766

Local jurisdiction issues: the Danziger Bridge, 2005. https://www.police1.com/officer-misconduct-internal-affairs/articles/5-ex-cops-sentenced-in-katrina-killings-case-lrtsflFs2hEpGb6b/

Recommendations from the 2011 USGS ARkStorm study are also recommended to you.

20

Banish Confusion

Examining the root causes, including messaging, and resolving them

"Light shone, and order from disorder sprung." —John Milton, Paradise Lost

There is a potentially serious issue with how the 2011 USGS ARkStorm Overview study report, and later reports, were misinterpreted in a dangerously rosy way in some quarters. I include this chapter because to ignore this problematic misunderstanding would undermine the purpose of this book. Briefly:

Messaging

The misunderstanding of the actual threat risk has two intertwined roots in the USGS ARkStorm report. First, the 'k' in the catchy, 'biblical' name 'ARkStorm' given to the computer-constructed storm and flood used in the study; second, the way that terms like 'levels' and 'event' were used (attached to '1000-year' terminology) in the written presentation, without an appreciation of how easily those terms could be misapplied to fundamentally inappropriate concepts. Some of these issues I covered early in this book, but I'll mention them again to keep this section clear.
- 'k' is used in the sciences as shorthand to represent the number 1000
- 'level' is a reference to a magnitude or volume (of precipitation, runoff, or flooding extent)
- 'event' is a thing that happens; in this case a thing described by its magnitude or volume, rather than its calendar date.

About events

Putting a calendar date on an 'event' seems normal for a birthday party, but inappropriate for an uncommon phenomenon like a possible 'extinction-level event.' We've learned to think of storms and floods as events that relate to calendars because of the mortgage-centric NFIP flood / property insurance framework that launched in the USA in the 1960s and then became pervasive. But when 'storm experts' refer to an 'event' or 'level' in 'X00-year' language, they are talking (in shorthand, to other experts) about the <u>magnitude</u> of the phenomenon, not its due-date. (Public officials may tend to go the other way.)

That 'k'

Some time ago I formed the view that the very catchy ARkStorm name for the 2011 megastorm study had done the public no favors. It does help the media sensationalize weather events in the same way that terms like 'bomb cyclone,' 'Arctic blast,' and 'polar vortex' do. Below I'll show you how that 'k' became a problem. But I recently came across this first-hand explanation of how the choice was made:

> "The program was called ARkStorm. The "AR" stands for atmospheric rivers, the meteorological phenomena behind the big storms, the "k" stood for "1,000" to suggest that we were looking at rare, big storms. (In fact, the "k" was somewhat arbitrary, but it allowed us to use cool graphics of arks.)" — Lucy Jones, Chief Scientist on the USGS MHDP ARkStorm study, writing in her 2018 book, <u>The Big Ones</u>.

Officially, the 'k' invoked an arbitrary magnitude (or size) number, 1000 (in a similar way as a Richter Scale number for earthquakes), that USGS stated was "<u>independent of time</u>." This was overlooked by some later writers. At the same time, USGS wrote about runoff stream flows, and flooding, that could approach "1000-year <u>levels</u>." (This is an abbreviated reference to <u>magnitude levels only</u>, communicated for perspective by using the familiar 'X00-years' magnitude-naming scheme, based on traditional probability estimates [see Chapter 3 on how needlessly confusing this is] used in simplified FEMA/NFIP approaches). It happened like this:

To provide this comparative magnitude calibration, in order to communicate the size of a megastorm to the public, and to public officials, USGS used a two-part approach. The USGS team first prepared (let's call this 'part 1') traditional, federal-standard-method storm frequency / probability curves, for various watersheds, based on observed 1917–2003 weather with no megastorms, just as

FEMA, USACE, and other agencies have done and still do. <u>Separately</u>, USGS then calculated (let's call this 'part 2') precipitation, runoff, and rough flooding levels, and impacts, in their ARkStorm model storm, and evaluated the resulting 'part 2' magnitude figures to see how they would <u>compare</u> to rainfall and flood magnitudes along the separate, standard 'part 1' probability curves. [Note: Two separate sets of results (parts 1 and 2) are being compared here, with respect only to <u>magnitude</u>, not time.] Then, USGS borrowed the 'X00-year' labels from the old-school method (part 1) to suggest the <u>magnitude</u> of the ARkStorm impacts (part 2), <u>not their frequency or probability</u>. This may have seemed straightforward to the professionals who prepared the study report, but the language used then and later left room for a serious misunderstanding.

That attempt at communicating a magnitude comparison, and the unfortunately brief language, was interpreted by readers and listeners in two absolutely different ways.

- USGS and its experts assumed that others would understand that a '1000-year level' referred to a <u>magnitude of the storm and its impacts</u> that resembled what had been estimated by (part 1) traditional sampling (too limited) and methods and 'X00' naming; levels that would have been traditionally predicted by federal-standard methods to be what 'ought to' happen on average only once in 1000 years. It was simply a way of saying, in effect, *a bucket of rainwater as big as the bucket you had imagined for your old, incorrect 1-in-1000-year storm / flood estimate.*

- <u>But</u> some readers, reporters, listeners and agencies fundamentally misunderstood this: they leapt to the conclusion that the convenient 'X00' language in the comparison USGS was making (about magnitudes, between two divergent technical approaches) could <u>only</u> refer to a 'time-stamped' probability-forecast result, and that therefore an ARkStorm-scale event could only happen (on average) once every 1000 years, exactly as the old methods would predict (that's the powerfully confusing effect of seeing everything through the pervasive time / risk concept and language adopted for the mortgage lending and insurance industries). This was in spite of the fact that USGS was saying clearly in their report and elsewhere that these megastorms were, historically, 1-in-100 to 1-in-200-year events (regionally) in California (or around 1-in-200-plus-year events for statewide or larger megastorms).

USGS study group members apparently remained unaware of the potential for misinterpretation going forward. In 2014, two participants in the 2010–2011 USGS ARkStorm study wrote that:

> "The "AR" stands for "Atmospheric River", the "k" for 1,000 (as the storm intensities, in some locale, might reach 1-in-1000 year **levels**), and, of course, "ARkStorm" is meant to summon visions of biblical-scale deluge, similar to the great flood of 1862."

To an expert, the context and meaning of 1-in-1000-year <u>levels</u> might be clear, but to others, it was not; neither was the separateness of the ARkStorm model from the old frequency estimation scheme.

On January 28, 2011, about two weeks after the ARkStorm study report was released and announced, Dr. Jeff Masters, on his 'Category 6' blog for www.wunderground/.com , wrote:

> "A group of scientists, emergency managers, and policy makers gathered in Sacramento, California earlier this month to discuss how the state might respond to a repeat of the 1862 rain event--the ARkStorm Scenario. The "AR" stands for "Atmospheric River", the "k" for 1,000 **(like a 1-in-1000 year event)**, and of course "ARkStorm" is meant to summon visions of biblical-scale deluge, similar to the great flood of 1862."

This problematic quote matches largely verbatim the later, 2014 quote from USGS team members that I presented above. The one difference between the two quotes is the annoyingly unclear quip "<u>like a 1-in-1000 year event</u>," which doesn't unambiguously state what it means (though invoking probability). 'Like' could mean 'in other words,' or 'like' could mean 'otherwise comparable to.' And, frankly, anyone invoking comparisons between two such fundamentally different technical approaches needs to go deeper to provide context and clarity… but the assumption that we all know what '1-in-1000-year' storm events are, and acceptance of the imagined reality and accuracy of such far-out estimates, and that time is the only way to think about their magnitude, and that all information has to be universally retrofit [the technical term is "bassackwardsly"] into the pre-existing frequency estimation framework, is now broadly entrenched.

Here are three examples of how the basic, unfortunate misunderstanding (optimistically understating the threat) started to spread; if you look at the agency sources below, you will understand the cause for concern:

> "It [an ARkStorm] comes around only once every 1000 years." —**Ventura County Watershed Protection District**, 2013

"ARkStorm is an extraordinarily rare event with an estimated annual chance of occurrence 1/1000." —**California Office of Emergency Services**, NCCFR Plan [Draft], 2016 [since omitted]

"However, the series of storms that led to the Great Flood of 1862 averaged precipitation levels that **records show only occur once every 500 to 1,000 years**." —the community contributed Wikipedia article on the Great Flood of 1862 stated this misinformation for years, until corrected very recently in 2023. [To be clear, 'Records' don't 'show' this. This mis-statement combined (1) the familiar, fundamental misinterpretation of the USGS study results, which I explain above, while (2) misleading about 'records' and the actual methods and assumptions of the narrow (traditional, recent-observational) approach to flow-frequency estimation, and the meaning of its estimates. As of September 1, 2023, the original, persistent error is still being repeated on Wikipedia's 'Megastorm' page.]

I believe that USGS was looking not only for a 'familiar' verbal short cut with which to describe the <u>magnitude</u> of phenomena and impacts to their audience, it was also providing a shortcut to allow officials to conveniently view the extent of projected ARkStorm flooding on existing flood zone maps (assuming, it seems, that they would disregard the 'X00-year' or AEP probability labels). In fact Dettinger *et al.* wrote in a 2012 companion paper that the original ARkStorm study concept included new hydrology generating all new megastorm flood maps from scratch, but that work had to be scaled back, so the alternative was to point to the existing 'X00-year' flood zone maps. It's my view that they should have taken more care with how they worded those comparative statements for non-experts. For example, I might have written:

"The ARkStorm has a magnitude producing levels of precipitation, runoff, and flooding comparable to what would <u>otherwise, previously,</u> have been estimated to occur with only a 0.1–0.2% annual probability (meaning a hypothetical event predicted—by traditional methods based on limited samples of 20th-century weather data—to occur, on average, once in any [500–] 1000 years); however we know from the geological record that storms like the ARkStorm or the 1862 megastorm have historically hit Northern California on average every 100–200 years, for example six times in the past 700 years, and statewide,

> *perhaps seven storms as big as or bigger than 1862 have arrived*
> *in the past 1800 years. The true event frequency up through the*
> *20th century has been in the range of 1-in-100 to –200 (or –300)*
> *years"*

Even experts have been left to struggle with this. It may be difficult to decide whether some later reports reflect a continuing misunderstanding, or whether the language and messaging issues are just stubbornly persistent. Consider the statement, by Sanders *et al.* in 2022, appearing to refer to the Great Flood (megastorm) *historical event* of 1861–62, but actually based on the (smaller, and possibly misunderstood) ARkStorm simulation made by the USGS team in 2010–11, in a form that I believe is too simplified:

> "The atmospheric event was characterized by a return
> period of 500–1,000 years and flooding of Los Angeles was
> characterized by a return period of 500 years." —Sanders *et*
> *al.*, 2022

As a fundamental reminder, <u>no</u> such calibrated return interval was proposed by USGS either for the 1861–62 storms or for the ARkStorm simulation. If this is not clear yet, please skip back a few pages and re-read. The phrase "was characterized by" is at least misleading.

Methodology

One key aspect of this communication issue is that different methods and approaches give different estimates of the frequency (recurrence interval) and annual-chance probabilities of megastorm-scale weather events. I think we will see progress toward some sort of reconciliation or synthesis of methods and estimates in the coming years; here are some hints about why that may happen.

There is an understated implication in the USGS ARkStorm study report, and in the storm simulation work of Swain, Huang and colleagues, including their new 'ARkStorm 2.0' initiative, one that is profound but only quietly inserted into their presentations of results: that the traditional, officially sanctioned and even officially required, standard 'historical-observational' methods of estimating storm precipitation, runoff, and flood event probabilities are missing something extremely important; consequently <u>the universally-accepted and promoted storm risk / recurrence estimates are consistently, inherently underestimates of actual event probabilities and risks</u>. Because, among other reasons, something important was left out. *USGS team muffling of this crucial point explains in part why the ARkStorm report had limited impact.*

Here's an abbreviated list of the most basic issues with the standard traditional estimation approach, which uses samples of weather data from limited periods in the 20th century, and lately, in some cases, the 21st:

- Samples are too small. Some NOAA/NFIP projections have been based on a 30-year data sample. FEMA has stated that 10 years is good enough. Small samples are not robust for reliably capturing variability, not to mention trends. Defining a 'thousand-year-flood' based on 10+ years of data is… odd.

- Samples are unrepresentative. Related to the first issue, samples that exclude relatively recent events or certain time periods (like wet or dry decades) that are distinctly different create a distorted picture of patterns, probabilities and magnitudes. No accepted traditional estimates have ever treated 1862 as anything more than a rare fluke that can be explained by manipulating only 'milder' 20th-century data (to push it out near the 1000-year prediction horizon). Omitting known (if incompletely known) events, and making no allowance or adjustment for them, is… odd.

- Weather is not all the same. Assuming for mathematical simplification that there is only one kind of storm or weather, and it comes in bigger or smaller versions (inversely proportional to likelihood), is a very strange proposition (especially if you are from the Midwest or Southeast). Different kinds of storms should have different probabilities. Defining one convenient (mathematically and otherwise) universal probability curve when in reality there may be a combination of multiple different undetermined probabilities for different kinds of weather events is… a very convenient source of possible error. And if (assuming for this argument) a megastorm sequence is a distinctly different kind of weather phenomenon, and because we have almost no observational data on them, then trying to make predictions about them <u>based only on other types of weather</u> is an extremely shaky proposition. (Newer simulation methods address this and other issues.)

- Trends can be overlooked. Increased attention is now being paid to changing-climate trends, which have gradually emerged in the data; however, this situation means that even a decent event estimate for today soon becomes a poorer one. More vexingly, even some recent state-sponsored studies <u>of climate change</u> have ignored these known trends, for example preferring instead to use 50-year-old 'snapshot' flood estimates, based on even older data (and methods), to represent what will happen to levees 80 years from now (that's a 130-plus-year blind spot), whereas more careful studies predict that storms, runoff and flooding will become different, and more extreme, in the coming decades. Some recent studies (and maps) have not caught up with our knowledge.

- Note also that some contributing factors like pluvial flooding impacts have been left out of official FEMA flood zone mapping; this is another accepted source of local-scale risk underestimation (see Chapter 3, and Sanders *et al.*, 2022).

Two common features apply across this short list of issues with the standard methods: the choices are convenient or expedient, and they all have tended to produce <u>underestimates</u> of risks ['nobody likes a party pooper']. These issues are beginning to be discussed less quietly, and in some cases now are appearing in mainstream media reporting. And that brings us back to misunderstanding, misinformation, and confusion; what is the basis for what we are being told?

I'm going to have faith that you have absorbed the points I've tried to make above: that the standard risk estimation methods, still officially employed to this day, have issues, and that it has been difficult to clearly communicate alternate scientific findings, in part because the official framework is still so entrenched in mortgage-based thinking and practices from the 20th century. With that, I'd like to close with a review of an important recent paper (August 12, 2022) that not only raises again the alarm about megastorms and megafloods, but highlights a new and more versatile approach to estimating future recurrence intervals and magnitudes, not just for megastorms but for the entire range of storms and weather (including droughts) that occurs in California.

New methods

Rather than use the traditional estimation method based on a limited sample of mostly 20th century weather observations, the work from UCLA by Daniel Swain and colleagues uses the most detailed and up to date computer models of global atmospheric and oceanic circulation to artificially generate (in this case, by Huang & Swain in 2022) 400 years' worth of realistic simulated weather years that could be expected to occur at any time in a given 10-year period and climate up through 2080 or potentially beyond (in the computer simulations, the climate is kept steady during each 400-years run, to provide an in depth picture of what any of those 10 years could look like). 400 years of 'spontaneous' weather (but with the resulting probabilities and magnitudes arising from the decade-specific climate conditions) is a robust sample including droughts, megastorms, and everything in between. By using the same approach on a 10-year period in the recent past, with known weather and climate records, it was (and is) possible to reality-check this computational-simulation approach;

there was a good agreement. To the extent that the model approaches reality, and depending upon assumptions about the predicted future climate (primarily, global temperature), this method provides a large, robust, representative sample of 'plausibly expected winters' for the present period and for the latter part of this century—in a plausible future—from which event probabilities and magnitudes can be extracted. I'm really happy to see this new research and its potential to avoid the problems with both the traditional observation-based flood / flow estimation methods and with the 'one-off' reconstructed scenario developed for the original ARkStorm study.

For example, their best estimate, based on their results and current trends, is that (in most likely numbers) between now and 2100 California might have around five events reaching at least the magnitude of smaller megastorms here, perhaps three of which might reach into the range of the ARkStorm model, and/ or with two potentially becoming even larger. The exact intensity and impact ranges of these storms are not spelled out in this aggregated probability forecast. That forecast assumes that greenhouse gas emissions and global temperatures will continue to follow recent trends; even if we step on the CO_2 brakes today it would take decades to begin to slow warming down and decrease the predicted risk from megastorms and other intensifying weather.

Here's my review of the important 2022 paper by Huang & Swain. Because this report received so much media attention (deserved), it's worth taking a few minutes to understand what's in this report. The review I provide here leans a bit toward the technical side, more than the typical news reports did, as it covers several important technical points from this study, setting the stage for their forthcoming publications; I hope the gist will come through to all readers (and to you detail-oriented folks).

Huang, Xingying, and Swain, Daniel L. 12 August 2022. Climate change is increasing the risk of a California megaflood. Science Advances 8:32. https://www.science.org/doi/10.1126/sciadv.abq0995

Overview: The authors position their new modeling work as an "ARkStorm 2.0" study, a project that will span multiple papers, a follow-up to the 2011 USGS ARkStorm scenario, but using newer climate and weather models and simulation methods to generate new digital megastorms and storm data. There are actually two new detailed model storm scenarios, each selected from one or the other set of 400 weather-year simulations: ARkHist, based on climate from 1996–2005, and ARkFuture, based on predicted climate in 2071–2080 (under the RCP8.5 'business as usual' GHG scenario). By evaluating a robust set of simulations, in contrast to the single reconstructed simulation of the 'ARkStorm 1.0' scenario, a probabilistic assessment of event storm frequencies and AEPs, return intervals, range of magnitudes, etc. can be derived. That is a big step forward. The analysis of the 400 '1996-2005 climate' simulations and comparison to data from around that time period provided a reality check.

While results for the ARkHist simulation (most relevant to the present day) are presented, the emphasis is consistently placed on changing climate and the increased magnitudes for effects of an event (but note: a much rarer event!) occurring in the late 21st century simulations; that time frame fits a more pragmatic planning horizon / scenario, for example in infrastructure investment and land use planning, as well as pointing to a better benchmark for adequate emergency response preparation. That said, the two-storms comparative framing of the paper—one good example is found in figures 3C and 3F—could create a misimpression in a casual reader:

The criteria for selecting the two model megastorm events are clearly explained in Methods; less obviously, <u>the ARkHist and ARkFuture storms have two very different probabilities</u>, and any drawn inference that they provide an apples-to-apples comparison of trends attributable solely to climate change would be incorrect. Fundamentally, two hand-picked independent simulations, however related, will not be directly linked to each other. A reading of this paper that does not delve into the details of the methods could miss this point. The paper states that

> "Last and most critically, we design and implement two separate scenarios—ARkHist and ARkFuture—with the combined aim of **comparing** a "lesser" present era severe storm sequence to a much more intense but physically plausible future sequence amplified by climate change."

Why this comparison was desirable is unclear to me; setting two event bracket points could be useful but not comparative. This passage does not dispel the possible impression that amplification by climate change is what distinguishes the future-period storm from the historical-period one. Neither does referring to "projected **increases** in ARkFuture runoff," for example, which would imply a linkage to ARkHist. A clearer explanation is found here:

> "Therefore, we manually selected the respective ARkHist and ARkFuture events from among the top three ranked events such that each would bring a high level of impacts to the entire state rather than just a portion of the region. In so doing, we ultimately select the second ranked event for ARkHist (calendar date range: 9 February 2002 to 12 March 2002 in ensemble member #20) and the third ranked event for ARkFuture (calendar date range: 11 January 2072 to 11 February 2072 in ensemble member #2). Further analysis suggests that **the**

selected ARkHist event has an approximate RI of ~85 years in the 1971–2020 era climate, and the ARkFuture event has an approximate RI of ~333 years in a 2051–2100 era high warming climate and is empirically unprecedented (*i.e.*, a >400-year RI) in the 1971–2020 era climate (fig. S11)."

The ARkHist storm event would have had a once-in-about-85 years occurrence probability expectation in the 1971–2020 period, whereas the ARkFuture storm event, to compare apples to apples, would have had a less than once-in-400-years expected occurrence probability during that same period (compressing down to an RI of ~333 years during the second half of the 21ˢᵗ century). Perhaps obviously, 'event' here might best be understood in terms of <u>magnitude</u>; the primary ranking criterion for choosing among the 800 simulations was the amount of cumulative 30-day <u>statewide</u> precipitation (see date ranges stated above).

One important point: At least three of the 800 simulations, which were not selected, had higher statewide precipitation that was not balanced from north to south, meaning that some of the simulations had substantially greater regional precipitation than what was observed in ARkHist or ARkFuture. Other simulations with somewhat lower statewide totals may have depicted similarly intense regional-scale impacts. To recap this point, the two featured simulations were chosen in part because they produced 30-day precipitation totals that were heavy in <u>both</u> Northern and Southern California (that pattern, not the case in all simulations, fit the authors' study requirements for storm events having widespread impacts); for that reason, <u>regional</u> return interval and magnitude indications for similar storm events <u>in-region</u> were evidently, respectively shorter and greater. Emergency planners, take note!

Note that although the authors use the term "30-day megastorm sequence," these 30-day periods are not 30-day storms, they are 30-day sampling period 'chunks' extracted from full data on 400 simulated wet seasons; storm activity including megastorms could span longer (or shorter) periods than 30 days. Similarly, precipitation and runoff calculations, noted below, are capped at those 30-day 'input' levels, although these models found that megastorm periods are often associated with extra-wet run-up and tail-off periods, as in 1862. Such 30-day estimates therefore provide <u>minimums</u> within the bigger picture of a full wet season (apparently the promised hydrological workups of one or more simulations will account for run-up, base flows, and other conditions beyond 30-day precipitation).

Examining that parameter, the ARkHist scenario was associated with ~447 mm (17.6") of cumulative 30-day statewide precipitation; for ARkFuture that number is ~586 mm (23.1"). That may not seem like much, but it is a statewide average; broad areas will receive much more precipitation. Statewide, those two figures bracket a range of about 45 to 60 cubic miles of precipitation, of which some amount will immediately become surface runoff. Regarding the two selected simulations, the following results are presented:

> "In both ARkHist and ARkFuture, 30-day cumulative precipitation is extremely high. In ARkHist, we find broad regions exceeding 500 mm [19.7"] of cumulative precipitation, with widespread areas exceeding 1000 mm in the Sierra Nevada (SN) and more isolated pockets exceeding 1000 mm [39.4"] in the Coast Ranges, Transverse Ranges, and far southern end of the Cascade Range (domain maximum of ~2150 mm [84.6"]; Fig. 2A). In ARkFuture, spatial patterns of event total precipitation are similar but are uniformly characterized by heavier accumulations, with broad areas in both northern and southern California exceeding 700 mm [27.6"] and widespread areas in the abovementioned mountain areas above 1400 mm [55.1"] (domain maximum of ~3200 mm [126"]; Fig. 2B). We note that these values are comparable to maximum precipitation informally reported during the GF1862, which exceeded 2500 mm in at least two locations on the SN western slope over a slightly longer (~40-day) period (6)." [Furthermore, the high Sierra could receive 35' of snow in the stronger storm sequence.]

I'll note again that at least some number of simulations had more extreme impacts at regional (north or south) scale; those were not discussed by the authors. Keep in mind that Huang and Swain selected two simulations (from 800) based on <u>statewide</u> high-magnitude precipitation that affected both Northern and Southern California, which is relevant to scope of catastrophe. In the precipitation forecasts quoted above, the numbers they cite therefore may not always be upper limits, locally, even within the universe of the simulations they constructed. This is true not only spatially, but also in time beyond 30 days as noted earlier.

The two simulated '2.0' storm events are suggested to be in the same general range as the real 1862 event, perhaps bracketing it (additional work with hydrological models could refine those comparisons). In a garbled quote from the Los Angeles Times, "It would also probably be "bigger in almost every respect" than what scientists have come to call the "ARKStorm scenario" of 1862, said climate scientist Daniel Swain, co-author of the study published Friday in the journal Science Advances." (Presumably, the ARkFuture scenario was being referred to as "it" here, followed by a comparison to the proxy 2011 ARkStorm scenario for an event smaller than 1862).

Translating that precipitation into runoff is more complicated and deserves the greater attention these authors and collaborators propose to give it in future. Runoff efficiency, the fraction of precipitation that becomes streamflow in a given period, is predicted in this 2022 paper to range from ~0.19 to ~0.29 in the smaller and larger ARkStorm 2.0 scenarios, respectively.

[Note: The two numbers above suggest that runoff efficiency should be highest with higher precipitation intensity, also true when soils are saturated, particularly under megastorm conditions and the preceding relatively wet run-up period; for example, reservoir operating regulations build real-time soil moisture data and thus anticipated runoff efficiency into their models for predicting inflow dynamics and managing flood control 'buffer' capacity requirements. Flint *et al.* (four former and current USGS scientists) reported in 2021 that, while averaged runoff efficiencies in the Sierra Nevada Mountains have trended downward over the past 50 years, from about 0.45 to 0.19, apparently associated with drier soil conditions, within that timeframe there have been events (as in 1974) in which 71% of precipitation rapidly became runoff. During the large storm years 1986 and 1997, Sierra runoff efficiencies for overall wet season precipitation were 0.48 and 0.44 respectively. The last year with 40% runoff efficiency was 2017, a year with strong AR storms, in which the overflow emergency at the Oroville Dam occurred (in part due to underestimated runoff inflows). I'll suggest that <u>local</u> models of runoff behavior in Sierra watersheds under ultra-wet megastorm conditions should incorporate or examine scenarios with runoff efficiencies extending at least into the 0.4-0.5 range, higher than the presumably statewide average values given by Huang & Swain. Snow accumulation and rain-on-snow melting will both also alter runoff fractions in short sampling windows.]

Some hours of runoff from precipitation greater than 10 mm (0.39") / hour are predicted, a statistic that locally must also consider runoff efficiency, area, and aspects of hydrology. For perspective <u>only</u>, 10 mm / square mile equals ~21 acre-feet; how this translates to runoff will be interesting to explore.

Also for perspective on precipitation intensity is this quote:

> "Oakley *et al.* [2018] (40) conducted a literature review on published hourly rainfall rates in California and/or similar Mediterranean climate regions thought to be sufficient to trigger shallow landslides and debris flows in susceptible terrain, noting a range (5 to 20 mm/hour) that encompasses our HPH threshold (10 mm/hour) in the present study. These findings, therefore, likely have large implications from a flash flood and debris flow risk perspective."

Returning to the topic of frequency, or recurrence interval (RI) estimates, the ARkHist storm event said to have lately had an RI of ~85 years (an estimate averaged over the past five decades) is depicted in Figure 5A to have an estimated expectation of cumulative event probability, for the period beginning in 1920, of 1 event by the year 2020. In other words, having one megastorm like the ARkHist simulation would have been a likely expectation during the past 100 years (not to mention since 1862); in a sense it's 'lucky' that we had none. However, the trend is upward; under the RCP8.5 GHG climate warming assumption, between 2022 and 2100 more than three such megastorm events are likely, or, if counting from 1920, almost 4.5 such events overall would be a likely cumulative expectation. For larger megastorms, for which an RI of 200 years in the 1995–2005 period was calculated, an expectation of about two such events between now and 2100 is calculated (based on their Figure 5A). For smaller megastorms, perhaps at the lower limit for what might be called a megastorm, for which an RI of 50 years in the 1995–2005 period was calculated, a likely expectation of almost three such events between now and 2080, and perhaps four or more by 2100, is calculated.

Note that those event expectations are not independent and additive; they are called "events equal or greater in magnitude" to / than those three defined 'exceedance thresholds.' An event that exceeds the smaller ('50y') and ARkHist ('85y') magnitudes and meets or exceeds the larger ('200y') intensity threshold would tick all three boxes in the forecast; a bigger event presumably also accounts for one event in each smaller category. Following that reasoning, under the RCP8.5 scenario, the most likely total number of megastorm events affecting California from now through 2100, having a mix of magnitudes and different probabilities, would be approximately five. It's not clear whether regional megastorms would be in addition to these estimates, however; ARkHist is a statewide event. Regional-scale megastorms might increase these numbers, or perhaps might belong to the smaller or '50y' class that was depicted.

While describing RIs and event probabilities, as here, it may make sense to associate these events on trendlines by emphasizing their initial RI estimates; however, in general, I'd prefer to avoid the shifting-RI nomenclature for such events; to me it would seem more useful to describe, for example, a "400 mm / 30 d" event, as the RI estimates will be continually shortening during this century. At a minimum, it would have been useful here to have the range of 30-day cumulative precipitation levels, at least, and perhaps size of impact area, stated for the 50- and 200-year RI events.

Commendably, rain vs snow and rain-on-snow effects are clearly accounted for in these simulations; also, uncertainty about significant 'run-up' conditions before arrival of the megastorm proper is acknowledged. Interestingly, years with megastorms are likely to be wet years before and/or after the sampling period (30 days here) containing the megastorm proper.

Also, just between the lines, this paper presents annual likelihood and RI estimates, for megastorm events, that are not a part of the traditional observational based, AEP-linked flow frequency and floodplain mapping conventions.

"…we leverage the large sample size afforded by large ensemble climate model simulations to draw upon **a much wider range of physically plausible event sequences that [than] are available by considering the roughly century-long observational record alone…**" [That evident typo, 'that' for 'than,' could have blurred this key point.]

Therefore, these megastorm events entail risks that exist <u>in some overlapping, enhanced combination with</u> the widely-adopted storm and flood risk estimates, the latter used for example in reservoir inflow frequency estimates, AEP-based flood zone maps, and several other surface water study projections. The authors do not even invoke that traditional framework. *I see this as a softly-voiced nudge to those who prepare hydrological projections and estimates in California and the West, gently packaged within an assessment of climate change impacts.* At some point, perhaps someone will overlay RI or AEP curves from 'traditional 20th century hydrology observations' with the same curves derived from simulations associated with the climate of, say, 1996–2005, to finally portray what the traditional approaches, for example in flood zone mapping, may have missed. And, of course, this study implies, as did earlier ones, that a new, synthetic approach to storm recurrence frequency, flood probability and risk estimation must be implemented.

This is a very important study from a leading team with experience in this field. This is a fine first installment in the ARkStorm 're-visitation' I've been hoping for, but one using more elegant methods and new information.

* * *

I used a fair bit of ink in this chapter because confusion and misinformation could have the single greatest negative impact on whether we and our governing agencies prepare adequately for a real threat, or not. Lives, and much of everything else here, are at stake. Clarity, and ink, are cheap in comparison.

* * *

In conclusion

I'd like us to be safe, starting with becoming well-informed. So, I wrote this book, and I want to wrap up the main narrative line by making a few points.

- A future megastorm would / will be a big deal; it may be more likely and more destructive than a 7.8-8.0 magnitude earthquake.
- Presently, we are not well prepared as a society to withstand the full scope of its impacts.
- Much current infrastructure may be overwhelmed by the flood volumes and other impacts; emergency response services may be overwhelmed by the scope of the disaster.
- It is challenging to find good estimates of extreme storm risk / frequency predictions (though this may be changing); some widely used methods may ignore or underestimate megastorm risks.
- Some newer approaches suggest that the real risk is substantial and increasing rapidly.
- New information also indicates that "whiplash" weather reversal from drought to AR storms including megastorms is a real but deceptive phenomenon that must be anticipated.
- It has been difficult to assess where on the 'radar' of local, state and federal agencies these specific risks are being seen (this has been improving) and how detailed any response planning might be.

Agencies like USGS, USACE, Cal OES and CA DWR take these threats (especially flooding) seriously. Leading research teams are sounding alarms about impacts, and the year to year odds and risks (and issues with estimates). For all these reasons, individual and community-level awareness and preparedness is prudent, and may someday provide people with crucial resilience and protection. Credible assurances from public officials, that these extreme weather risks are well understood, and that fully adequate public safety and other measures are being implemented, are a reasonable expectation from a concerned public. Guidance on and support for individual and community preparedness would also be welcome.

I hope you have found this book to be useful. If so, please let others know. If you are not saturated yet, the many references collected in this work can take you on some deeper dives into particular topic areas.

* * *

Further reading

https://www.wunderground.com/blog/JeffMasters/the-arkstorm-californias-coming-great-deluge.html

https://www.wunderground.com/blog/weatherhistorian/californias-superstorm-the-usgs-arkstorm-report-and-the-great-flood-.html

Dettinger, M., and D. Cox. Planning for the Atmospheric River threat, by USACE Silver Jackets Quarterly Newsletter (The Buzz), January, 2014: 8–9. https://usace.contentdm.oclc.org/utils/getfile/collection/p16021coll8/id/2106

Flint, Lorrie, Alan Flint, Michelle Stern and Joe Hevesi.
2021. What Will Happen When it Rains?
Runoff Efficiency using the BCM. [PowerPoint presentation] https://www.watereducation.org/sites/main/files/file–attachments/flint_wow2021.pdf?1637189936

Epilogue

"In retrospect, hindsight was overrated."

Acronyms and Abbreviations

"The long and the short of it…" —Idiom

Occasional quoted abbreviations, if not found below, are defined in the original documents.

ACE—Annual Chance of Exceedance; see AEP; = 1/estimated recurrence interval
AEP—Annual Exceedance Probability; a frequency or return-interval estimate
a-f—acre-foot (a unit of volume)
AFB—Air Force Base
AFDC—Alternative Fuels Data Center (US)
AIR—AIR Worldwide Corporation (now Verisk)
AP—Associated Press
AR—Atmospheric River (defined in book)
ASL—Above Sea Level

BAU—Business-as-usual
BAM—Best Available Map(s)
BC—British Columbia (Canada)
BLM—Bureau of Land Management (US)
BRIC—Building Resilient Infrastructure and Communities (FEMA grant program)
BTS—Base Transceiver Stations

C—Celsius ('Centigrade:' temperature scale)
CA—California
CA4_CCA—California's Fourth Climate Change Assessment (2018)
CA DWR—California Department of Water Resources
CalEPA—California Environmental Protection Agency
Cal Guard—California National Guard (comprising three distinct forces)
Cal OES—California Governor's Office of Emergency Services
Caltrans—California Department of Transportation
CBC—Canadian Broadcasting Corporation
CCLT—California Council of Land Trusts

CDAA—California Disaster Assistance Act
CDFA—California Department of Food and Agriculture
CDT—Central Distribution Terminal
CEC—California Energy Commission
CEII—Critical Energy / Electric Infrastructure Information
CERT—Community Emergency Response Team (Federally managed program)
CFF—California's Flood Future (report, 2013)
cfs—cubic feet per second (flow rate)
cfh—cubic feet per hour (flow rate)
CHP—California Highway Patrol
CMD—California Military Department (see Cal Guard)
CNG—California National Guard
CNN—(National cable news network ID)
CPUC—California Public Utilities Commission
CSG—California State Guard (California Defense Force): State-controlled CMD branch
CSWC—California State Warning Center
CSIWG—Climate-Safe Infrastructure Working Group (California)
CV—California Volunteers
CVFPB—Central Valley Flood Protection Board
CVFPP—Central Valley Flood Protection Plan (2017, 2022)
CVP—Central Valley Project
CVHS—Central Valley Hydrology Study (2015)
CVIFMS—Central Valley Integrated Flood Management Study (2015)
CW3E— Center for Western Weather and Water Extremes (at Scripps)
CWS—California Warning System

d—day (time)
DHS—Department of Homeland Security (US)
DOD—Department of Defense (US)
DOT—Department of Transportation (US)
DRC—Disaster Recovery Center (CA)
DSOD—California Division of the Safety of Dams

EBS—Emergency Broadcast System (also EANS)
EIA—Energy Information Administration (US)
EMA—Emergency Management Agency (CA)
ENSO—El Niño Southern Oscillation
EOC—Emergency Operations Center
ESRD—Emergency Spillway Release Diagram (dam overflow protocol document)
EV—Electric Vehicle

F—Fahrenheit (temperature scale)
FCO—Flood Control Outlet (normally the main dam spillway)
FEMA—Federal Emergency Management Agency
FHBM—Flood Hazard Boundary Maps
FIRM—Flood Insurance Rate Maps
FIFO—"First in, first out"
FIRO—Forecast-Informed Reservoir Operations
FOC—Flood Operations Center (CA / federal facility in Sacramento)
FOUO—For Official Use Only
fps—feet per second (velocity)
FSF—First Street Foundation
FSIVA—Full Spectrum Integrated Vulnerability Assessment (team: CNG)

gal—gallon (volume)
GEV—Generalized Extreme Value (distribution)
GG—Golden Gate
GHG—Greenhouse Gas
GPA—Grade Point Average

ha—hectare (land area)
HAZUS-MH—Software to estimate potential disaster losses (FEMA)
HGMP—Hazard Mitigation Grant Program (FEMA)
HMP—Hazard Mitigation Plan (Standard: for levees, 1' freeboard during 100-year flood; federal PL84-99 is 1.5')
h—hour (time)
hrs—hours
HHS—Health and Human Services
HTF—High-tide Flood

IAP—Incident Action Plan
IC—Incident Commander
IC4U—Incident Commander's Command Control Communications and Computers Unit
ICP—Unified Incident Command Post
ICS—Incident Command Structure
IDF—Intensity-Duration-Frequency (curve)
IPCC—Intergovernmental Panel on Climate Change
ISP—Internet Service Provider
IVT—Integrated Vapor Transport
IWM—Integrated Water Management (term from CA DWR)
IWV—Integrated Water Vapor

JFHQ—Joint Force Headquarters
JIC—Joint Information Center

kg—kilogram (a unit of mass)
km—kilometer (distance)
KM—Kinder Morgan (company)
kph—kilometers per hour
kWh—kilowatt-hour (a watt is a unit of power; 1 kWh = 1000 watts delivered
     for 1 hour)

LA—Los Angeles
LAC—Local Assistance Center
LAR—Lower American River
LEO—Law Enforcement Officer
LFPZ—Levee Flood Protection Zone
LP3—Log-Pearson Type III Probability Distribution
LPG—Liquefied Petroleum Gas

m—meter (distance); minute (time)
m3/s—cubic meters per second (velocity)
MHDP—Multi Hazard Demonstration Project USGS)
mi—mile (distance)
mi^3—cubic mile (volume)
min—minutes (time)
MOT—Marine Oil Terminal(s)
MPF—Maximum Possible Flood (USACE term)
mph—Miles per hour
MRE—Meal Ready to Eat
MYTEP —Multi-Year Training and Exercise Plan

NBI—National Bridge Inventory (database, from DOT)
NCCFRP—Northern California Catastrophic Flood Response Plan (2018;
     FOUO / restricted)
NCPA—Northern California Power Agency
NFIP—Federal National Flood Insurance Program
NGO—Non-Governmental Organization
NIMS—National Incident Management System
NOAA—National Oceanic and Atmospheric Administration
NoD—North of Delta
NPR—National Public Radio
NPS—National Park Service
NREL—National Renewable Energy Laboratory (US)

NS—Nova Scotia (Canada)
NW—Northwest
NWS—National Weather Service

OHS—Office of Homeland Security (CA) (since folded into Cal OES)
OA—Operational Area (including counties)

PBJ—Peanut Butter and Jelly (sandwich)
PDO—Pacific Decadal Oscillation
PDQ—Pretty Damn Quick
PFD—Personal Flotation Device
PG&E (PGE)—Pacific Gas and Electric, "Northern California's primary energy utility"
PMF—Probable Maximum Flood (USACE term); see MPF
PMP—Probable Maximum Precipitation (USACE term)
POTS—Plain Old Telephone Service
PSPS—Public Safety Power Shutoff

RCP—Representative Concentration Pathway (a GHG concentration trajectory: IPCC)
RI—Return Interval
RV—Recreational Vehicle

s—second (a unit of time)
SCR—Santa Clara River
SE—Southeast
SEMS—State Emergency Management System
SEP—State Emergency Plan
SFB—Space Force Base
SFHA—Special Flood Hazard Area
SHMP—State Hazards Mitigation Plan (2018)
SHS—State Highway System (= Caltrans responsibility)
SLR—Sea Level Rise
SMUD—Sacramento Municipal Utility District, a local energy provider
SN—Sierra Nevada
SoE—State of Emergency
SPF—Standard Project Flood (USACE term)
SPFC—State Plan of Flood Control (component of CVFPP)
SPS—Standard Project Storm (USACE term)
SR—State Route (highway)
SWP—State Water Project

TAMP—Transportation Asset Management Plan (California; Caltrans)
TFS—Transportation Fuels Sector
THIRA—Threat and Hazard Identification and Risk Assessment
ToC—Time of Concentration
TPW—Total Precipitable Water
TTE—Tabletop Exercise

UC—University of California
UCG—Unified Coordination Group (state / federal catastrophic incident management)
UCIP—Utility Crossing Inventory Program
UCLA—University of California, Los Angeles
URL—Uniform Resource Locator; a web address
USACE—U.S. Army Corps of Engineers
USB—Universal Serial Bus (older computer connector now used for device charging)
USBR—U.S. Bureau of Reclamation; "Reclamation"
USFS—U.S. Forest Service
USGS—United States Geological Survey
U.S.—United States; also designates federal highway system routes

V2G—Vehicle-to-Grid
V2H—Vehicle-to-Home
VCPWA—Ventura County Public Works Agency
VIC—Variable Infiltration Capacity (hydrological model)

WCM—Water Control Manual (USACE term)
WV—West Virginia
WWTP—Wastewater Treatment Plant
WWWD—What Would Water Do?

Acknowledgements

I gratefully thank the early readers of sections of this work, and of early full-length drafts, for their time and efforts, and their useful comments and edits. They include: LMC, RM, LT, LE, JB, CL, and GQ (who also forwarded many useful news reports). Of course, any infelicitous turns of phrase, errors, or interpretations are my own responsibility.

I thank Jeremy Malamed and the Ledger-Dispatch of Jackson, Amador County, for publishing in 2020 early versions of four early chapters of this book. The role of local newspapers in getting the word out on important topics is vital. They are also among the best records of the events of 1862.

I thank Neal Swain and the UC Press for clarifying the copyright status of the journal entries of William H. Brewer, from which I borrowed several invaluable excerpts. For the source I used the UC Press publication, "<u>Up and Down California in 1860–1864</u>," by William H. Brewer (Fourth Edition, 2003).

I thank Drs. Anne Wein and Jeff Peters of USGS for permission to use Peters' map rendering of ARkStorm flood depth data.

I thank Mark Yashinsky for helpful correspondence and for his very useful, detailed blog on bridges in this area.

I thank Nancy Ward and Jun Kinoshita of Cal OES for access to the NCCFRP and other documents, and to the latter for further helpful correspondence.

Finally, I'd like to thank the many friends who listened to me talk so often and earnestly about extreme weather over the past four years, as this book was writing itself in my head. Maybe now I'll taper off.

About the Author

To understand the outlook I brought to this project, here is a note about some events and experiences that have shaped my views and my attitudes.

For starters, I was switched at birth, with another newborn, in the hospital. It's a somewhat elaborate story (thanks, Mom), too long for this book, and it was resolved fairly swiftly. I have to hope I was switched back correctly, or at least optimally. The point is: things happen.

One of my great-greats was Jacob Hochstetler, an Amish Mennonite immigrant whose pacifism became a famous example in 1657, in Pennsylvania, when he forbade his family to defend themselves against an attack by the original inhabitants. The result was several deaths, capture, and enslavement. My line is descended from John, a son on a neighboring farm who had to watch the whole bloody scene. Possibly my pragmatism is inherited from John, and a proactive stance taken from the lesson. One only has so many cheeks to turn; there are limits.

My paternal firefighter grandfather survived the big 1906 earthquake, and then fought the fires in San Francisco for many days, while my grandmother and their four young children heeded his snap assessment and immediately fled across the Bay 'on the last ferry' to Oakland with cash kept on hand for such emergencies(!), walked about four miles, started asking around about places for sale, and put money down on the next Kerrigan home while their doomed old one in San Francisco faced the spreading fires. That same grandfather died in 1919, when my father was three, from the flu pandemic, while serving as an ambulance responder after San Francisco had rescinded its unpopular mask mandate too soon.

In more recent decades, several family members, friends, and neighbors have been burned out of their homes in the Oakland hills, the Santa Barbara hills, and in multiple fires in the Sierra. As I proofread these words, the air is full of smoke (from the Electra Fire, this time); my go-bags are in the car; an evacuation order could be expanded my way at any time.

My father had to watch his Japanese-American friends—American citizens—be interned in camps during the second world war, while he worked as a welder to build ships for the Navy. He came close to being trapped in the collapse of the elevated roadway of the Nimitz Freeway in Oakland, during the

1989 Loma Prieta earthquake. A friend had his house knocked apart by that same quake (never build on an epicenter!).

One of my early indelible memories is of a morning drive to the hospital (the same one) with my father, in April, 1958, through a flooded intersection in Oakland; the water was about two feet deep in my memory, and seemed likely to float us in our Chevy, but I suppose it could have been less.

When I was 19 I entered public service in a role that included public safety responsibilities and could have required me to lead wildfire evacuations, so, during a drought, I familiarized myself with the network of non-public forest roads where I was based, and identified best route options. Fortunately, that need did not come to pass (then); I assisted with only a smattering of injury-rescues, car collisions, smaller fires... and one of the catastrophic winter storms of that decade. Yet my perspective was forever changed. I am in no way a disaster response professional. Still, from that long-ago public work I've taken with me throughout my life a public safety and preparedness outlook. I look around, assess situations, and think ahead.

From 1974 I entered formal training as a scientist, and have been a working scientist, and occasional educator, from 1979. The Ph.D. came in 1989.

I've had several of my own close calls, too close, too many, and experiences that life did not lead me to expect or prepare for. Four years ago I found myself sprinting through an old grove of desert cottonwoods as a no-warning, apparent microburst (extreme vertical winds) started tearing it down. The fact that I'm still here after assorted slings and arrows leads me to wonder whether I might have some purpose to advance, namely, to encourage you:

Be smart (or at least, not foolish). Be aware. Be informed. Be prepared. Be proactive.

Things happen. Some can be anticipated. Do that. Please.